AI for Risks

Series Editors

Risks are widespread in human society, such as in the financial field (various investment risks), in technical fields (risks brought by emerging technologies), in social fields (political risks), and in all aspects of our lives (health risks, natural environment risks, etc.) At the same time, the inherent links between various risks generate systemic risks. The major challenge today is not to deal with new types of risks, but to focus more on those risks that are difficult to distinguish effectively and timely, or risks that have emerged in a different way from the past.

This series of books aims to strengthen discussions on frontier hot topics across disciplines, that is, using AI technologies to solve risks problems that exist in the environment, healthcare, technology, and financial fields. The scope of it focuses on the implementation of artificial intelligence technology in dealing with risks, such as risk prediction, assessment, and mitigation. It includes monographs, edited volumes, textbooks and proceedings etc. on the application of artificial intelligence in risk management in the fields of social media, healthcare, the public sector, financial technology, and regulatory technology.

Xiyuan Ma · Desheng Wu

Financial Fraud Detection Using Machine Learning

Springer

Xiyuan Ma
Institutes of Science and Development
Chinese Academy of Sciences
Beijing, China

Desheng Wu
University of Chinese Academy of Sciences
School of Economics and Management
Beijing, China

ISSN 2731-6327 ISSN 2731-6335 (electronic)
AI for Risks
ISBN 978-981-95-0839-6 ISBN 978-981-95-0840-2 (eBook)
https://doi.org/10.1007/978-981-95-0840-2

The Chinese Academy of Science President's International Fellowship Initiative (CAS PIFI) Intenational Outstanding Team Project under Grant 2024PG0013; The Specific Research Fund of the Innovation Platform for Academicians of Hainan Province under Grant YSPTZX202210.
This work was supported by National Natural Science Foundation of China (72210107001), the Chinese Academy of Science President's International Fellowship Initiative International Outstanding Team Project (2024PG0013), the Specific Research Fund of the Innovation Platform for Academicians of Hainan Province (YSPTZX202210).

This Springer imprint is published by the registered company Springer Nature Singapore Pte Ltd.
The registered company address is: 152 Beach Road, #21-01/04 Gateway East, Singapore 189721, Singapore

Preface

With the increasing complexity of economic transactions, business model and ownership structures, financial process and accounting treatment are becoming more multifaceted, which creates greater operable space for financial fraud. Corporate financial fraud not only directly undermines the quality of financial information, but also damages the reputation of managers and organizations, potentially accelerating their descent into financial distress. The resulting chain reactions can even trigger systemic risks. However, in practice, financial fraud techniques have become increasingly sophisticated, flexible and concealed, making financial fraud detection significantly more challenging. Simultaneously, the rapid development of machine learning and other data mining techniques provides more effective tools for financial fraud detection. Therefore, how to enhance the detection of financial fraud leveraging advanced machine learning quantitative tools has become a critical concern for both academia and industry.

The combination of machine learning and financial fraud detection is still faced with batches of challenges due to the ambiguous definition of fraud, the scarcity of sample data, and the redundancy of influencing factors. This book aims to improve the detection ability of financial fraud and further advance the theoretical and empirical applications of machine learning techniques in financial fraud detection. This book comprehensively examines the scope and motivations of financial fraud committed by publicly listed companies, employs differentiated data processing and feature selection approaches and explores novel financial fraud detection metrics, in order to achieve precise modeling of fraudulent activities in the Chinese context. Specifically, based on the systematical review of related studies, this book addresses the key issues of financial fraud detection from data preprocessing, indicator systems, feature selection, model construction and empirical analysis, combined with classical accounting theories and data mining methods, which is divided into four aspects as follow:

This book establishes the essential theoretical framework of the whole book through six chapters (Chap. 2–7), beginning with financial fraud research analysis based on bibliometrics and knowledge mapping to make theoretical and empirical definitions of financial fraud in corporate finance literature. After systematically analyzing the nature of financial fraud and defining the research scope through a taxonomical hierarchy of two distinct categories of fraudulent behaviors in Chinese listed companies, we trace the theoretical evolution of financial fraud motivations to guide our feature selection methodology. The discussion then advances to a comprehensive comparative analysis of financial fraud litigation and enforcement mechanisms between China and the United States, contributing to forensic accounting, before culminating in the technical and methodological foundations of fraud detection, which encompasses advanced resampling techniques, sophisticated feature selection methodologies, and various detection models that integrate traditional econometric approaches, contemporary machine learning algorithms, and state-of-the-art deep learning architectures to provide a robust analytical framework.

Following the theoretical foundation, this book advances to practical applications through two empirical studies (Chaps. 8 and 9) examining effective financial fraud detection mechanisms. The final chapter (Chap. 10) synthesizes classical case studies and presents evidence-based recommendations for fraud prevention.

Specifically, in Chap. 8, the public enforcement for listed companies disclosed by supervisory authorities is used as proxy for financial fraud. What is more, a multi-dimensional financial fraud detection indicator system is constructed with the domain knowledge of accounting to develop a highly imbalanced large-sample financial fraud dataset. Imbalanced machine learning models are explored by incorporating data resampling techniques and compared to find the best one. The empirical results show that the traditional Gaussian Naive Bayes algorithm outperforms other machine learning models and imbalanced machine learning models exhibit superior performance compared to traditional models, with the Gaussian Naive Bayes algorithm integrated with the ClusterCentroid resampling method achieving the best performance in financial fraud detection. Additionally, we innovatively incorporate litigation-related factors and verifies their feature significance in Chinese context using machine learning methods, which emphasizes the importance of optimizing the legal environment.

Chapter 9 in this book contracts the wide range of the identification criteria for financial fraud to only include significant accounting fraud within general regulatory violations in the research framework. The financial fraud detection model is systematically optimized across raw data, modeling methods, and feature selection, aiming to identify major accounting fraud effectively. In terms of the raw data, significant accounting fraud is proxied by fraudulent misstatements resulting in substantial fines imposed by regulatory authorities. Furthermore, following the GONE theory (Greed, Opportunity, Need, and Exposure), the original features are divided into five categories: Greed, Opportunity, Need, Exposure and Others. A paired small financial fraud dataset is constructed to validate the effectiveness of the GONE framework in financial fraud detection and the significance of "Need" variables. In terms of modelling methods, this chapter demonstrates the superiority of random forest (RF) and gradient boosted decision tree (GBDT) models to detect significant accounting fraud. Moreover, an innovative two-stage feature selection method combining machine learning and Pearson correlation analysis is introduced to further enhance the discriminatory power of above-mentioned machine learning models for financial fraud detection.

Overall, this book designs a financial fraud analysis framework tailored to Chinese capital market to effectively detect fraudulent companies using machine learning, considering scenario-based factors such as original dataset, feature selection and model construction, in order to timely detect financial fraud and effectively improve capital market governance. The book highlights that financial fraud in Chinese publicly listed companies is primarily driven by internal financial condition and external legal environment, which underscores the urgent need to establish a more comprehensive regulation system at both institutional and managerial levels to strengthen the prevention and control of fraudulent activities in the multi-tier capital market.

Beijing, China

Xiyuan Ma
Desheng Wu

Acknowledgements

This work is supported in part by National Natural Science Foundation of China (NSFC) under Grant 72210107001, in part by the Chinese Academy of Science President's International Fellowship Initiative (CAS PIFI) International Outstanding Team Project under Grant 2024PG0013, in part by the Specific Research Fund of the Innovation Platform for Academicians of Hainan Province under Grant YSPTZX202210. The authors are deeply grateful to many individuals and organizations who provided generous support and guidance, which helped the completion of this book.

Contents

Chapter 1
Introduction

1.1 The Nature of the Problem

1.1.1 The Current Trend of Financial Fraud

The evolving complexity of modern economic activities has led to increasingly sophisticated business models, intricate equity relationships, and complex financial processes and accounting practices, creating expanded opportunities for financial malfeasance. Contemporary corporate financial fraud has become notably more flexible and concealed, presenting unprecedented challenges to existing regulatory frameworks (Huang et al. 2021). This growing challenge is evidenced by the data disclosed by PricewaterhouseCoopers (PwC) in 2022, which revealed that 48% of companies worldwide have encountered various forms of fraud, with financial fraud emerging as the most pervasive and detrimental category (Yuan et al. 2022). The risk of financial fraud among listed companies shows a concerning upward trend, with fraudulent activities becoming more prevalent over time (Association of Certified Fraud Examiners 2023). Particularly troubling is the diminishing effectiveness of traditional fraud detection models in addressing these evolving challenges, as they struggle to adapt to increasingly complex and dynamic business environments.

Therefore, financial fraud detection remains a critical concern that commands sustained attention from diverse stakeholders, including investors, audit institutions, regulatory authorities, and other market participants since the accurate detection and prevention of financial fraud is fundamental to ensuring the sustainable, high-quality development of both listed companies and capital markets. This research examines financial fraud behaviors within Chinese listed companies through a comprehensive analysis of regulatory penalty documents issued by the China Securities Regulatory Commission (CSRC) and its affiliated institutions from 2006 to 2022, as shown in Table 1.1. The analysis reveals that financial violations constitute the predominant category of infractions, encompassing four main types: delayed disclosure,

X. Ma and D. Wu, *Financial Fraud Detection Using Machine Learning*, AI for Risks,
https://doi.org/10.1007/978-981-95-0840-2_1

false or misleading statements, material omissions, and general accounting misconduct. Meanwhile, the scope of these violations is substantial. By the end of 2021, approximately 3572 companies listed on China's A-share market had been subject to regulatory penalties, with a total of 9176 documented violation cases. Notably, more than half of all Chinese listed companies have been involved in various types of regulatory infractions. What is more, industry-specific analysis as illustrated in Fig. 1.1 indicates that violation rates are particularly concentrated in several sectors, including electronic equipment, pharmaceuticals, chemicals, manufacturing, and real estate.

Figure 1.2 illustrates the temporal evolution of both the number of listed companies and their corresponding violation rates from 2006 to 2022. Overall, the Chinese stock market has experienced substantial growth, with the total number of listed companies reaching 5039 by 2022. The violation rate trajectory exhibits two distinct growth phases. During the initial phase (2008–2012), while the number of listed companies remained relatively stable at approximately 2500, the violation rate showed a consistent upward trend, escalating from 3.94% in 2008 to 10.59% in 2012. Following a brief decline to 8.14% in 2013, the market entered a second growth phase, culminating in a historical peak of 12.26% in 2015. The post-2015 period marked a turning point, characterized by enhanced regulatory oversight. This decline in violations was particularly pronounced following two significant regulatory reforms including the implementation of the revised Securities Law of the People's Republic of China (hereafter "Securities Law") in 2019 and the introduction of the "Opinion on Strict Implementation of Delisting System" (hereafter "New Delisting Rules") in 2014. These regulatory initiatives, coupled with improved market supervision and governance mechanisms, contributed to a substantial reduction in the violation rate, which decreased to 5.64% in 2022, a level comparable to the low rates observed in 2010.

While the overall violation rate has shown a downward trend, the severity and sophistication of violations among listed companies have intensified markedly. Financial fraud persists as one of the most serious forms of corporate misconduct,

Table 1.1 Types of violations of listed companies in China (2006–2022)

Violation events	Counts	Proportion	Violation events	Counts	Proportion
Delayed disclosure	2440	33.04%	Others	161	2.18%
Misleading disclosure	1473	19.95%	Unauthorized Change in Fund Usage	72	0.97%
Material omissions	1472	19.93%	Illegal Stock Trading	55	0.74%
General accounting misconduct	557	7.54%	Falsification of Assets	46	0.62%
Assets misappropriation	482	6.53%	Insider Trading	4	0.05%
Irregular guarantees	327	4.43%	Illegal Investment	1	0.01%
Fictitious profits	295	3.99%	Fraudulent Listing	0	0.00%

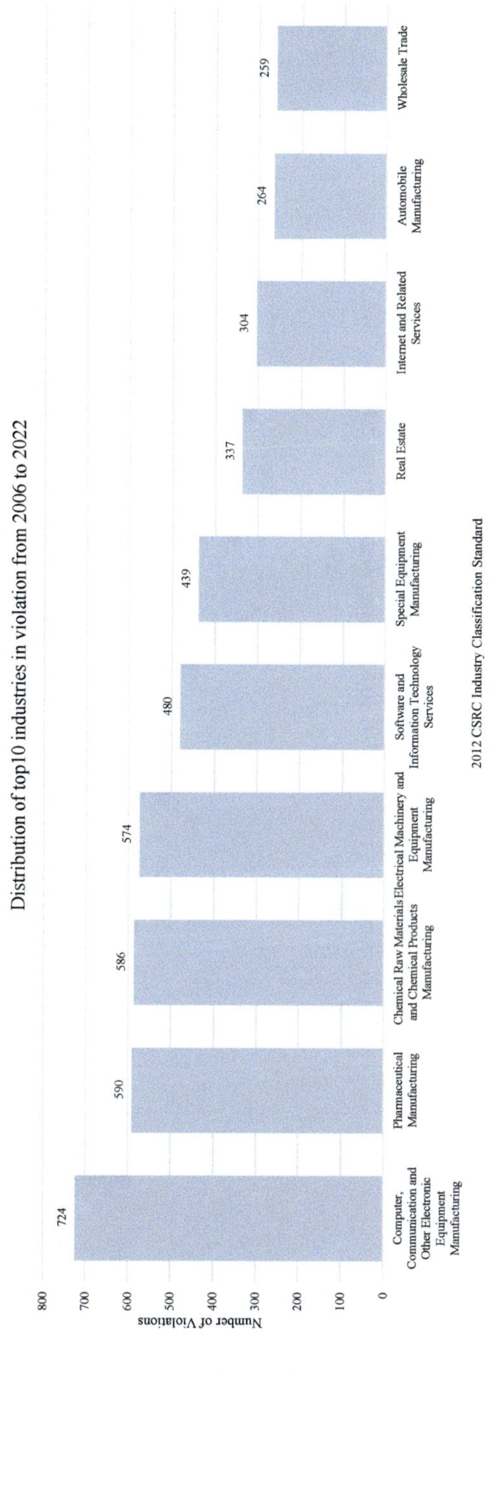

Fig. 1.1 Distribution of top10 industries in violation from 2006 to 2022

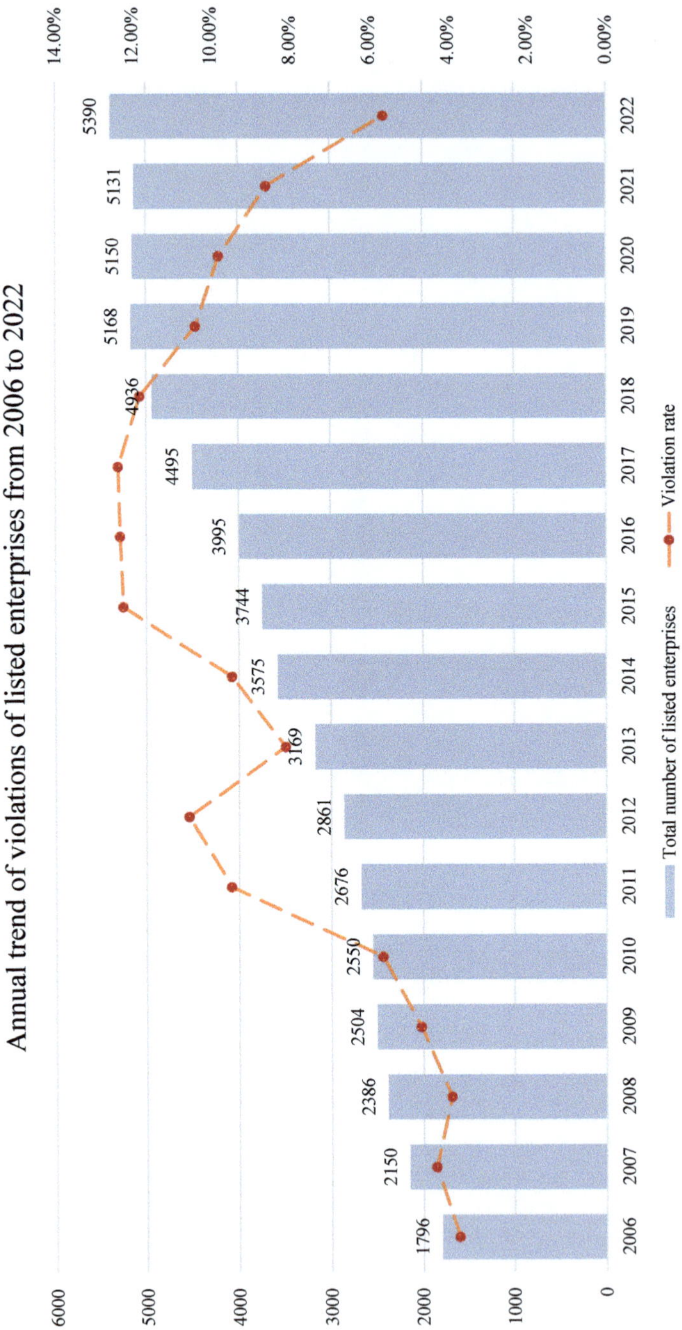

Fig. 1.2 Annual trend of violations of listed enterprises from 2006 to 2022

with numerous Chinese listed companies since 2020 becoming embroiled in cases that have significantly undermined market confidence. Several high-profile cases underscore the magnitude of this issue. For example, Kangde Xin (002450.SZ) was delisted following the discovery of RMB 11.5 billion in fraudulent activities; Luckin Coffee (LKNCY) fabricated RMB 2.2 billion in revenue; Fushun Special Steel (600399.SH) inflated profits by RMB 1.9 billion; Xinlv Shares (834632.SZ) overstated revenue by RMB 900 million; and most notably, *ST Kaile (600260.SH) engaged in systematic fraud totaling over RMB 50 billion during 2016–2020. The scale and frequency of these financial fraud cases have raised serious concerns about market integrity.

The complexity of financial fraud stems from its potential to infiltrate every aspect of business operations, from initial transactions and raw data collection through to accounting documentation and final financial statement preparation. Moreover, the comprehensive nature of modern business processes, encompassing initial recognition, subsequent measurement, and financial presentation, creates multiple vulnerabilities where fraudulent activities can occur. Financial fraud cases among Chinese listed companies typically exhibit distinct patterns such as prolonged duration of fraudulent schemes, substantial scale of financial manipulation, involvement of multiple parties, increasingly sophisticated concealment techniques and so on. These multifaceted characteristics, combined with the systematic nature of such fraud, not only complicate detection and verification efforts but also pose a significant threat to the sustainable development and integrity of capital markets.

1.1.2 Research Background

The detection of financial fraud has emerged as a critical focus in academic research, garnering significant attention from scholars worldwide. This growing interest is reflected in the substantial body of influential studies published in premier international accounting journals, including the Review of Accounting Studies, The Accounting Review, and Contemporary Accounting Research (Dechow et al. 2011; Purda and Skillicorn 2015; Karpoff et al. 2017; Amiram et al. 2018; Donelson et al. 2021; Dyck et al. 2024). The escalating importance of this field is further evidenced by the dramatic increase in research output across major international academic databases, particularly the Science Citation Index (SCI) and Social Sciences Citation Index (SSCI). Notably, the volume of published research in this domain demonstrated remarkable growth, with publications in 2021 reaching six times the level observed in 2007, as shown in Fig. 1.3.

In response to the recurring financial fraud cases among listed companies in China's capital markets, scholars in China also have intensified their research efforts in critical areas including financial fraud detection, financial distress prediction, and financial risk management. This heightened academic focus is evidenced by the substantial growth in research publications indexed in the Chinese Social Sciences

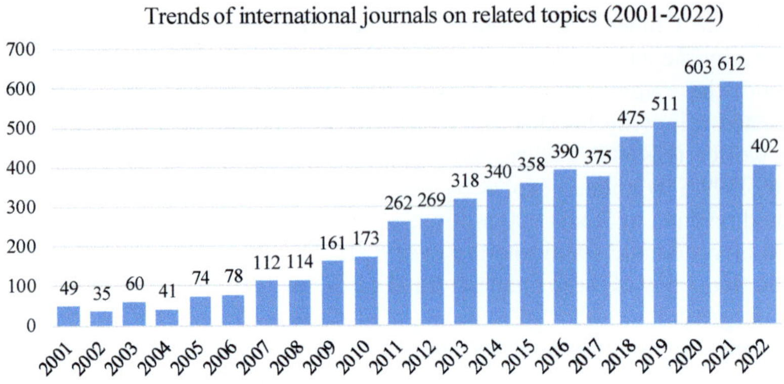

Fig. 1.3 Trends of international journals on related topics (2001–2022)

Citation Index (CSSCI) database, as illustrated in Fig. 1.4. The increasing scholarly attention to this domain is particularly reflected in the publication trends of China's premier academic journals, including Management World, Economic Research Journal, Chinese Journal of Management Science, Auditing Research, Accounting Research, and Financial Research. These prestigious publications have featured a growing body of sophisticated analyses examining various aspects of financial fraud and its detection mechanisms (Wang et al. 2015; Yao and Zhao 2016; Xu et al. 2018; Chen et al. 2021; Huang et al. 2021; Xiu et al. 2021; Yang et al. 2022).

Current research in financial fraud detection primarily advances through two complementary approaches inlcuding the development of innovative indicators and the refinement of detection models, both contributing to comprehensive research frameworks. However, several critical areas still present opportunities for enhancement. First, there remains significant potential to strengthen the theoretical foundation

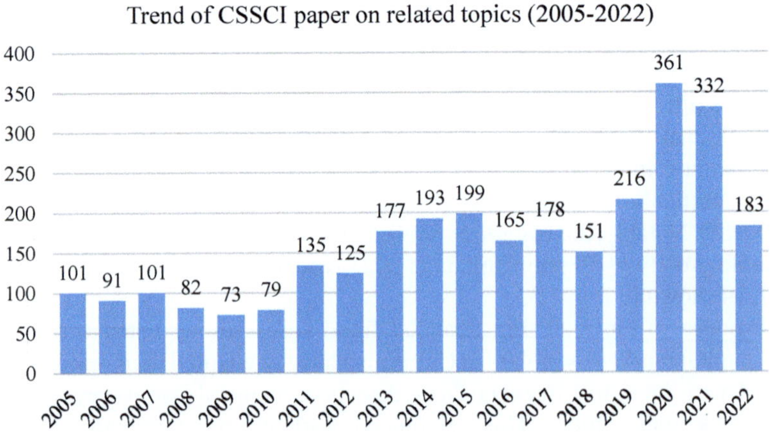

Fig. 1.4 Trend of CSSCI paper on related topics (2005–2022)

of fraud detection frameworks by integrating fundamental accounting principles and fraud theories, thereby improving their explanatory power. Second, the emerging capabilities of machine learning and ensemble learning techniques offer promising avenues for expanding variable selection, developing more sophisticated detection models, and conducting multifaceted performance comparisons. Third, the strategic selection and implementation of feature selection methodologies could not only enhance financial fraud detection accuracy but also provide deeper insights into how individual features contribute to the identification of financial fraud. Fourth, given the constantly evolving nature of financial fraud motivations, there is a pressing need to develop novel research perspectives to better understand and investigate emerging patterns of corporate financial misconduct.

This book presents a comprehensive theoretical and empirical framework for effective financial fraud detection by integrating three crucial elements including theoretical foundations with practical experience, financial data with business processes, and machine learning with advanced data mining techniques. First, we establish a robust financial fraud detection indicator system grounded in fundamental accounting and fraud theories to analyze how specific signals contribute to financial fraud detection, thereby enriching empirical evidence and providing theoretical support for regulatory bodies and managers in their corporate fraud monitoring efforts. Additionally, we introduce a severity-based classification of financial fraud, distinguishing between general violations and more serious fraudulent activities. By leveraging a sophisticated combination of resampling techniques, feature selection methods, and ensemble learning algorithms, we develop machine learning models capable of precisely detecting financial fraud across the severity spectrum. These models, rigorously validated for stability, generate detailed corporate information quality profiles at the micro level. This multifaceted approach ultimately enhances the efficiency and effectiveness of financial risk management frameworks.

The practical implications of this framework offer significant value across multiple stakeholder groups. For corporate managers, the comprehensive financial risk management and early warning system serves as a proactive tool, enabling the implementation of remedial measures before financial conditions deteriorate, thereby supporting more informed and precise decision-making processes. For investors and creditors, the sophisticated financial fraud detection system provides deep insights into business operations, enabling timely identification of fraudulent activities and facilitating financial risk mitigation through the systematic detection and avoidance of high-risk enterprises. Perhaps most significantly, for regulatory bodies and external auditors, the proposed financial fraud detection models and research perspectives substantially enhance financial fraud detection capabilities. By strategically focusing investigative resources on companies flagged by the model, regulators can substantially streamline their oversight processes. This targeted approach effectively addresses several longstanding challenges in regulatory supervision, including high operational costs, extended investigation cycles, and delayed response times, ultimately leading to more efficient and effective regulatory oversight.

1.2 Research Content

This research investigates the detection of financial fraud within complex data scenarios characterized by high dimensionality, heterogeneous information sources, and dynamic market conditions. The main research contents are as follows:

1.2.1 Theoretical Foundations of Financial Fraud

This section establishes the essential theoretical framework of the whole book, spanning six chapters (Chap. 2–7). The discussion initiates with text mining and visualization analysis of financial fraud researches in international core journals to find valuable rules and patterns in this kind of research. Then the theoretical and empirical definitions of financial fraud is explained using financial distress as a benchmark given the intrinsic interconnections between these phenomena in corporate finance literature. Through systematic analysis of the nature of financial fraud, we define the specific scope of this study, which encompasses a taxonomical hierarchy of two distinct categories of financial fraudulent behaviors observed in Chinese listed companies, structured in a hierarchical framework from broad to narrow classifications. Furthermore, we conduct a chronological analysis of the theoretical evolution underlying financial fraud motivations, synthesizing various scholarly perspectives that provide the theoretical guidance for feature selection methodology.

The book then presents a comprehensive comparative analysis of financial fraud litigation and enforcement mechanisms between China and the United States, contributing substantively to the evolving domain of forensic accounting. The final segment elaborates on the technical and methodological foundations of financial fraud detection, encompassing advanced resampling techniques, sophisticated feature selection methodologies, and a spectrum of detection models. These models integrate traditional econometric approaches through statistical regression analysis, contemporary machine learning algorithms, and state-of-the-art deep learning architectures, providing a robust analytical framework for fraud detection and classification.

1.2.2 Financial Fraud Detection Based on Litigation and Resampling Methods

This study examines financial fraud risk within listed companies by analyzing general violations documented by regulatory bodies, leveraging an extensive and highly imbalanced dataset that spans from 2006 to 2021. The dataset encompasses over 40,000 sample records with 68 distinct feature indicators, enabling a comprehensive investigation of financial fraud risk patterns among listed companies. The research framework is firmly grounded in fundamental accounting theories, particularly double-entry bookkeeping and accounting information systems theory, establishing clear logical relationships between accounting indicators and financial fraud. This theoretical foundation is enhanced by the integration of non-financial information and key litigation variables specifically characteristic of financial fraud patterns in Chinese listed companies. Finally, this study produce a comprehensive feature framework that encompasses seven critical dimensions, including solvency, profitability, and corporate governance, with each financial fraud detection feature systematically ranked according to its relative importance in identifying fraudulent activities.

Methodologically, this research content implements various resampling methods, including Cluster Centroids, Synthetic Minority Over-sampling Technique-Tomek Links (SMOTE-Tomek Links), Synthetic Minority Over-sampling Technique (SMOTE) and its derivatives, Tomek Links, Adaptive Synthetic Sampling (ADASYN), Random Under-sampling (RUS), and Random Over-sampling (ROS), combined with multiple machine learning algorithms, including Gaussian Naïve Bayes (GaussianNB), Logistic Regression (LR), Decision Tree (DT), Support Vector Machine (SVM), Random Forest (RF), Adaptive Boosting (AdaBoost), and Gradient Boosting Decision Tree (GBDT). The empirical results reveal that without feature selection, the Cluster Centroids-integrated Gaussian Naïve Bayes algorithm achieved optimal performance with a 99.4% financial fraud detection rate. Moreover, the innovative incorporation of litigation indicators significantly improved model performance, with SMOTE-integrated Gaussian Naïve Bayes algorithm showing a 56.21% increase in recall rate, demonstrating the crucial role of litigation-related indicators in financial fraud detection within capital markets in China, with varying impacts observed across different machine learning models.

1.2.3 Financial Fraud Detection Based on Feature Selection and the GONE Framework

This study explores the role of ensemble learning models in financial fraud detection through the lens of feature selection methods and the GONE (Greed, Opportunity, Need, Exposure) theoretical framework. Building upon the financial fraud detection indicator system established in the previous chapter, this study categorizes all indicators into five categories according to GONE theory, encompassing Greed, Opportunity, Exposure, Need, and Others. Unlike the previous research focusing on broad financial fraud risk, this study specifically examines severe accounting fraud cases in the Chinese market using a paired-sample dataset. This research methodology also employs seven machine learning models including, GaussianNB, DT, SVM, RF, GBDT and AdaBoost, with optimal hyperparameters determined through Cross-Validation (CV) and Grid Search (GS) techniques. Empirical result shows that the RF model outperformed other algorithms, accurately identifying 90% of fraudulent samples, while Need-related variables consistently showed the highest contribution to fraud detection across all models, aligning with findings by Huang et al. (2017). Only four feature indicators are consistently selected across all classifiers, including operating profit margin, owner's equity growth rate, cash ratio, and net assets per share, which correspond to common fraud techniques such as revenue inflation, profit manipulation, fictitious monetary funds, and asset inflation. Furthermore, a novel feature selection method based on average feature importance and Pearson correlation coefficients improved the G-means metric by 3% for GBDT, 3% for RF, and 5% for AdaBoost, enriching the empirical evidence of machine learning applications in financial fraud detection while highlighting the significance of feature selection and GONE theory in fraud identification.

1.3 Research Framework

This research substantially advances the empirical understanding of financial fraud detection within the Chinese context through multiple innovative approaches. By harnessing newly disclosed financial, non-financial, and textual data from listed companies, and integrating sophisticated machine learning algorithms, resampling techniques, feature selection methodologies, and text mining technique, this study makes significant contributions in both theoretical frameworks and methodological applications by developing a comprehensive indicator system and providing compelling empirical evidence from the Chinese market, particularly in the domains of indicator framework construction, feature selection optimization, and the application of hybrid machine learning techniques.

Firstly, this book begins with a macro analysis of financial fraud in listed companies supported by real financial fraud data from Chinese financial markets, which provides readers with a comprehensive understanding of its nature and the critical importance of timely and precise detection. So we can introduce the final objective of writing this book, to optimize the research framework and increase accuracy of financial fraud detection. Secondly, we address the definitional ambiguity and measurement complexity of financial fraud encountered in previous research, aiming to guide readers to the specific and well-defined scope for our investigation that serves as the cornerstone of this study. Furthermore, we present and elaborate on the foundational theories that have shaped this domain, constructing a theoretical framework essential for understanding the empirical analyses in subsequent chapters. This theoretical foundation encompasses not only classical theories explaining motivation to conduct fraudulent behavior but also incorporates relevant legal and litigation frameworks, alongside technical methodologies covering data preprocessing, feature selection, and modeling approaches.

Additionally, this book establishes a comprehensive financial fraud detection framework grounded in classical fraud theory and accounting principles. Beginning with broadly defined regulatory penalty events, it investigates optimal detection models through the application of imbalanced ensemble machine learning algorithms on Chinese datasets of listed companies, while empirically validating the

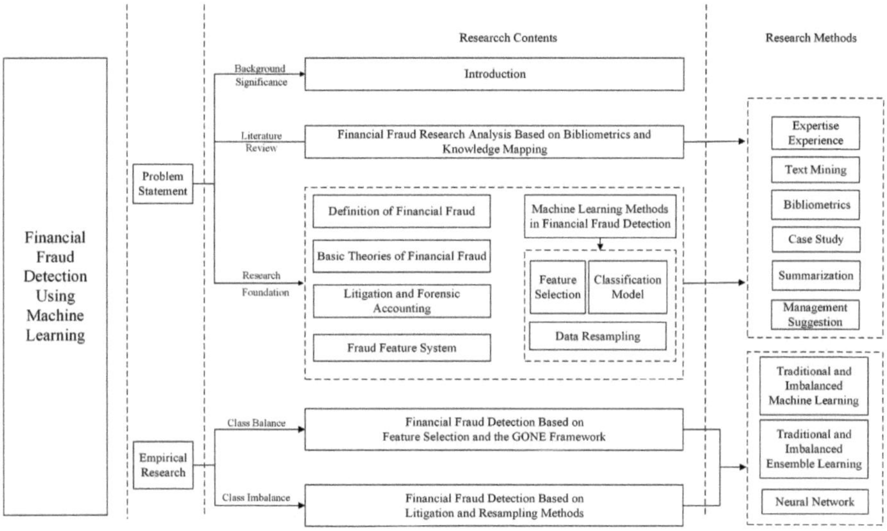

Fig. 1.5 The overall research framework

significant predictive power of litigation variables in financial fraud detection from a machine learning perspective. Furthermore, the study advances the understanding of the effectiveness and stability of the GONE theory in financial fraud detection through rigorous theoretical analysis. Through the implementation of sophisticated feature selection methodologies, it optimizes machine learning models, with particular emphasis on ensemble learning approaches, for detecting severe financial fraud cases. Notably, the research identifies the Need factor within GONE theory as the predominant driver of large-scale financial fraud, providing regulatory authorities with actionable insights for preventing severe fraudulent activities among listed companies. The integrated research framework of this book is illustrated in Fig. 1.5.

1.4 Innovation

This research advances the field of financial fraud detection among Chinese listed companies by introducing significant innovations across three key dimensions: modeling methodologies, dataset construction and variable selection, which provides novel analytical approaches for financial fraud detection while substantially enriching empirical evidence across multiple dimensions, particularly in empirical methodologies and indicator systems.

In terms of methodological innovation, this book introduces a sophisticated combination of resampling techniques and machine learning models to algorithmically address the challenges posed by extreme class imbalance in classification outcomes. It conducts a comprehensive comparative analysis of classification performance across conventional machine learning algorithms and ensemble learning approaches under diverse data scenarios, ultimately developing and validating optimal financial fraud detection models specifically calibrated for the Chinese context. Additionally, this research develops an innovative two-stage feature selection methodology, integrating Pearson correlation coefficients and feature importance scores, significantly improving the accuracy of machine learning models including RF, GBDT, AdaBoost, and DT in financial fraud detection, which demonstrates that the "feature selection + machine learning" approach represents a promising direction for financial fraud detection. Furthermore, machine learning methods are employed to synergistically examine the effectiveness of key indicators in detecting fraudulent behavior, thereby validating the robustness and stability of the constructed financial fraud detection indicator system.

Regarding innovations in research dataset and variables, this book first constructs a comprehensive multidimensional financial fraud detection indicator system through the integration of interdisciplinary theoretical frameworks, including classical financial fraud theory, forensic accounting theory, and accounting information systems theory, while systematically synthesizing knowledge from accounting, law, and economic management disciplines. Secondly, the empirical research employs a hierarchical approach to financial fraud datasets following a progressive relationship. It utilizes two distinct proxy variables for financial fraud identification: (1) general regulatory violations with potential financial fraud risk as disclosed by regulatory bodies, and (2) severe accounting fraud incidents encompassing false records, misleading statements, and material omissions. This methodological approach, structured on the principle of "from broad to narrow" classification, combined with China-specific financial fraud detection variables, substantially expands and enriches the empirical indicator system for financial fraud detection within the Chinese context.

1.5 Summary

To summarize, this chapter briefly introduces the research background, research significance, and research content of this book. Based on the detailed examination of actual situation of financial fraud among Chinese listed companies, we systematically analyze fundamental characteristics of Chinese financial fraud including temporal changes in the number of fraudulent enterprises, severity levels, and industry distribution patterns, in order to identify multiple challenges in financial fraud detection and establish an analytical framework that integrates both theoretical and empirical approaches for effective financial fraud detection. From an empirical perspective, financial fraud among Chinese listed companies exhibits complexity, concealment, and systemic characteristics, representing a significant component of financial risk.

In academic research, financial fraud detection remains a critical scientific inquiry that has garnered extensive attention. Accordingly, this book adopts a comprehensive analytical framework structured around four key aspects: definition and measurement of financial fraud, theoretical foundations of financial fraud detection, construction and application of detection models, and monitoring and response mechanisms for fraudulent activities. The whole chapter structure follows this research framework, employing an integrated methodological approach that combines resampling techniques, machine learning methods, and feature selection algorithms to enhance the accuracy of financial fraud detection.

References

Amiram D, Bozanic Z, Cox JD, Dupont Q (2018) Financial reporting fraud and other forms of misconduct: a multidisciplinary review of the literature. Rev Acc Stud 23:732–783

Association of Certified Fraud Examiners (ACFE) (2023) Report to the nations: 2023 global study on occupational fraud and abuse. https://www.acfe.com/fraud-resources/global-fraud-survey

Chen X, Jiang W, Xia W et al (2021) Review and contribution analysis of core hot topics in accounting research: 1980–2019. Account Res 04:10–22

Dechow PM, Ge W, Larson CR, Sloan RG (2011) Predicting material accounting misstatements. Contemp Account Res 28(1):17–82

Donelson DC, Kartapanis A, McInnis J, Yust CG (2021) Measuring accounting fraud and irregularities using public and private enforcement. Account Rev 96(6):183–213

Dyck, A., Morse, A., & Zingales, L. (2024). How pervasive is corporate fraud?. Review of Accounting Studies, 29(1), 736–769.

Huang SY, Lin CC, Chiu AA, Yen DC (2017) Fraud detection using fraud triangle risk factors. Inform Syst Front 19(6): 1343–1356.

Huang S, Zhou S, Ye F, Chen C (2021) Research on enterprise financial performance recognition under major public health emergencies: theoretical analysis of depreciation issues in the context of COVID-19. Account Res 03:3–10

Karpoff JM, Koester A, Lee DS, Martin GS (2017) Proxies and databases in financial misconduct research. Account Rev 92(6):129–163

Purda L, Skillicorn D (2015) Accounting variables, deception, and a bag of words: assessing the tools of fraud detection. Contemp Account Res 32(3):1193–1223

Wang H, Cao F, Ye K (2015) Supervision or tunneling: Large shareholders' shareholding ratio and stock price crash risk. Manag World (02):45–57+187

Xiu Z, Liu R, Yin J (2021) Financial fraud, supply chain concentration and corporate trade credit financing. Account Res 01:82–99

Xu W, Su L, Lv P et al (2018) The impact of delisting system reform on earnings management behavior of listed companies. Account Res 06:32–38

Yang S, Liu T, Shi Q (2022) Empirical accounting research: origin, development and reflection. Account Res 05:3–16

Yao Y, Zhao M (2016) Chinese-style risk disclosure, disclosure level and market reaction. Econ Res J 51(07):158–172

Yuan X, Zhao M, Liu H et al (2022) Screening and analysis framework of rural household poverty status characteristics: discussion on rural revitalization path selection in China. Chin J Manag Sci 30(12):234–244

Chapter 2
Financial Fraud Research Analysis Based on Bibliometrics and Knowledge Mapping

Over the past two decades, financial fraud research has experienced rapid development and been extensively applied across numerous sectors and scientific domains. This chapter employs CiteSpace and VOSviewer software to conduct text mining and visualization analysis of financial fraud researches in domestic and international core journals over the past 30 years. Through identifying core authors and institutions, research hotspots, research frontiers, and evolutionary trends, this chapter critically analyzes the current research landscape of financial fraud and prospects new research directions and finally concludes some valuable rules and patterns in this kind of research. First, as a classic research direction in management science, the international publication volume of financial fraud research demonstrates an increasing trend, forming a research distribution dominated primarily by China and the United States. Second, research perspectives predominantly concentrate on three dimensions including audit practices, legal regulations, and corporate governance, with emphasis on listed companies' motivations for financial fraud, legal liabilities, economic costs incurred when financial fraud is disclosed and punished, and litigation risks corresponding with concealed financial fraud behavior. Third, the research frontiers involve leveraging artificial intelligence technologies such as deep learning and large language models to construct multi-source heterogeneous fraud datasets to enhance the accuracy and effectiveness of financial fraud detection models. These preliminary research findings clarify the current state of financial fraud research, providing a foundational knowledge base for subsequent conceptualization, theoretical framework development, legal responsibility determination, and detection method optimization.

X. Ma and D. Wu, *Financial Fraud Detection Using Machine Learning*, AI for Risks,
https://doi.org/10.1007/978-981-95-0840-2_2

2.1 Introduction

Bases on bibliometric methods, this chapter collects abundant and closely linked financial fraud-related literature textual data from Web of Science (WOS) and China National Knowledge Infrastructure (CNKI) databases to conduct comprehensive quantitative and qualitative description and analysis of the knowledge foundation and research themes of international financial fraud studies through year, author, nation (region), publication, institution, research domain, co-citation, keyword co-occurrence, and clustering analysis.

Research on financial fraud has explored multiple dimensions. However, existing studies still remain fragmented and lack a comprehensive research framework. In recent years, some scholars have attempted to integrate financial fraud research, but most investigations are predominantly confined to qualitative descriptive analysis, struggling to precisely delineate the origins, core issues, interconnections, and developmental trajectories of researches.

Bibliometric methods offer a quantitative approach to describe and evaluate published researches, providing a systematic, objective, and replicable review process (Donthu et al. 2021). Scholars have already applied this methodology to financial risk management research for quantitative analysis (Darmawati et al. 2025; Bahoo et al. 2024). Applying bibliometric methods to grasp the whole picture of financial fraud management research not only supplements and validates inferences of qualitative review but also quantitatively illuminates evolutionary trends of this field, presenting a more objective and comprehensive perspective on the developmental dynamics of financial fraud research for readers.

2.2 Data Collection

First, we collect related papers published in international journal by searching keywords on the titles and abstracts within the Web of Science Core Collection, specifically focusing on the Science Citation Index Expanded (SCI-EXPANDED) and Social Sciences Citation Index (SSCI). The searching strategy is that the Boolean operator "OR" is set as searching condition and "financial fraud", "accounting misconduct", "financial misconduct", "accounting fraud", and "accounting misstatement" are used as searching keywords. Only articles are retained in the final dataset. Simultaneously, a similar systematic search was performed in the China National Knowledge Infrastructure (CNKI) database to collect related Chinese academic literature. The keywords include "财务欺诈" (financial fraud), "财务造假" (financial falsification), "会计舞弊" (accounting misconduct), "财务舞弊" (financial misconduct), "会计欺诈" (accounting fraud), and "会计造假" (accounting falsification). The search was confined to academic journals within the Chinese Social Sciences Citation Index (CSSCI). We implement a meticulous screening process to further delete irrelevant papers following the initial retrieval. The final dataset for bibliometric analysis include 5109 international journal articles and 464 Chinese academic papers focusing on financial fraud from January 2000 to January 2025.

2.3 Analytical Strategy

CiteSpace, a Java-based information visualization software developed by the American research team dominated by Professor Chaomei Chen, integrates dual characteristics of graphical and bibliometric mapping (Chen et al. 2010). This sophisticated tool synthesizes multiple analytical approaches, including frequency analysis, clustering analysis, and social network analysis, enabling comprehensive scientific knowledge mapping. By leveraging CiteSpace, researchers can explore disciplinary frontier evolution, research hotspots, author clusters, and intricate interdomain relationships through advanced visualization techniques such as keyword co-occurrence networks, temporal zone networks, and emergence detection mechanisms. These analytical capabilities provide nuanced insights into research dynamics and emerging trends. VOSviewer complements CiteSpace by emphasizing distance, density, and hot/cold spot analysis. It effectively constructs cluster results among key nodes, offering clear visualizations of research domains, author communities, keywords, and thematic structures. The synergistic combination of these two tools facilitates deeper exploration of the essential characteristics and developmental trend of research theme.

In this study, we employed CiteSpace (version 6.3.R1, 64-bit) and VOSviewer to conduct comprehensive bibliometric analysis on financial fraud literature data and citation data. The overall research methodology encompasses objective statistics and cluster analysis as well as knowledge mapping visualization. In details, the statistical analysis centers on the publication volume, geographical distribution, journal source, author profiles, institutional contributions, keyword, co-occurrence patterns and citation networks. The knowledge mapping and visualization techniques are employed to explain the intrinsic intellectual linkages and structural relationships among scholarly publications, keyword networks, and citation references, thereby constructing a systematic literature review framework to facilitate a more comprehensive and nuanced comprehension of the research landscape and a more scientific assessment of financial fraud research dynamics and potential future research frontiers.

2.4 Statistics Analysis

2.4.1 *Temporal Distribution*

Figure 2.1 illustrates and compares the annual distribution of domestic and international financial fraud research literature. The scholarly exploration of financial fraud commenced in 1992, with an average of 1–3 publications annually before 1997. A significant acceleration in literature volume occurred post-1998, particularly after the Enron scandal in 2001, which established financial fraud as a persistent research focal point. Therefore, the time research of this study is restricted to the period between January 2000 and January 2025. During this time interval, international publications demonstrate a consistent upward trend and the publication volume reaches to the highest 707 articles in the year of 2024, with an average of 27 annual publications and an impressive compound growth rate of 130%. In contrast, Chinese academic research exhibits more volatile characteristics. During the period from the year of 2000 to 2012, the whole trend is characterized by rapid and oscillating growth with publication volume escalating from 3 articles in 2000 to 31 in 2012. The annual growth rate on average is 60% and the absolute volume published annually is approximately 25, which reflects heightened academic and regulatory focus on financial fraud in China and the research output in this field reaches to the peak in the year of 2012. Since 2012, the publication volume has exhibited a marked decline, with merely six articles being published by 2018. Following 2019, a modest resurgence in research output was observed, with publication numbers stabilizing around 20 articles annually during the period 2020–2023. Notably, article count again decreased to 7 in 2024. Comprehensively, the time series analysis confirms that the Chinese literature in this domain demonstrates a fluctuating downward tendency over the past decade, contrasting with the steady international research momentum.

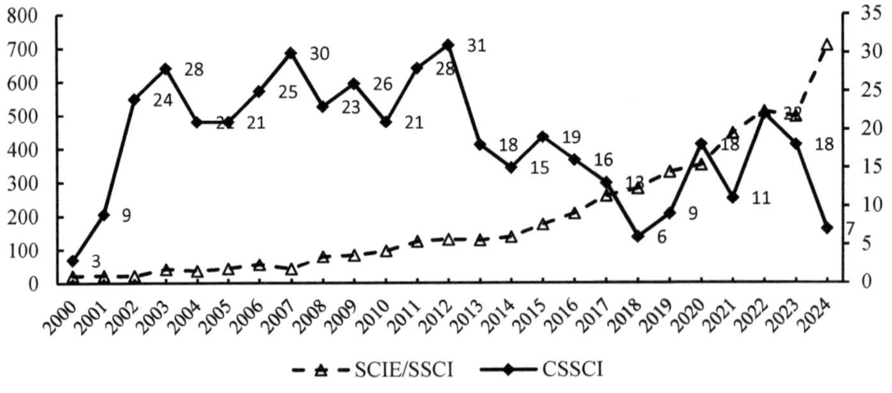

Fig. 2.1 Annual distribution of Chinese and International financial fraud literature. *Notes* SCIE is the abbreviation of the Science Citation Index Expanded. SSCI is the abbreviation of the Social Sciences Citation Index. CSSCI represents the Chinese Social Sciences Citation Index

2.4.2 National Distribution

This section conducts a comprehensive analysis of international financial fraud research, focusing on publication volume, collaborative networks, and cumulative citation times across different countries and regions. Currently, there are 116 countries and regions which have contributed to financial fraud research and generate some papers with direct or indirect impacts. Table 2.1 provides detailed publication data for the top 10 countries ranked by total publication output. When considering the publication volume, China and the United States dominate by collectively accounting for 49.3% of the total global research publications, with the United Kingdom ranking third. Regarding citation frequencies, the United States significantly outperforms other nations, followed by China and the United Kingdom. Despite the research output of China is competitive by the absolute publication volume, its research impact or innovation capacity as measured by total citation frequencies, remains considerably lower than the United States. In terms of international research collaboration, the top three countries are the United States, China, and the United Kingdom in sequence.

Moreover, 47 countries with more than 15 publications were selected from all 116 countries and regions to construct national collaboration networks based on publication and citation, as illustrated in Figs. 2.2 and 2.3. The size of node represents the volumes of publication or citation, while edges indicate collaborative relationships between nodes. Notably, China and the United States demonstrate pronounced advantages in both publication and citation, with the United States particularly distinguished by its exceptionally prominent citation network. Comprehensively, the current international landscape of financial fraud research predominantly centers on China and the United States, with substantial contributions from secondary core nations including the United Kingdom, Canada, Australia, Germany, Spain, the Netherlands, and France. Figure 2.4 presents the ranking of top 25 countries with highest citations at the national level between 2000 and 2025. We segment the

Table 2.1 Analysis of national publication output, citation frequency, and collaboration link

Rank	Countries	Documents	Citations	Total link strength
1	USA	2022	72,624	763
2	CHINA	893	16,375	465
3	ENGLAND	464	9127	369
4	AUSTRALIA	322	6831	273
5	CANADA	250	7916	229
6	GERMANY	214	4438	184
7	SPAIN	178	2665	97
8	ITALY	153	3221	133
9	BRAZIL	147	3059	42
10	NETHERLANDS	141	3544	127

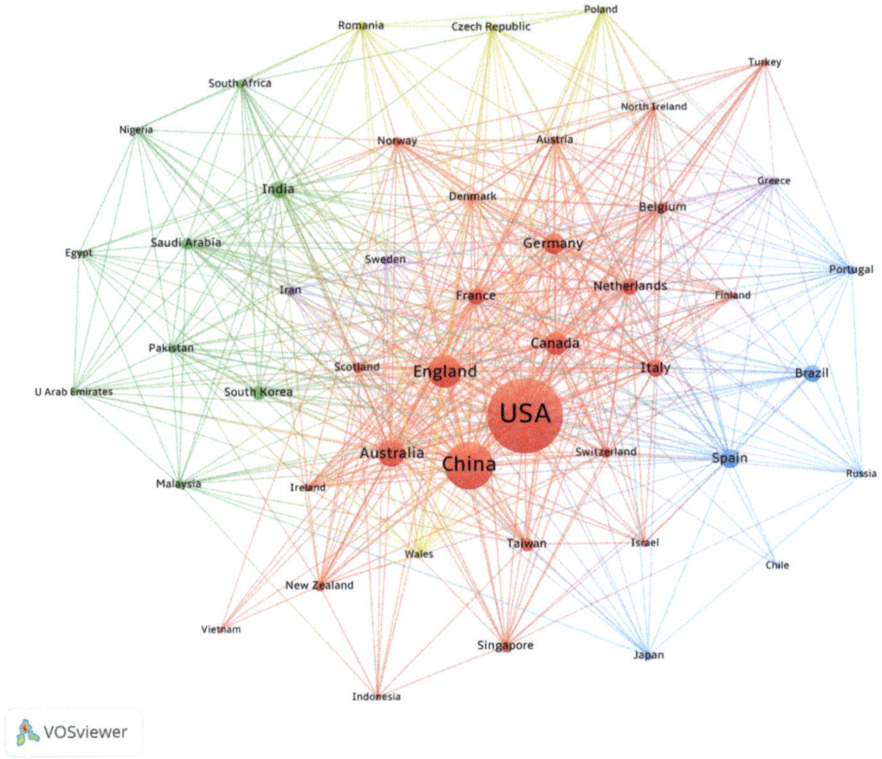

Fig. 2.2 Co-occurrence network visualization of countries based on publication output

whole time period into three distinct periods: 2000–2011, 2012–2021, and 2022–2024. During the first phase, the United States maintained an overwhelmingly dominant position. In the second phase, European countries such as Sweden and the Netherlands experienced exponential growth in literature citations. The third phase witnessed the emergence of developing nations including China, Vietnam, Egypt, and Thailand as significant academic contributors, markedly enhancing their scholarly influence.

2.4.3 Distribution of Journals and Research Domains

The corpus of international financial fraud research is distributed across 1749 journals, with an average publication output of 3.45 articles per journal. Among these, 236 journals have published five or more articles on this research theme. According to the number of publication output, the top ten most prolific journals in this field includes Journal of Business Ethics (158 articles), Accounting Review (119 articles), IEEE Access (91 articles), Contemporary Accounting Research (84 articles),

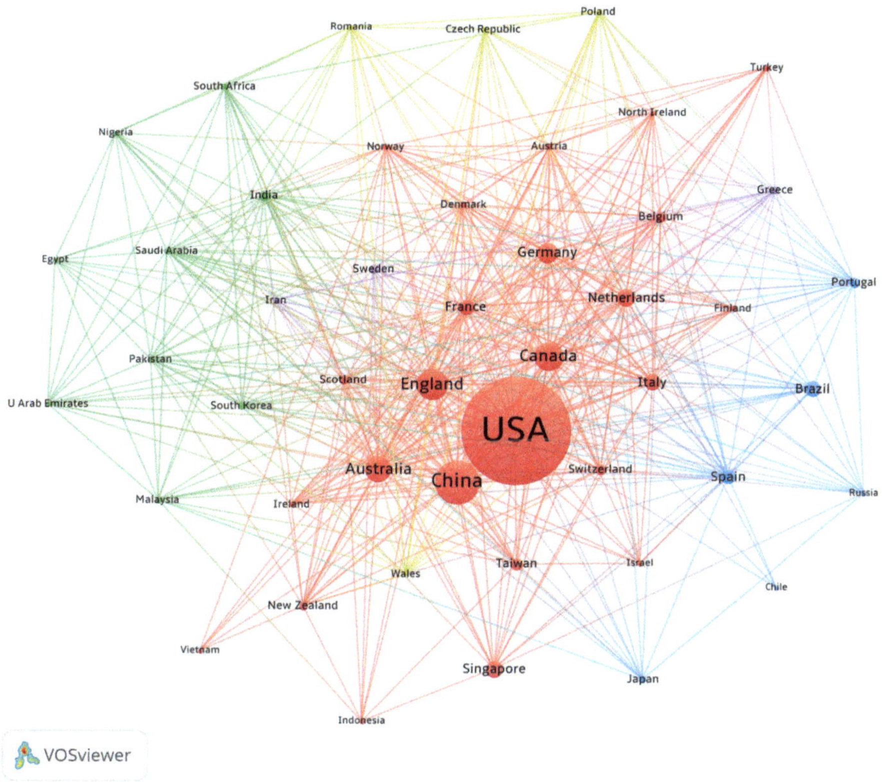

Fig. 2.3 Co-occurrence network visualization of countries based on citations

Auditing-A Journal of Practice & Theory (80 articles), Accounting Horizons (62 articles), Expert Systems with Applications (55 articles), Sustainability (50 articles), Journal of Accounting Research (49 articles), and Accounting, Organizations and Society (42 articles). The research content primarily falls within the domains of accounting, auditing, business ethics, engineering technology, artificial intelligence, and sustainable development. This distribution reflects an interdisciplinary convergence trend that builds upon traditional accounting and auditing foundations while being enhanced by artificial intelligence technologies. Table 2.2 shows the list of research domains accounting for more than 1% of total publications. 30.6% of English papers are categorized under Business & Economics, followed by Computer Science (6.3%), Government & Law (5.9%) and Criminology & Penology (4.4%).

The Chinese financial fraud research is distributed across 20 journals, with an average publication output of 23 articles per journal. Each of these journals has published five or more articles on this subject matter. Accounting Research leads with 40 publications, followed by Journal of Shanxi University of Finance and Economics

Fig. 2.4 Top 25 countries with the strongest citation bursts. *Notes* Top 20 countries with the strongest citation bursts by CiteSpace. Each rectangle represents a year. Green rectangles indicate the time interval, and red rectangles indicate the duration of the burst from the beginning to the end

(33 articles) and Auditing Research (29 articles). Additionally, numerous influential research in this domain has been published in Statistics & Decision (16 articles), Auditing & Economic Research (14 articles), Management World (7 articles), and Journal of Management Sciences in China (5 articles). Figure 2.5 depicts the disciplinary distribution of CSSCI-indexed literature. The research in this database

Table 2.2 Distribution of research areas in English Literature

Research areas	Count	Proportion (%)
Business and Economics	1565	30.6
Computer Science	323	6.3
Government and Law	299	5.9
Criminology and Penology	224	4.4
Business and Economics; Social Sciences - Other Topics	188	3.7
Food Science and Technology	148	2.9
Computer Science; Engineering; Telecommunications	106	2.1
Science and Technology - Other Topics	81	1.6
Computer Science; Engineering	78	1.5
Psychology	71	1.4
Business and Economics; Public Administration	68	1.3
Computer Science; Engineering; Operations Research and Management Science	55	1.1

is predominantly concentrated in the domain of management, encompassing sub-disciplines such as business economics (197 articles/21.74%), accounting (173 articles/19.09%), finance (116 articles/12.8%), investment (114 articles/12.58%), securities (108 articles/11.92%), and auditing (62 articles/6.84%). Meanwhile, a smaller proportion of research has been published in the domains of automation technology, law, and media and communication.

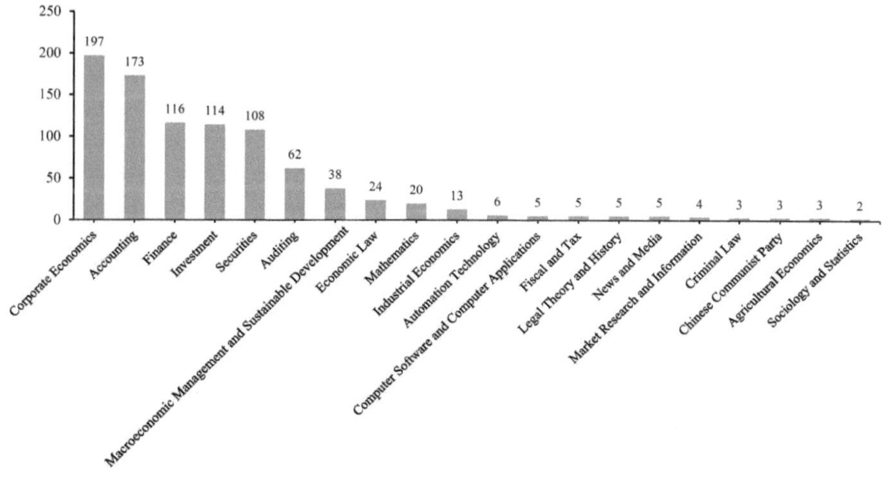

Fig. 2.5 Disciplinary distribution of CSSCI literature

2.4.4 Distribution of Institution

This section analyzes publication output, collaboration relationships, and total citation frequencies for 3905 institutions involved in financial fraud research from the international level. Table 2.3 presents detailed data for the top 20 institutions ranked by total publication output. First, in terms of publication volume, the differences between institutions are relatively small, ranging between 30 and 50 papers. Among the top 10 institutions by publication count, Arizona State University with 49 publications, Indiana University with 47, and University of Illinois with 46 are top three institutions and they are all from the United States. Only two institutions out of ten are from China: Shanghai Jiao Tong University and Xiamen University, both with 32 publications. Meanwhile, three institutions are from Australia: University of Portsmouth (37), Monash University (37), and Macquarie University (34). The remaining institutions are all from the United States. Regarding citation frequency, University of Washington (USA), despite ranking only 11th in publication count, accumulatively received 5024 citations, demonstrating the remarkable research impact far exceeding other institutions in the financial fraud domain. American institutions maintain absolute advantage in terms of research influence. Only Hong Kong Polytechnic University and Shanghai Jiao Tong University show strong international competitiveness when considering citation frequency, ranking 8th and 14th respectively. Especially the Hong Kong Polytechnic University has achieved 1796 citations based on only 32 publications, indicating high publication quality. In terms of collaborative relationships, the top three institutions are University of Chicago, University of Washington, and Texas A&M University. Overall, international financial fraud research is predominantly conducted by institutions from the United States, followed by China and Australia.

We further select 45 institutions with more than 26 publications from all 3905 institutions to generate an institutional co-occurrence network as illustrated in Fig. 2.6. These 45 institutions are comprised by 29 (64.44%) from the United States, 7 (15.56%) from China, and 6 (13.3%) from Australia. Notably, publications from Chinese institutions are predominantly concentrated after the year of 2019. The Chinese institutions ranked by publication volume are Shanghai Jiao Tong University, Xiamen University, Tongji University, City University of Hong Kong, Hong Kong Polytechnic University, Southwestern University of Finance and Economics, and Sun Yat-sen University in sequence. When ranked by total citation count, the order shifts to: Hong Kong Polytechnic University, Shanghai Jiao Tong University, Sun Yat-sen University, Southwestern University of Finance and Economics, City University of Hong Kong, Tongji University, and Xiamen University.

Figure 2.7 presents density visualizations based on citation volume and publication count, where darker regions indicate higher concentrations of publications or citations. This visualization further confirms that while publication volumes across institutions show minimal variance (as shown in the right picture), citation metrics demonstrate significant disparities (as shown in the left picture). Institutions such as the University of Washington, Texas A&M University, and the University of Chicago

Table 2.3 Institutional publication output, citation frequency, and collaboration analysis

Rank	Organization	Documents	Citations	Total link strength
1	Arizona State Univ	49	1481	14
2	Indiana Univ	47	2244	19
3	Univ Illinois	46	1693	15
4	Texas A&M Univ	45	3438	19
5	Univ Texas Austin	42	2033	19
6	Univ Chicago	41	2411	23
7	Michigan State Univ	40	1498	13
8	Univ Portsmouth	38	781	2
9	Monash Univ	38	637	16
10	Harvard Univ	37	2345	13
11	Univ Washington	36	5024	20
12	Univ Penn	36	1778	11
13	Macquarie Univ	34	722	7
14	Univ Minnesota	33	1788	9
15	Univ Michigan	33	1705	8
16	Univ Alabama	33	1264	5
17	Shanghai Jiao Tong Univ	32	1620	15
18	Northeastern Univ	32	1424	12
19	Univ Nevada	32	582	10
20	Xiamen Univ	32	507	7

exhibit substantially higher research impact than other institutions, appearing as deep red regions in the density visualization.

2.4.5 Co-Authorship Network Analysis

International research on financial fraud began in 1992 when AUDITCHECK, a statistical-based hybrid "neural network" microcomputer system are firstly introduced and utilized by accounting firms to analyze financial statements of audited companies (Marose et al. 1992). This system is essentially a model that verified the consistency of reconciliation relationships between income and balance sheet accounts. In 1995, Hill first demonstrated the validity of applying Benford's Law to accounting data for fraud detection. In the same year, Coakley pioneered the application of Artificial Neural Network (ANN) technology for pattern recognition in audit signals generated during analytical procedures. This approach enabled more reliable detection of significant errors while providing reasonable explanations

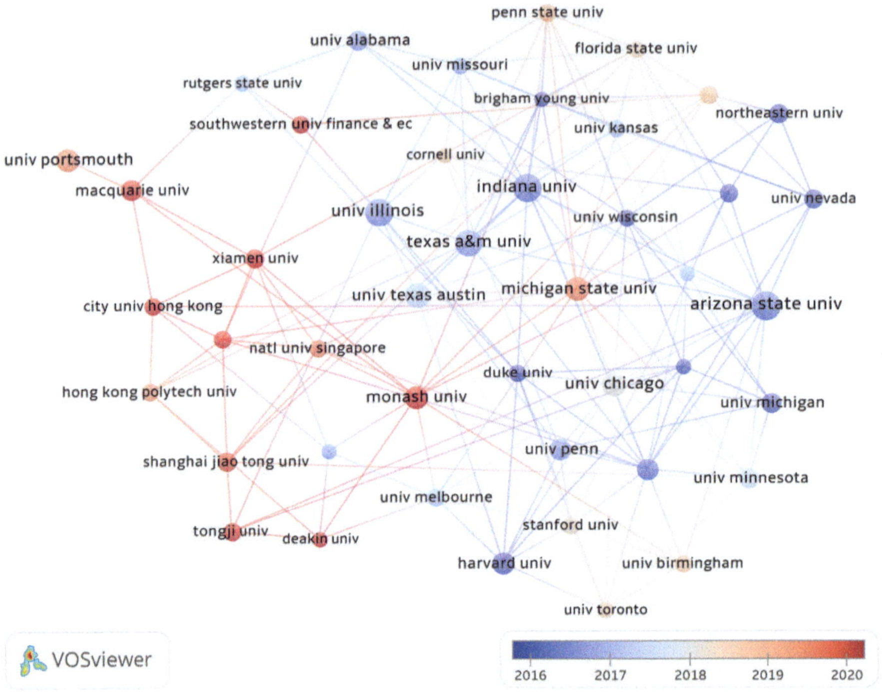

Fig. 2.6 Institutional co-occurrence network

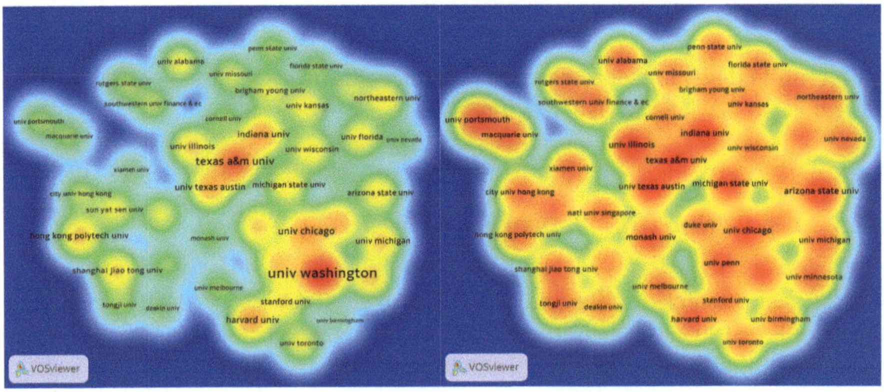

Fig. 2.7 Institutional density visualization based on citations (left) and publications (right)

for discrepancies, thus enhancing the performance of identifying material misstatements in financial accounts. Hansen et al. (1996) employed a generalized qualitative-response model (EGB2) comprising probit and logit models to assist auditors in assessing fraud risks during audit planning. They emphasized that failure to predict fraud when present (Type II error) typically resulted in exceedingly high litigation costs for companies. Davis et al. (1997), in an article published in the European Journal of Operational Research, first applied Artificial Intelligence (AI) techniques by integrating Expert Systems (ES) and Neural Networks (NN) to assist auditors in evaluating audit risk. The Accounting Review published two seminal articles in financial fraud in 1998 that first explored the relationships between fraud and auditor litigation (Bonner et al. 1998) and insider trading (Summers and Sweeney 1998). Early fraud research primarily focused on audit risk (Houston et al. 1999).

Figure 2.8 presents the co-authorship network of researchers who have published articles on financial fraud topics in international journals, which effectively captures the distribution nature of research efforts in this domain. This visualization illustrates collaboration networks among highly productive authors, where node size represents publication volume, connecting lines indicate collaborative relationships, and line thickness reflects collaboration intensity. The network analysis reveals that international scholars conducting financial fraud research predominantly organize into small team rather than big team. The academic landscape in this field is characterized by numerous but fragmented research teams, with no evident economies of scale yet emerging.

To provide a more detailed illustration, we examine several small but exemplary research teams that have made significant contributions to the field of financial fraud research. First, Professor Dain C. Donelson's team from the University of Wisconsin-Madison represents a notable collaborative cluster, having published 13 relevant articles between 2015 and 2024 with 248 total citations. Eight of these publications appeared in premier accounting journals including Review of Accounting Studies, Contemporary Accounting Research, and Accounting Review. Their research primarily examines financial statement fraud from the perspective of enforcement actions such as securities litigation and tax prosecution. Another significant group is led by Marguerite DeLiema from the University of Minnesota Twin Cities, with 14 publications focusing on financial fraud risks targeting elderly populations. Additionally, Dan Amiram's team from Tel Aviv University concentrates on measuring the magnitude of financial statement error and gains from financial statement misconduct. Their three high-quality studies have all been published in the top-tier journal Reviews of Accounting Studies, accumulating 266 citations.

The research team led by Mark Cecchini at Consiglio Nazionale delle Ricerche (CNR) published two foundational articles in the financial fraud domain in 2010, which are published in Management Science and Decision Support Systems respectively and have garnered 345 cumulative citations. Their pioneering works introduced support vector machine kernel functions for financial applications and first incorporated textual data from Management Discussion and Analysis (MD&A) sections into fraud detection datasets, aiming at enhancing the accuracy of financial fraud detection (Cecchini et al. 2010a, b). Patricia M. Dechow's research team at the University of Southern California focuses on earnings management and methods for detecting or predicting material accounting misstatements. Their research published in The Accounting Review and Journal of Accounting Research has accumulated an impressive 6205 citations. The team led by Johan L. Perols from the University of

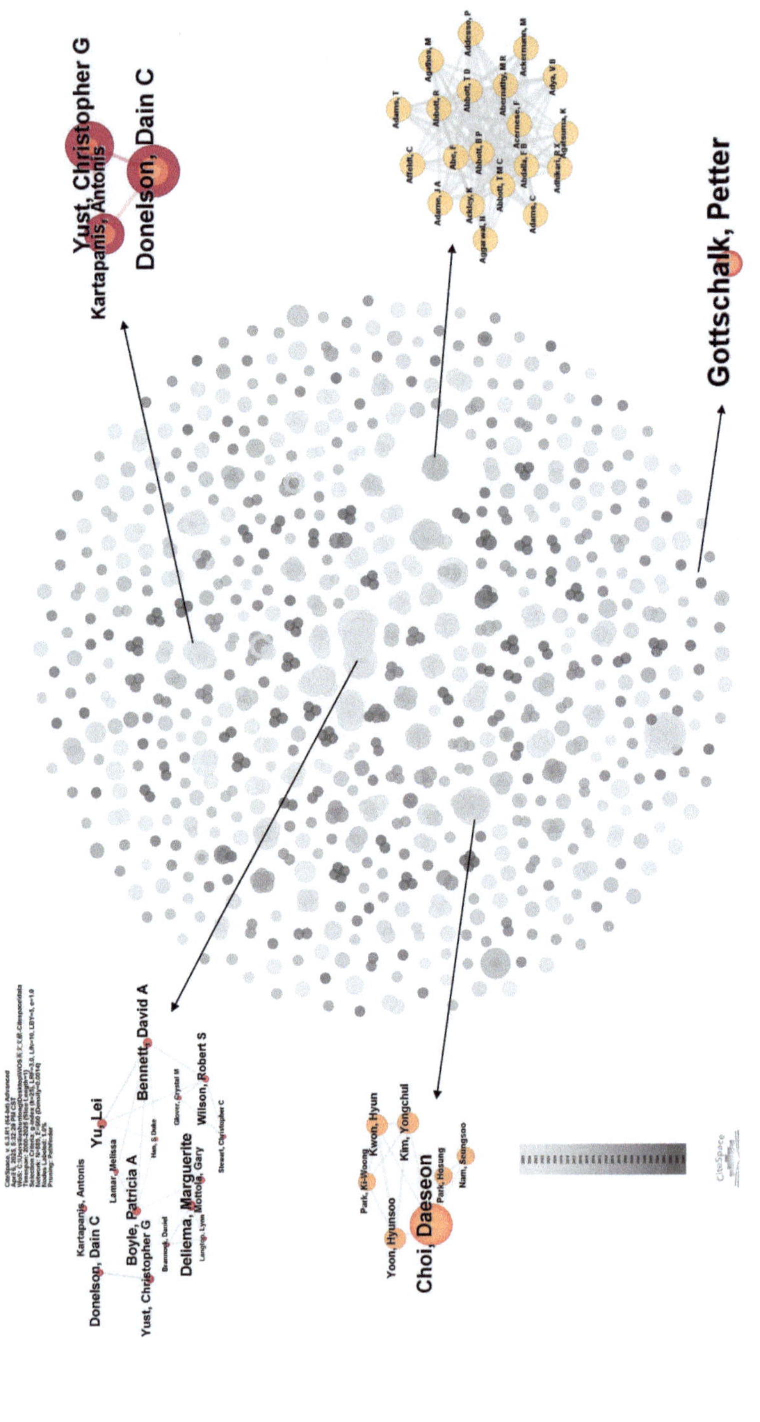

Fig. 2.8 Co-authorship network of financial fraud research in international journals

San Diego deeply investigates the relationship between earnings management and financial statement fraud, employing statistical and machine learning methods to detect fraudulent financial statements and comparing their performance comprehensively. Jonathan M. Karpoff's team from the University of Washington has published seven articles exploring various types of financial misconduct, their proxy variables, databases, and the impact of financial fraud on stock markets. Their work appears exclusively in leading finance and accounting journals, including Journal of Finance, Management Science, Review of Accounting Studies, The Accounting Review, Journal of Financial Economics, and Journal of Corporate Finance, accumulating 1700 citations.

In 2018, Wei Dong from the University of Science and Technology of China collaborated with Professor Zhongju Zhang from Arizona State University to publish "Leveraging Financial Social Media Data for Corporate Fraud Detection" in the Journal of Management Information Systems. Their research expanded traditional fraud detection databases by incorporating financial social media data, garnering 140 citations for this single publication. Professor Yang Bao from the Antai College of Economics and Management at Shanghai Jiao Tong University published a highly influential article in the Journal of Accounting Research in 2020. This study employed machine learning methods to develop state-of-the-art fraud prediction models for identifying financial fraud among U.S. public companies, accumulating 202 citations to date.

2.4.6 Citation Analysis

Financial fraud research encompasses various research objects including earnings management, financial statement preparation, internal control, and corporate governance. It employs computer technology, econometric models, and expert experience as methods or tools for fraud detection, ultimately aiming to achieve early warning and identification of fraudulent financial behavior. References constitute the core knowledge foundation of one research. Setting the minimum citation threshold at 75, 50 articles out of 199,170 cited works meet this criterion. After removing entries with missing values, 46 articles with more than 75 citations are retained to construct the co-citation network shown in Fig. 2.9. Table 2.4 presents information about the top 20 most-cited references, including titles, authors, and publication dates, providing readers with a comprehensive understanding of the foundational literature in this domain. Highly cited literature primarily addresses conceptual definitions, measurement methods, databases, detection techniques, influencing factors, and economic and social costs of financial fraud through numerous empirical studies investigating important explanatory variables such as executive compensation, corporate litigation, stock price volatility, and audit quality, all of which have significantly advanced the development of financial fraud research.

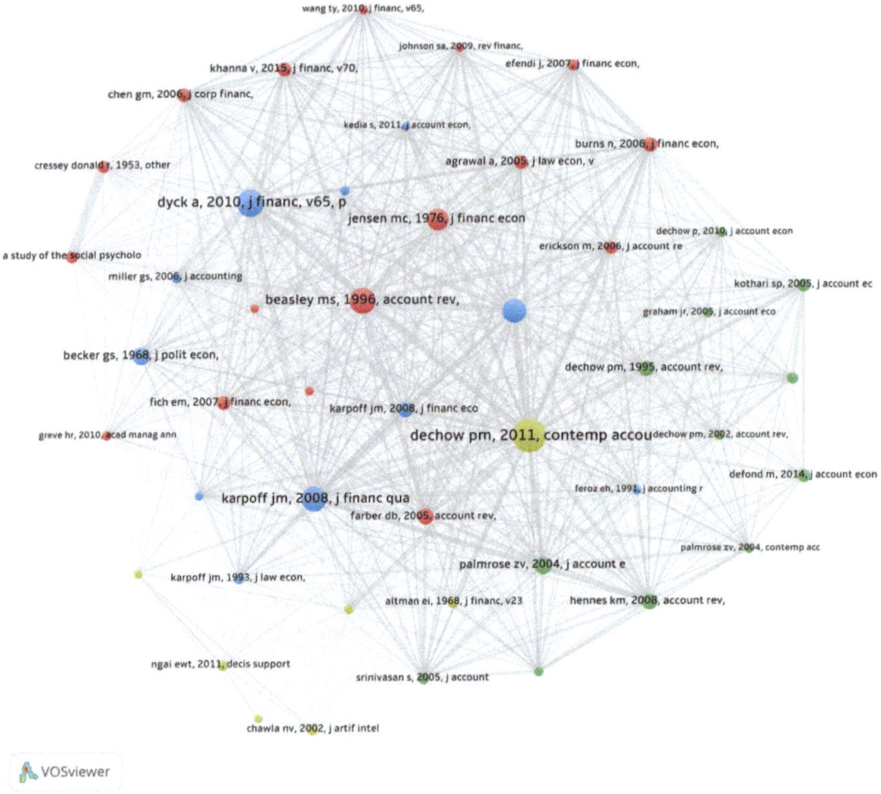

Fig. 2.9 Co-citation network of references in international financial fraud research

2.4.7 *Keywords Co-Occurrence and Clustering Analysis*

Next, this chapter conducts a co-occurrence and clustering analysis of keywords in financial fraud research, with results shown in Fig. 2.10. Modularity Q, a network modularity evaluation metric, indicates significant clustering structure when $Q > 0.3$. The Silhouette index evaluates the reliability of clustering results, with values > 0.7 representing highly reliable clustering. In our analysis, Modularity $Q = 0.3844$ and Silhouette $= 0.7787$, indicating that the co-occurrence network clustering has excellent structure and validity.

Based on high-frequency keywords (Table 2.5) and the clustering map, financial fraud research can be classified into five major categories:

(1) Financial Fraud Detection Methods

Representative words in Clusters #2 and #4 include audit planning, professional skepticism, fraud risk, decision making, auditor liability, machine learning, artificial intelligence, anomaly detection, data models, classification algorithms, deep

Table 2.4 Top 20 cited references by international papers

Rank	Cited reference	Google citation	WOS citations	Total link strength	Title	Journal
1	Dechow et al. (2011)	2668	284	1400	Predicting material accounting misstatements	Contemporary accounting research
2	Dyck et al. (2010)	2498	234	1061	Who blows the whistle on corporate fraud?	The Journal of Finance
3	Beasley (1996)	7393	215	1147	An empirical analysis of the relation between the board of director composition and financial statement fraud	Accounting Review
4	Karpoff et al. (2008)	1742	213	1163	The cost to firms of cooking the books	Journal of financial and quantitative analysis
5	Dechow et al. (1996)	6968	204	1284	Causes and consequences of earnings manipulation: An analysis of firms subject to enforcement actions by the SEC	Contemporary accounting research
6	Jensen and Ruback (1983)	8290	182	719	The market for corporate control: The scientific evidence	Journal of Financial economics
7	Becker (1968)	27,738	155	500	Crime and punishment: An economic approach	Journal of Political Economy
8	Palmrose (2004)	1777	143	839	Determinants of market reactions to restatement announcements	Journal of accounting and economics
9	Farber (2005)	1893	136	803	Restoring trust after fraud: Does corporate governance matter?	The Accounting Review
10	Karpoff et al. (2008)	1014	133	782	The consequences to managers for financial misrepresentation	Journal of Financial Economics

(continued)

Table 2.4 (continued)

Rank	Cited reference	Google citation	WOS citations	Total link strength	Title	Journal
11	Hennes et al. (2008)	1218	130	790	The importance of distinguishing errors from irregularities in restatement research: The case of restatements and CEO/CFO turnover	The Accounting Review
12	Dechow, et al. (1995)	16,063	129	649	Detecting earnings management	Accounting Review
13	Burns and Kedia (2006)	1889	122	804	The impact of performance-based compensation on misreporting	Journal of financial economics
14	Fich and Shivdasani (2007)	1357	118	666	Financial fraud, director reputation, and shareholder wealth	Journal of financial Economics
15	Chen et al. (2006)	1436	117	600	Ownership structure, corporate governance, and fraud: Evidence from China	Journal of corporate finance
16	Agrawal and Chadha (2005)	2725	115	771	Corporate governance and accounting scandals	The Journal of Law and Economics
17	Khanna, et al. (2015)	760	115	639	CEO connectedness and corporate fraud	The Journal of Finance
18	Kothari et al. (2005)	10,570	113	550	Performance matched discretionary accrual measures	Journal of accounting and economics
19	DeFond and Zhang. (2014)	4087	110	322	A review of archival auditing research	Journal of accounting and economics
20	Erickson et al. (2006)	1111	108	763	Is there a link between executive equity incentives and accounting fraud?	Journal of accounting research

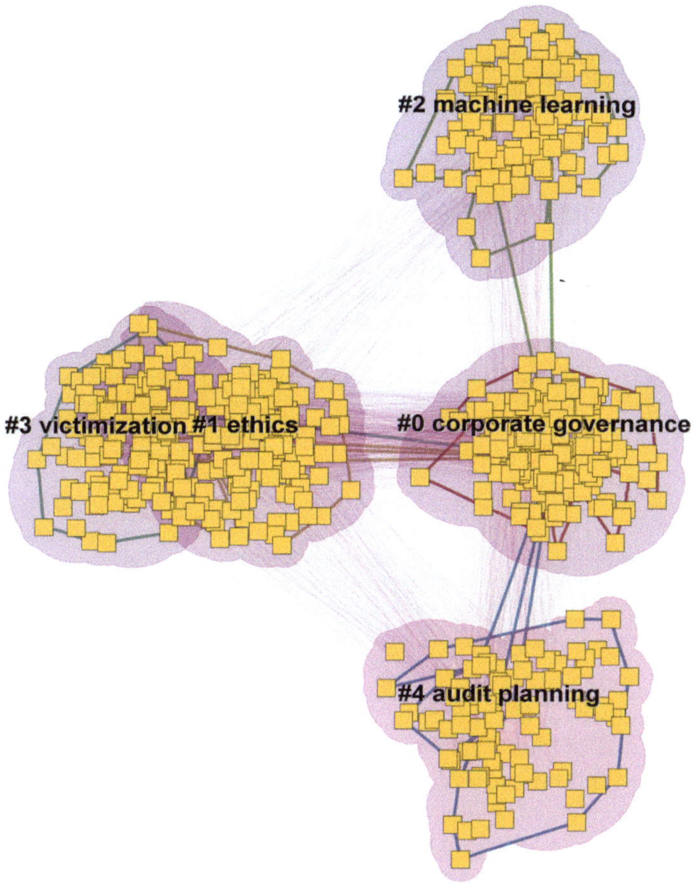

Fig. 2.10 Keyword clustering map of researches on financial fraud in international journals

learning, blockchain technology, real-time systems, and feature extraction. These clusters primarily focus on detection methods for financial fraud. Early research treated financial fraud in public companies as a source of audit risk, requiring auditors to implement professional audit procedures to identify potential fraudulent financial activities and fulfill their audit responsibilities. This process mainly relied on work experience and professional judgment of auditors. Over time, detection methods for financial fraud have become more diverse, with data-based anomaly detection methods gradually gaining prominence, including artificial intelligence technologies such as machine learning and deep learning.

(2) Concept and Origins of Financial Fraud

Representative terms in Clusters #1 and #3 include corporate misconduct, whistle-blower programs, gambling attitudes, audit committee, risk factors, financial exploitation, white-collar crime, regulation, misconduct, materiality, and financial

Table 2.5 Keywords of financial fraud from international journals

KeyWords	Count	KeyWords	Count	KeyWords	Count	KeyWords	Count
Corporate governance	343	Governance	189	Compensation	115	Decision making	81
Impact	331	Consequences	179	Ownership	110	Law	81
Performance	326	Machine learning	177	Classification	109	Perceptions	79
Quality	289	Behavior	154	Misconduct	106	Cost	72
Fraud detection	283	Crime	143	Corporate fraud	98	Corporate social responsibility	71
Management	253	Determinants	139	Reputation	95	Internal control	69
Earnings management	241	Market	136	Identification	93	Deep learning	69
Information	228	Incentives	136	Organizations	88	Corruption	68
Risk	217	Financial fraud	132	Board	85	Directors	67
Model	212	Disclosure	128	Firm performance	85	Trust	67

crime. These clusters define what constitutes financial fraud while explaining the fundamental causes of fraudulent financial behavior. The definition of financial fraud derives from legal norms and auditing practices, though no consistent authoritative definition has yet emerged. While moral and legal constraints can effectively inhibit fraudulent behavior, the combined influence of factors such as "motivation/pressure," "excuses/rationalization," and "opportunity" can still lead to the occurrence of fraud. This research stream has developed classic theoretical frameworks explaining the behavioral logic of financial fraud, including the Fraud Triangle theory, the GONE (Greed, Opportunity, Need, Exposure) theory, the Diamond theory, the Pentagon theory, and the Hexagon theory.

(3) Financial Fraud and Corporate Governance

Representative terms in Cluster #0 include corporate governance, compensation, costs, corporate fraud, financial constraints, short selling, and management emphasis. Financial fraud behavior typically occurs at the company level, with publicly listed companies being the primary research subjects in this field. Existing research confirms that financial fraud risk can affect corporate performance indicators such as company reputation, stock prices, and financing costs. Meanwhile, corporate governance indicators significantly influence the frequency of financial fraud, specifically including management ownership percentage, equity balance, property rights nature, internal controls, internal control quality, personal ethics, and executive compensation.

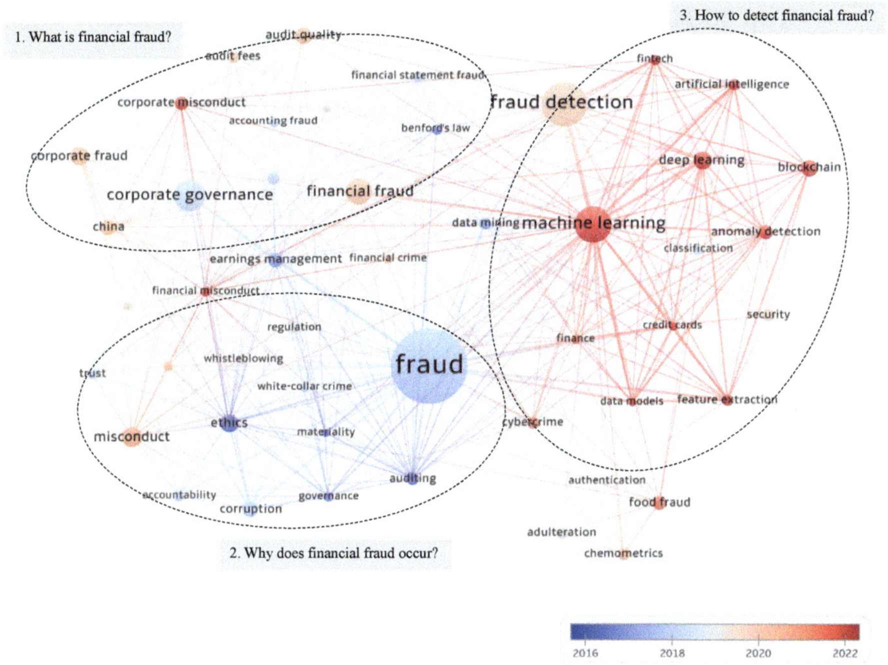

Fig. 2.11 Co-occurrence network map of keywords in international financial fraud research

Furthermore, we selected 49 keywords with frequencies exceeding 28 occurrences to establish a co-occurrence network, as shown in Fig. 2.11, with clustering results largely consistent with Fig. 2.10. Additionally, we created a keyword burst map to explore changing research trends in this field. Figure 2.12 displays the top 30 keywords with the highest burst strength and their corresponding time spans. Before 2020, research content emphasized audit experience, legal provisions, policy systems, and enterprise management, with detection methods primarily focused on traditional data analysis. After 2020, there has been greater emphasis on emerging research points such as integrated development of algorithmic models, the functional role of social media, and corporate and individual social responsibility, placing higher demands on computer skills and professional knowledge of scholars in this field.

2.5 Summary

As global financial markets continue to evolve, there is growing recognition of the importance of financial risk management. Financial fraud early warning systems, functioning as risk discovery mechanisms, enable companies to anticipate and address potential financial misconduct. This chapter aims to explore research concept

Top 30 Keywords with the Strongest Citation Bursts

Keywords	Year	Strength	Begin	End
act	2000	9.43	**2000**	2015
experience	2000	8.32	**2000**	2013
judgments	2002	8.81	**2002**	2015
accounting restatements	2003	9.34	**2003**	2017
corporate governance	2002	5.52	**2006**	2010
litigation	2007	10.37	**2007**	2017
data mining	2007	5.8	**2007**	2015
empirical analysis	2009	6.2	**2009**	2018
compensation	2006	7.23	**2010**	2015
politics	2010	5.29	**2010**	2016
equity incentives	2011	6.1	**2011**	2015
behavior	2002	5.71	**2011**	2017
law	2008	9.89	**2013**	2018
audit committee	2002	5.76	**2017**	2019
research misconduct	2018	5.74	**2018**	2021
system	2016	5.26	**2019**	2022
algorithm	2020	7.19	**2020**	2023
deep learning	2020	5.4	**2020**	2025
victims	2021	7.52	**2021**	2025
social media	2021	5.91	**2021**	2025
professional skepticism	2017	5.11	**2021**	2022
feature extraction	2021	6.01	**2022**	2025
media	2022	5.46	**2022**	2025
credit card fraud detection	2023	8.27	**2023**	2025
artificial intelligence	2020	6.8	**2023**	2025
smote	2023	6.69	**2023**	2025
graph neural network	2023	5.84	**2023**	2025
responsibility	2019	5.48	**2023**	2025
social responsibility	2020	5.47	**2023**	2025
ensemble learning	2023	5.15	**2023**	2025

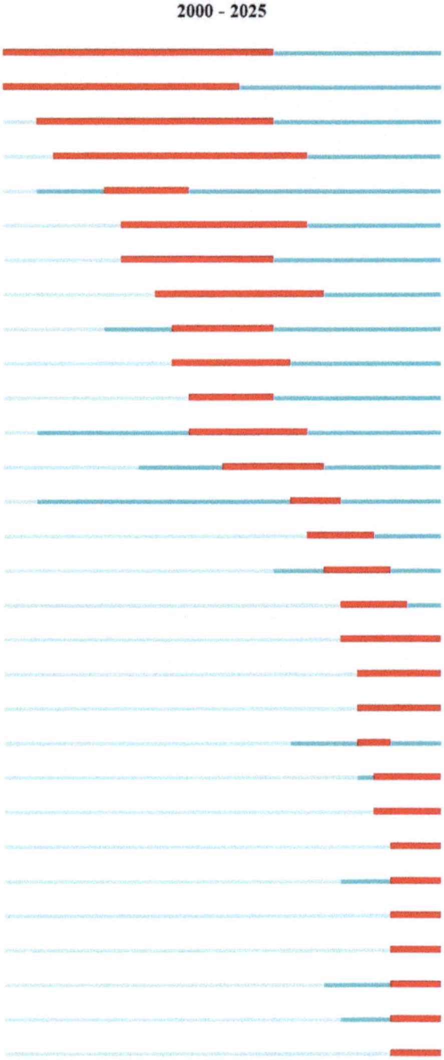

Fig. 2.12 Top 30 keywords with the strongest citation bursts

hotspots and the evolution of research directions in financial risk management and early fraud detection through bibliometric analysis. The academic literature review focused on English publications indexed in the Web of Science (WOS) database between 2000 and 2025. Bibliometric analysis and network mapping of selected articles were conducted using CiteSpace and VOSviewer software, providing a comprehensive analysis of the current state and academic evolution of financial fraud research while highlighting significant trends and future directions.

This study reveals a transition in financial fraud detection methods from traditional statistical approaches to advanced machine learning and AI technologies. Neural networks, random forests, and XGBoost have emerged as key technologies for establishing classification/detection/warning systems and implementing big data analysis, data mining, and text mining. Innovations such as attention mechanisms and LSTM models have improved detection accuracy. Future research will further incorporate and integrate external environmental factors including policy elements, legal environments, social responsibility factors, and media supervision to promote comprehensive risk management. Additionally, the research emphasizes the importance of interdisciplinary collaboration and advanced data analytics in this field. Moving forward, scholars should enhance their skill levels, improve their understanding of how recent disruptive technological developments affect finance, and elevate the quality of research in this domain.

References

Bahoo S, Cucculelli M, Goga X, Mondolo J (2024) Artificial intelligence in finance: a comprehensive review through bibliometric and content analysis. SN Bus Econ 4(2):23

Bonner SE, Palmrose ZV, Young SM (1998) Fraud type and auditor litigation: an analysis of SEC accounting and auditing enforcement releases. Account Rev 73:503–532

Cecchini M, Aytug H, Koehler GJ, Pathak P (2010a) Detecting management fraud in public companies. Manag Sci 56(7):1146–1160

Cecchini M, Aytug H, Koehler GJ, Pathak P (2010b) Making words work: using financial text as a predictor of financial events. Decis Support Syst 50(1):164–175

Chen C, Zhang J, Vogeley M (2010) Making sense of the evolution of a scientific domain: a visual analytic study of the Sloan Digital Sky Survey research. Scientometrics 83(3):669–688

Darmawati D, Mediawati E, Dewi ARS (2025) Bibliometric analysis of digital financial reporting: a comprehensive review of research trends and emerging topics. J Bus Econ Manag 26(1):49–68

Davis JT, Massey AP, Lovell RE II (1997) Supporting a complex audit judgment task: an expert network approach. Eur J Oper Res 103(2):350–372

Hansen JV, McDonald JB, Messier WF Jr, Bell TB (1996) A generalized qualitative-response model and the analysis of management fraud. Manag Sci 42(7):1022–1032

Houston RW, Peters MF, Pratt JH (1999) The audit risk model, business risk and audit-planning decisions. Account Rev 74(3):281–298

Marose RA, Rothenberg D, Sankaran S (1992) Knowledge based decision support system for accounting auditors. In T. Jelassi, MR. Klein, & WM. Mayon-White (Eds.), Decision Support Systems: Experiences and Expectations (pp. 201–213). North-Holland

Summers SL, Sweeney JT (1998) Fraudulently misstated financial statements and insider trading: an empirical analysis. Account Rev 73:131–146

Chapter 3
The Definition of Financial Fraud

3.1 Definition of Financial Fraud

The global economy faces unprecedented risks due to a series of "black swan" and "gray rhino" events, including the COVID-19 pandemic, the Russia-Ukraine conflict, and global debt peaks. The heightened uncertainty in the economic environment has increased the likelihood of businesses falling into financial distress, which in turn can trigger financial fraud. There is a close relationship between financial distress and financial fraud, as Companies experiencing financial distress often have the "Pressure", as illustrated in the Fraud Triangle Theory, to manipulate financial statements to present a more favorable financial performance. Cao et al. (2023) studied the relationship between financing constraints and financial fraud, finding that firms with limited access to financing are more likely to commit fraud and less likely to be detected. Rosner (2003) examined 293 bankrupt U.S. firms and found that manipulative activities, including not only accounting and revenue manipulation but also business fabrication significantly increased within the five years prior to bankruptcy.

Habib et al. (2013) analyzed financial distress among New Zealand firms during the global financial crisis and discovered that managers often overconfident to window dressing financial statements to navigate temporary financial difficulties. However, as financial conditions continued to deteriorate, managers realized that short-term earnings management could no longer resolve the current financial distress and they then resorted to financial fraud, which was more likely to occur in small and medium-sized enterprises (SMEs). Specifically, there is a positive relationship between the degree of financial distress and the occurrence likelihood, severity and concealment of fraudulent activities. Perols and Lougee (2011) further demonstrated that fraudulent firms are more likely to engage in earnings management. Overall, financial distress and financial stability significantly influence financial fraud.

Kukreja et al. (2020) examined the effectiveness of the Beneish M-score and Altman Z-score models to detect material misstatement, finding that the financial distress index of Altman Z-score is more effective than the fraud index of Beneish

X. Ma and D. Wu, *Financial Fraud Detection Using Machine Learning*, AI for Risks,
https://doi.org/10.1007/978-981-95-0840-2_3

M-score in financial fraud detection. Additionally, Aviantara (2023) observed that companies classified into the safe zone based on the Altman Z-score have lower the Beneish M-score and Dechow F-score, indicating that financially healthy firms have a significantly lower probability of committing fraud. When firms enter financial distress, the barriers to financial fraud will diminish, which offers more opportunities for managers to engage in more aggressive accounting manipulations such as accounting restatements and financial fraud (Aviantara 2023). Based on Financial Crime Theory, Halteh and Tiwari (2023) deeply explored the vicious cycle relationship between financial distress and financial fraud. This kind of relationship is that financial distress increases the propensity for financial fraud, which, in turn, fails to eliminate negative profitability and further exacerbate financial distress. To conclude, both financial fraud and financial distress are mutually influenced as major sources of financial risk in publicly listed companies and they have biased definitions in different researches. Following we will systematically analyze the theoretical definitions and practical measurement of financial fraud and financial distress with subtle differences.

We summarized the classical definition of financial distress. As a dynamic process, financial distress is delineated by scholars with different stages, including temporary cash flow difficulties, debt default, business failure, and finally corporate bankruptcy. For example, Fisher (1933) regarded financial distress as the microeconomic driving force of systematic financial crisis, that is, companies with high debt to equity ratio may not afford their short-term liability, which will trigger repayment crisis and ultimately leads to bankruptcy. Altman (1968) only included enterprises entering statutory bankruptcy into the scope of financial distress. Gordon (1971) put forward a comprehensive financial distress theory that could explain the asset pricing, capital structure, cost analysis, and financing conditions. Carmichael (1972) combined financial distress with characters of insufficient liquidity and equity, inability to repay maturing loans, and failure to financing. Blum (1974) was the first to establish a theoretical framework for financial distress prediction and introduce cash flow to demonstrate that whether a company falls into financial distress depends on the size of current assets, the degree of debt financing, and the condition of its capital structure.

Jones and Hensher (2004) proposed that the whole process of financial distress experienced the following four stages. First, when the company is insolvent with negative book value of net assets, it enters the stage of accounting bankruptcy. Second, when the company fails to fulfill its debt obligations, named as debt default, it enters technical bankruptcy stage. Third, the company and its creditors file for bankruptcy in court, marking the stage of statutory bankruptcy. Finally, after bankruptcy liquidation, if the company remains unable to pay its creditors, it collapses. Kim and Upneja (2014) defined financial distress as the inability to meet debt obligations to creditors and suppliers. Zhang and Wang (2020) characterized financial distress as a dynamic process from a breakdown in the financial chain, debt default, to ultimately corporate bankruptcy. Wu et al. (2022) emphasized that financial distress can be predicted before the stages of insolvency and bankruptcy, since it includes several stages including financial deterioration, managerial remediation, continued deterioration, insolvency, and the declaration of bankruptcy.

The definition of financial fraud (or financial misconduct and falsification) is ambiguous in judicial and academic fields. Only when misrepresentation meets the standard of materiality, intent and economic loss simultaneously, it can be judged as financial fraud (Amiram et al. 2018). However, the corresponding judicial interpretations vary across legal and economic contexts. This section, we summarize and compare the detailed judicial interpretations of financial fraud in China and the United States respectively.

In U.S., the statutes related to financial fraud include Section 17(a) of the Securities Act of 1933, Section 10(b) of the Securities Exchange Act of 1934, Rule 10b-5 under the Securities Exchange Act, Section 13(b) of the Exchange Act, the Foreign Corrupt Practices Act (FCPA), and Case Law (Amiram et al. 2018; Klimczak et al. 2022). In Section 13(b) of the Exchange Act, financial misrepresentation is defined as a violation of the basic principle that the representation of accounting records, books, and financial statements should be accurate, reasonable, and fair to reflect real transaction. However, not all financial misrepresentations are financial fraud and only 75% of financial misrepresentation cases are enforced by the U.S. Securities and Exchange Commission (SEC) due to financial fraud from the year of 1978 to 2015 (Amiram et al. 2018). An intentional material misstatement or omission in financial statements is regarded as fraud by auditors as the provision in the Statement on Auditing Standards No. 99 (SAS 99) of the American Institute of Certified Public Accountants (AICPA) and the Auditing Standard No. 2401 (AS 2401) of Public Company Accounting Oversight Board (PCAOB). The 2023 Fraud Risk Management Guide issued by the Association of Certified Fraud Examiners (ACFE) used the similar identification criteria of financial fraud.

In Chinese Law system, the judgement criteria of financial fraud is more suitable for the local context. The 2019 revised Securities Law collectively defines false records, misleading statements and material omissions as financial misrepresentation. Provisions of the Supreme People's Court on Several Issues Concerning the Trial of Civil Compensation Cases for Misrepresentation in the Securities Market announced in 2022 gives a relatively explicit definition of financial misrepresentation as well as the standards and procedures for determining materiality, causality, fault, responsible parties, and loss assessment. Among these provisions, misleading statements and material omissions primarily refer to the concealment or omission of major events, while false records are defined as "material mis-recording of relevant financial information disclosed."

Accounting Standards regulated by the Ministry of Finance grant more discretion for financial statements preparers, allowing them to engage in certain levels of earnings management within standard permission for profit smoothing. Once the earnings management exceeds the allowable boundaries, it turns to be fraud. However, the scope of permission is hard to define, creating a gray zone between earnings management and financial misconduct. To distinguish financial fraud from earnings management, the following four elements must be satisfied for financial fraud, including materiality, intentionality, causality, and resulting economic loss.

No. 1141 of Chinese Auditing Standards for Certified Public Accountants defines financial fraud as an intentional act to obtain improper or illegal benefits through deception by management, governance, employees, or third parties of an audited entity. In auditing practice, the manipulation, falsification or alteration of accounting records and documents, the deliberate omission of significant transactions and false disclosures that lead to material misstatements in financial statements are defined as fraud by auditors. Based on the above illustration, this book explains the relation network of earnings management, financial misconduct, misrepresentation, and financial fraud, to construct a judgment process of fraudulent behavior, as shown in Fig. 3.1.

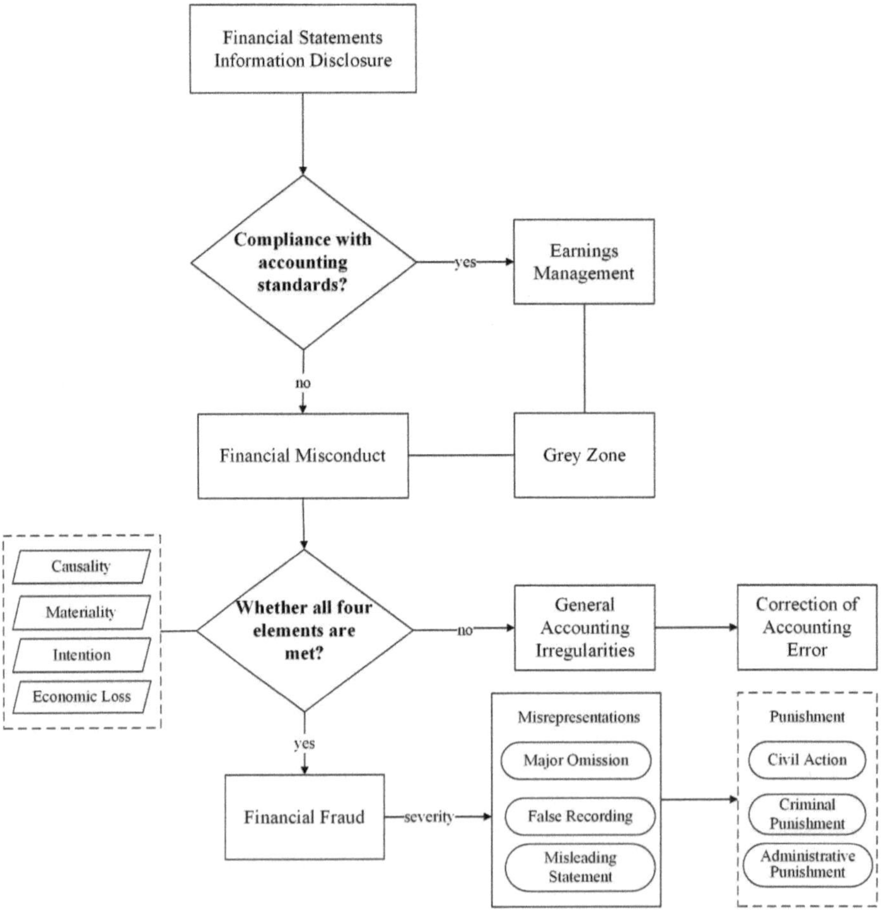

Fig. 3.1 The judgment process of financial fraud

3.2 Measurement of Financial Fraud

In addition to the ambiguous definitions of financial fraud and distress, they are also represented by various measurements in empirical studies. In terms of financial distress, the commonly used measurement is whether publicly listed companies can repay maturing debt (Beaver 1966; Mohammed 2016; Ninh et al. 2018). Additionally, financial ratios with a manually defined threshold are also used to measure financial condition of the company. For instance, Ninh et al. (2018) classified Vietnamese listed companies as financially distressed when the ratio of earnings before interest, taxes, depreciation, and amortization (EBITDA) to interest payments was less than 1, and as financially healthy when the ratio exceeded 1. Campbell et al. (2008) argued that firms experience financial distress when their net operating cash flow after interest payments is negative. Habib et al. (2013) used the indicator of working capital and net loss within one year as proxies for financial distress. Furthermore, Ni et al. (2023) enumerated various signs of financial distress by severity, including declining stock prices, asset sales-out, corporate restructure, debt restructure, and qualified audit opinions.

Moreover, other studies directly employ financial distress indices as proxy measures, such as the Altman Z-score (Altman 1968), Ohlson O-score (Ohlson 1980), and Zmijewski score (Zmijewski 1984). In international financial distress researches, "bankruptcy" related indicators are dominant identification criteria for financial distress (Altman 1968; Jones and Hensher 2004; Barboza et al. 2017). However, in China, rare of publicly listed companies declared bankruptcy. Therefore, using bankruptcy as a marker of financial distress is not entirely applicable in Chinese context. Chinese scholars widely use the label of ST (Special Treatment) or *ST as the dominant distinction criteria in empirical studies, while its accuracy as a classification tool is still under question.

In terms of financial fraud, there is significant measurement differences between China and the United States in empirical research. In the United States, the Accounting and Auditing Enforcement Releases (AAERs) issued by the Securities and Exchange Commission (SEC) is a commonly used proxy variable for financial fraud in the U.S. context (Cecchini et al. 2010; Perols et al. 2017; Bao et al. 2020). These publicly listed companies disclosed in AAERs are identified as having engaged in fraudulent activities as defined under Section 17(a) of the Securities Act of 1933, as well as Sections 13(b)(5), 13(b)(2)-1, and 10(b)-5 of the Securities Exchange Act of 1934. AAERs, as public enforcement, are always combined with private enforcement from Securities Class Actions (SCAs) to represent accounting fraud samples, and the enrichment of fraud samples will reduce both Type I and Type II errors in some degrees (Donelson et al. 2021).

Additionally, fraud information is also sourced from other prominent databases including the U.S. Government Accountability Office (GAO), the Audit Analytics (AA) and the Stanford Securities Class Action Clearinghouse (SCAC). GAO investigative reports provide valuable insights for researchers to analyze regulatory enforcement and compliance to enhance fraud detection. SCAC provides comprehensive information including detailed case summaries and litigation trends on federal securities class action lawsuits since the enactment of Private Securities Litigation Reform Act (PSLRA). The Audit Analytics (AA) database contains financial restatements with detailed information about accounting adjustments due to errors, noncompliance with accounting standards, or identification of fraudulent activities. Any research relying on single source of fraud information may suffer from sample selection bias and the integrated use of multiple databases should be encouraged to broaden the scope of fraud sample data (Karpoff et al. 2017; Blackburne et al. 2021).

Compared to the United States, China as an emerging economies with lower enforcement efficiency, has more measurement errors in fraud data (Hass et al. 2016). Their financial fraud research typically collects violations issued and penalized by regulatory agencies such as the China Securities Regulatory Commission (CSRC), the Ministry of Finance, and stock exchanges as well as media fraud reports from the WIND, CSMAR and CNRDS Database to extract fraudulent samples that meet the corresponding research definition. For example, most studies extracted five types of financial violations including profit overstatement, asset overstatement, false recordings, material omissions, and inaccurate disclosures as fraud samples (Liao et al. 2019; Li et al. 2024). Xiu et al. (2021) incorporated two additional violations, delayed disclosures and improper accounting treatments, to measure financial fraud. Qian and Luo (2015) only included false financial information disclosures and material misstatements in their financial fraud prediction research. Li et al. (2020) excluded insider trading, illegal stock trading, stock price manipulation, and unauthorized guarantees from violations issued by CSRC. Lin et al. (2015) used litigation cases suspected of fraud disclosed by Taiwan's Securities and Futures Bureau and the Securities and Futures Investors Protection Center as proxy variables for financial fraud. Ye et al. (2022) defined transaction-based and accounting-based financial fraud based on auditing standards. Ren et al. (2021), Yuan et al. (2022), and Xu et al. (2023) broadened the scope of financial fraud by utilizing risk events (Red Flags) closely linked to financial fraud as criteria for identifying fraud samples.

Based on above-mentioned financial fraud definition and measurement, the proportion of financial fraud samples in China ranges from 10 to 15%, apparently higher than the 1–3% in the United States (Liao et al. 2019). Specifically, Xu et al. (2023) reviewed related researches in China from 2009 to 2018, finding that the overall fraud rate among listed companies was approximately 12%. Chen et al. (2006) analyzed the condition of fraudulent companies across various industries in China between 1999 and 2003 and found that except for the real estate industry with an extremely high fraud rate of 21.05%, fraud rates in other industries ranged from 8.79 to 13.84%. Ren et al. (2021) examined the relationship between analyst forecasts and corporate fraud using 13,068 samples from 2008 to 2019, of which 1907 observations (14.59%) are fraud, and the highest fraud rate is 18.57% in 2018. Hass et al. (2016) studied the impact of equity incentives for managers and supervisors on corporate fraud in China and reported an actual average fraud rate of 15.1% between 2000 and 2010. Similarly, Luo et al. (2020) and Gupta et al. (2020) investigated the gender

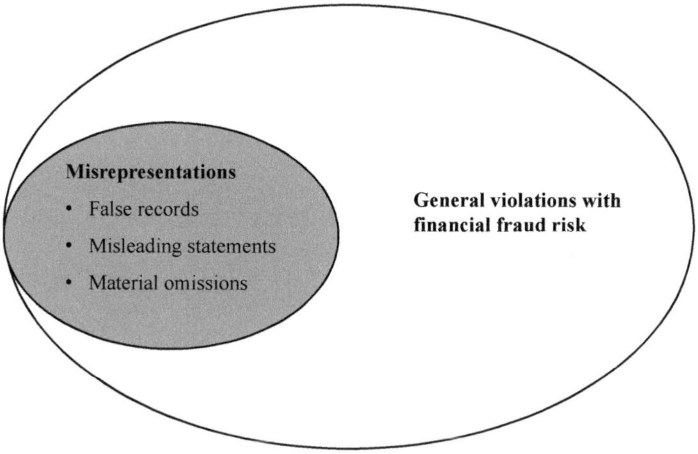

Fig. 3.2 Relationship of two types of financial fraud

influence of Chief Financial Officer (CFO) on financial fraud and used a fraud rates of 11% in their studies.

3.3 Summary

To summarize, the definition of financial fraud originates from laws and regulations, highlighting the material misstatement, intentional deception, and caused economic losses with differentiated judicial interpretations across countries. What is more, financial distress evaluating liquidity by comparing asset and liability, also a key driver of financial fraud. Both financial fraud and financial distress are important components of financial risk. In China, empirical research on financial fraud focuses on public enforcements instead of private enforcements since the private enforcement mechanism still remain in its infancy with limited data available for empirical studies. With the China-specific class action system evolving, fraud samples in China will incorporate more private enforcements.

This book aims to detect two types of "broad-to-narrow" financial fraud in Chinese listed companies. First, the broad financial fraud includes all violations penalized by the CSRC with financial fraud risk (Li et al. 2020; Ren et al. 2021; Yuan et al. 2022; Xu et al. 2023), which is used to construct a large-scale dataset for empirical analysis in Chap. 8. Second, the narrow financial fraud includes material misrepresentations with massive fine, which is used to create a smaller matched dataset in Chap. 9. The inclusion relationships among these three types of financial fraud are illustrated in Fig. 3.2.

References

Altman EI (1968) Financial ratios, discriminant analysis and the prediction of corporate bankruptcy. J Finance 23(4):589–609
Amiram D, Bozanic Z, Cox JD, Dupont Q (2018) Financial reporting fraud and other forms of misconduct: a multidisciplinary review of the literature. Rev Account Stud 23:732–783
Aviantara R (2023) Scoring the financial distress and the financial statement fraud of Garuda Indonesia with «DDCC» as the financial solutions. J Model Manag 18(1):1–16
Bao Y, Ke B, Li B, Yu YJ, Zhang J (2020) Detecting accounting fraud in publicly traded US firms using a machine learning approach. J Account Res 58(1):199–235
Barboza F, Kimura H, Altman E (2017) Machine learning models and bankruptcy prediction. Expert Syst Appl 83:405–417
Beaver WH (1966) Financial ratios as predictors of failure. J Account Res 4:71–111
Blackburne T, Kepler JD, Quinn PJ, Taylor DJ (2021) Undisclosed SEC investigations. Manag Sci 67(6):3403–3418
Blum M (1974) Failing company discriminant analysis. J Account Res 12:1–25
Campbell JY, Hilscher J, Szilagyi J (2008) In search of distress risk. J Finance 63(6):2899–2939
Cao Y, Zhang Z, Peng K, Zhou Y (2023) The establishment of circuit courts and corporate fraud. Emerg Markets Finance Trade 59:2600–2616
Carmichael DR (1972) Auditor's reports—a search for criteria. J Account 134(03):67
Cecchini M, Aytug H, Koehler GJ, Pathak P (2010) Detecting management fraud in public companies. Manage Sci 56(7):1146–1160
Chen G, Firth M, Gao DN, Rui OM (2006) Ownership structure, corporate governance, and fraud: evidence from China. J Corp Finance 12(3):424–448
Donelson DC, Kartapanis A, McInnis J, Yust CG (2021) Measuring accounting fraud and irregularities using public and private enforcement. Account Rev 96(6):183–213
Fisher I (1933) The debt-deflation theory of great depressions. Econom J Econom Soc 1:337–357
Gordon MJ (1971) Towards a theory of financial distress. J Finance 26(2):347–356
Gupta VK, Mortal S, Chakrabarty B, Guo X, Turban DB (2020) CFO gender and financial statement irregularities. Acad Manag J 63(3):802–831
Habib A, Uddin Bhuiyan B, Islam A (2013) Financial distress, earnings management and market pricing of accruals during the global financial crisis. Manag Financ 39(2):155–180
Halteh K, Tiwari M (2023) Preempting fraud: a financial distress prediction perspective on combating financial crime. J Money Laund Control 26(6):1194–1202
Hass LH, Tarsalewska M, Zhan F (2016) Equity incentives and corporate fraud in China. J Bus Ethics 138:723–742
Jones S, Hensher DA (2004) Predicting firm financial distress: a mixed logit model. Account Rev 79(4):1011–1038
Karpoff JM, Koester A, Lee DS, Martin GS (2017) Proxies and databases in financial misconduct research. Account Rev 92(6):129–163
Kim SY, Upneja A (2014) Predicting restaurant financial distress using decision tree and AdaBoosted decision tree models. Econ Model 36:354–362
Klimczak KM, Sison AJG, Prats M, Torres MB (2022) How to deter financial misconduct if crime pays? J Bus Ethics 179(1):205–222
Kukreja G, Gupta SM, Sarea AM, Kumaraswamy S (2020) Beneish M-score and Altman Z-score as a catalyst for corporate fraud detection. J Invest Compliance 21(4):231–241
Li J, Sun H, Chang Y et al (2024) Financial fraud identification considering multiple semantic associations of audit elements. J Manag Sci 27(03): 58–70
Li J, Wu Y, Lei Y, Huang Y (2020) Effective early warning indicators and artificial intelligence models for listed companies' violations based on deferred tax changes. J Financ Res 08:149–168
Liao L, Chen G, Zheng D (2019) Corporate social responsibility and financial fraud: evidence from China. Account Finance 59(5):3133–3169

Lin CC, Chiu AA, Huang SY, Yen DC (2015) Detecting the financial statement fraud: the analysis of the differences between data mining techniques and experts' judgments. Knowl-Based Syst 89:459–470

Luo J, Peng C, Zhang X (2020) The impact of CFO gender on corporate fraud: evidence from China. Pac Basin Finance J 63:101404

Mohammed S (2016) Bankruptcy prediction by using the Altman Z-score model in Oman: a case study of Raysut cement company SAOG and its subsidiaries. Australas Account Bus Finance J 10(4):70–80

Ni D, Lim MK, Li X, Pan K (2023) Monitoring corporate credit risk with multiple data sources. Ind Manag Data Syst 123(2):434–450

Ninh BPV, Do Thanh T, Hong DV (2018) Financial distress and bankruptcy prediction: an appropriate model for listed firms in Vietnam. Econ Syst 42(4):616–624

Ohlson JA (1980) Financial ratios and the probabilistic prediction of bankruptcy. J Account Res 18:109–131

Perols JL, Lougee BA (2011) The relation between earnings management and financial statement fraud. Adv Account 27(1):39–53

Perols JL, Bowen RM, Zimmermann C, Samba B (2017) Finding needles in a haystack: using data analytics to improve fraud prediction. Account Rev 92(2):221–245

Qian P, Luo M (2015) Financial fraud prediction model for Chinese listed companies. Account Res (07):18–25+96

Ren L, Zhong X, Wan L (2021) Missing analyst forecasts and corporate fraud: evidence from China. J Bus Ethics 181(1):171–194

Rosner RL (2003) Earnings manipulation in failing firms. Contemp Account Res 20(2):361–408

Wu D, Ma X, Olson DL (2022) Financial distress prediction using integrated Z-score and multilayer perceptron neural networks. Decis Support Syst 159:113814

Xiu Z, Liu R, Yin J (2021) Financial fraud, supply chain concentration and corporate trade credit financing. Account Res 01:82–99

Xu X, Xiong F, An Z (2023) Using machine learning to predict corporate fraud: evidence based on the gone framework. J Bus Ethics 186(1):137–158

Ye Q, Ye F, Huang S (2022) Construction of financial fraud identification framework: based on accounting information system theory and big data perspective. Account Res 03:3–16

Yuan X, Zhao M, Liu H et al (2022) Screening and analysis framework of rural household poverty status characteristics: discussion on rural revitalization path selection in China. Chin J Manag Sci 30(12):234–244

Zhang J, Wang D (2020) Financial distress warning: concept definition and theoretical analysis. Finance Econ 12:61–69

Zmijewski ME (1984) Methodological issues related to the estimation of financial distress prediction models. J Account Res 22:59–82

Chapter 4
The Basic Theory of Financial Fraud

The dominant directions in financial fraud detection include optimizing features, enhancing data processing, and modelling. This chapter reviews the evolution of theories of financial fraud motivation, together with fundamental accounting and management theories such as the double-entry bookkeeping and financial reporting, and the theory of accounting information systems, to systematically explore the driving force of financial fraud and extensively provide theoretical guidance for feature selection. These theories explored in this chapter is shown in Fig. 4.1.

4.1 Evolution of Fraud Motivation Theories

Generally, fraud motivation theories have evolved from the Fraud Triangle, GONE (Greed, Opportunity, Need and Exposure) Theory, Diamond Theory, Pentagon Theory, and Hexagon Theory. Firstly, the Fraud Triangle, introduced by Cressey (1953), is one of the most widely used frameworks in fraud research. In this theory, financial fraud is explained as an outcome of the interaction of Motive/Pressure, Rationalization, and Opportunity and the stability of the triangle can be disrupted by weakening the power of any factor, thereby reducing the occurrence rate of financial fraud. Among these three factors, the existence of Opportunity is the beginning point while Motive/Pressure and Rationalization further encourage fraudsters to commit fraud. Building on the Fraud Triangle, Bologna et al. (1993) introduced the GONE Theory by incorporating the factor of Exposure to account for external regulatory influences. The other three factors were defined as Greed (corresponding to Rationalization/Attitude in the Fraud Triangle), Opportunity, and Need (corresponding to Motive/Pressure in the Fraud Triangle).

In practice, when management has direct or indirect "greedy" desires for substantial wealth (e.g., performance incentives, initial public offering, or stock issuance), it generates a "Need" for fraud and their discretionary power, combined with weak

X. Ma and D. Wu, *Financial Fraud Detection Using Machine Learning*, AI for Risks,
https://doi.org/10.1007/978-981-95-0840-2_4

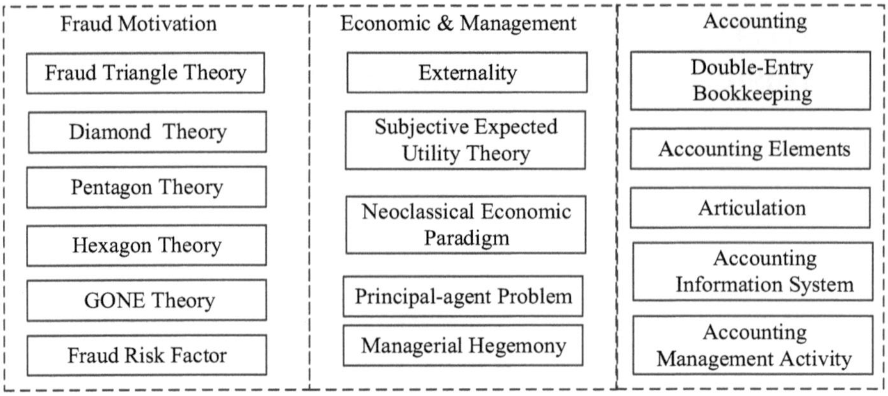

Fig. 4.1 Theoretical framework of financial fraud

internal controls, also creates opportunities and ultimately, fraudulent behavior will be more likely to occur if the associated exposure risk diminishes due to weak regulatory oversight or lenient punitive measures (Xu and He 2021). Hong et al. (2012) examined the individual effects of Greed, Opportunity, Need, and Exposure on financial fraud. Their findings revealed positive correlations between the degree of individual greed, organizational need, and fraud opportunities with the likelihood of fraud, while an inverse relationship was observed between the level of exposure and the likelihood of fraud. Moreover, Bologna et al. (1993) introduced the Fraud Risk Factor Theory which classifies fraud risk factors into two types: independent individual risk factors, driven by personal ethics, and general risk factors at the organization level, influenced by external environmental conditions. Subsequently, Wolfe and Hermanson (2004) argued that only when the perpetrator possesses the ability to rationalize fraudulent behavior within their surrounding environment, fraud can be successfully executed. Therefore, they added the factor of Competence into the Fraud Triangle theory to build the new Theory of Diamond Fraud.

Lou (2004) proposed a fraud model tailored to the Chinese market, comprising Culture (encompassing social and organizational culture), Opportunity, Motive, and Trade-off. In environments with weak internal controls, self-interested management is more likely to conceal unfavorable information (Song et al. 2017). The Association of International Bank Auditors and Compliance Professionals (AIBACP) reported that 62% of banking fraud in 2010 was primarily caused by arrogance or greed of senior management, often manifesting as management overriding internal controls. Based on this statistics results, Horwarth (2010) introduced the factor of Arrogance, representing managerial traits, and developed the Pentagon Theory of Fraud. Later, Vousinas (2019) expanded this framework by adding the factor of Collusion to propose the Hexagon Theory of Fraud, which emphasized the critical role of intentional collusion among two or more individuals to deceive third parties.

Secondly, economic and management theories have also been employed to explain financial fraud. Becker (1968) was the first to employ the externality theory in economics to explain the influence of financial fraud and other violations. Based on the cost–benefit principle, rational individuals are more likely to commit financial fraud when the net present value (NPV) is positive. Following utilitarian thinking, the neoclassical economic paradigm regards financial fraud as a rational decision-making process with the positive NPV. The Subjective Expected Utility (SEU) theory further explains that financial fraud is aimed at maximizing SEU under uncertainty (Savage 1972). Furthermore, from the perspective of managerial hegemony theory, the inherent principal-agent problem due to information asymmetry weakens the control of shareholders and boards of directors and the effectiveness of internal control system, creating more opportunities for financial fraud (Zhang et al. 2022).

Currently, there is no consensus on the financial fraud detection indicator system for in empirical research. The research direction is to innovate non-financial variables, textual variables, and other novel indicators. In addition to traditional financial indicators, the financial fraud detection power of several non-traditional indicators have been verified, including raw accounting data (Cecchini et al. 2010), deferred income tax anomalies (Li et al. 2020), distribution of numbers (Amiram et al. 2015), operational efficiency (Brazel et al. 2009), the degree of earnings management (Shang 2020), corporate governance (Ran et al. 2023), industry prosperity (Yuan et al. 2020), macroeconomic conditions (Povel et al. 2007), religious beliefs (Hasan et al. 2023), organizational culture (Perols et al. 2017), national culture (Shen et al., 2019), and corporate reputation (Song et al. 2017).

In detail, industries with low prosperity, such as chemicals, agriculture, fisheries, and pharmaceuticals have higher occurrence likelihood of fraud (Yuan et al. 2020). As well, Povel et al. (2007) simulated the relationship between macroeconomic conditions and fraudulent behavior, revealing that fraud increases during economic booms, peaks at the end of the boom, and is uncovered during subsequent recessions. Understanding the inherent link between financial fraud and economic cycles will be conducive to fraud prediction. Alongside this, a positive corporate citizenship image has a moderating effect on financial fraud, reducing its frequency and severity (Song et al. 2017). All these academic findings underscore the significance of each variable for financial fraud detection.

Overall, the evolution of fraud motivation theories, along with economic and management theories, provides a comprehensive understanding of drivers of financial fraud and establishes a robust theoretical foundation for analyzing fraudulent behavior and selecting fraud detection variables (Hong et al. 2012; Lin et al. 2015; Gepp et al. 2021; Ye et al. 2022). Among these, the Fraud Triangle Theory and the GONE Theory remain the most widely utilized frameworks.

4.2 Double-Entry Bookkeeping and Financial Reporting

Double-entry ledger accounts refer to various types of accounting books under double-entry bookkeeping. This double-entry bookkeeping system is a scientific methodology to record the funds movement using accounting language based on the accounting equation: "Assets = Liabilities + Equity" (Zeng 2020). There is an inherent articulation among various accounting elements which evolve into specific accounting subjects and then consolidate into five main account categories: assets, liabilities, equity, costs, and income, finally forming financial statements (Ge & Gao 2013). The preparation of financial statements using the double-entry bookkeeping enhances the fairness, accuracy and transparency of financial information while also helping to prevent financial fraud.

For example, when an accounting entity purchases raw materials with cash, processes them into finished goods, sells the goods, and receives cash, a complete fund circulation cycle is achieved. Each economic transaction is accompanied by a cash flow encompassing the raising, allocation, utilization and consumption of cash as well as the conversion of non-monetary assets into cash. Even though fund-related activities have become increasingly complex, the fundamental principle based on the accounting equation remains unchanged. Businesses must maintain the dynamic balance of debit and credit within the double-entry bookkeeping system. Any change in one accounting item must trigger a corresponding change in another related accounting item. The occurrence of a transaction often involves changes in multiple accounting subjects.

The articulation and cross-validation within financial statements provide essential reference for detecting financial fraud. As shown in Fig. 4.2, there are tight articulation between three financial statements, within the statements themselves, and between accounting items. In particular, the changes in assets and liabilities from the beginning to the end of a financial period, as presented in the balance sheet, can be explained by the changes shown in the cash flow statement and the income statement. For example, an increase in sales income on credit will result in a corresponding increase in accounts receivable on the balance sheet. Moreover, linkages also exist between accounting items or financial indicators that are not directly related or span across different periods. For instance, although revenue and long-term assets may not be directly connected, they can form a chain of cross-period relationships through multiple accounting items.

Since the primary goal of financial fraud is to overstate profits and revenue while understating costs (Liu et al. 2019), asset items that are closely linked to revenue and cost, such as cash, inventory, accrued items, and construction in progress, are tightly associated with financial fraud. Among these, construction in progress is particularly difficult to audit in detail due to its large amounts, long durations and flexible progress verification, making it a key accounting item used to conceal fraudulent behavior. Financial fraud cases like Wanfushengke, Beisheng Pharmaceuticals, Kangdexin, Erkang Pharmaceuticals, and Fushun Special Steel have all involved fraudulent activities related to construction in progress. Besides, an increase in revenue or gross profit margin is typically accompanied by a decrease in inventory, an increase in accounts receivable, and a decrease in advance payments. By cross-validating the articulation relationships between accounting items, anomalies in business operations and financial recording can be detected, allowing for a more accurate identification of fraudulent behavior.

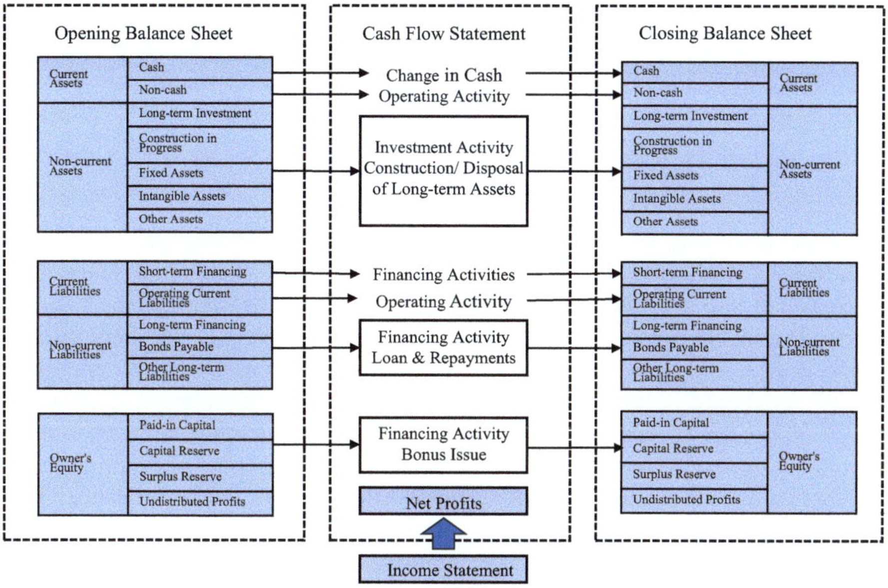

Fig. 4.2 Articulation between three financial statements

4.3 Theory of Accounting Information System

Absorbed findings from other disciplines such as finance, economics, and management, the discipline of accounting has developed several new research directions including earnings management, accounting information quality, accounting standards, internal controls, and audit quality (Yan 1984). In terms of the essence of accounting, there are two dominant viewpoints of the "Accounting Information System Theory" and the "Accounting Management Activity Theory" (Ge 2012). Specifically, scholars advocating for the "Accounting Information System Theory" thought that accounting is a financial information system, as a part of management information system that can accurately reflect the substance of economic transactions and (Jin et al. 2023). The core of an accounting information system is the financial statement, with off-balance-sheet disclosures (e.g., management accounting reports, performance forecasts, and other financial reports) serving as supplementary information (Ge et al. 2013). Accountants collect and integrate production and operations information into the accounting system for comprehensive processing, measure and evaluate economic activities and operational performance within the company to provide advisory services for management (Yan 1984).

As shown in Fig. 4.3, throughout the entire process of generating financial information, there are certain human estimation and judgment, such as accounting choices of measurement and asset valuation. Human manipulation, from the initial transactions and raw data to original vouchers, accounting ledgers, and ultimately the final financial statements, can affect the accuracy and rationality of transactions, data and

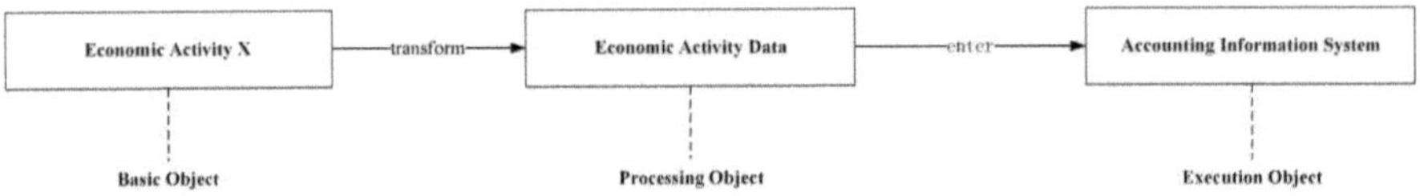

Fig. 4.3 Process of accounting information production

accounting treatment. The different stages of accounting information involve various types of fraud. For instance, transaction fraud often occurs when initial transactions are converted into raw data, such as the creation of fictitious transactions. Contract fraud may arise during the transition from raw data to accounting vouchers, such as falsifying sales contracts. Accounting fraud often happens when transitioning from original vouchers to accounting ledgers, including the overstatement of construction in progress, revenue recognition in advance, and manipulations involved in prepaid, accrued, deferred, or amortized accounting items. The accounting information generated from the accounting information system finally influences how financial statements are understood by their users (Ge et al. 2013).

Therefore, financial fraud detection requires a comprehensive analysis of each stage in the accounting information generation process to collect evidence and verify the economic substance of specific transactions, as well as to assess the truthfulness and fairness of the financial data. Based on control testing, substantive audit procedures—such as inspection, observation, interviews, confirmation, calculation, and analytical review—should be employed to conduct sample audits according to the principles of accuracy and reliability, with the goal of identifying potential fraud signals. Ye et al. (2022) were the first to apply double-entry bookkeeping and accounting information systems theory to integrate data from financial, tax, business, corporate governance, internal control, and numerical characteristics during the accounting information generation process. By leveraging expert experience and big data technology, they transformed fraud-related signals into quantifiable indicators, establishing an effective framework for fraud detection (Yang et al. 2022). Similarly, this book combines accounting theory with empirical research on financial fraud detection, offering both theoretical and empirical insights into microenterprise operations as well as macroeconomic management decisions.

4.4 Summary

This chapter summarizes classical theories of financial fraud from three perspectives. Firstly, from the perspective of causality, the Fraud Triangle theory and its evolved frameworks identify key driving factors of fraudulent behavior, such as pressure, opportunity, exposure, greed, collusion, arrogance, competence, and culture, viewing fraudulent behavior as a trade-off between these factors. These ideas are also supported by various economic and management theories, including NPV, SEU, and managerial hegemony theory. Secondly, the double-entry bookkeeping system describes how accounting information is generated and the articulation between accounting items, providing a general approach to detecting fraud. Thirdly, the theory of accounting information systems integrates accounting numbers with real transactions, offering a more systematic explanation of the occurrence of fraud. Even though an optimal financial fraud detection indicator system with multi-source information has not yet been established, these foundational fraud theories provide a broad understanding of this type of financial misconduct.

References

Amiram D, Bozanic Z, Rouen E (2015) Financial statement errors: evidence from the distributional properties of financial statement numbers. Rev Account Stud 20(4):1540–1593

Becker GS (1968) Crime and punishment: an economic approach. J Polit Econ 76(2):169–217

Bologna J, Lindquist RJ, Wells JT (1993) The accountant's handbook of fraud and commercial crime. Wiley, New York, NY

Brazel JF, Jones KL, Zimbelman MF (2009) Using nonfinancial measures to assess fraud risk. J Account Res 47(5):1135–1166

Cecchini M, Aytug H, Koehler GJ, Pathak P (2010) Detecting management fraud in public companies. Manage Sci 56(7):1146–1160

Cressey DR (1953) Other people's money: A study of the social psychology of embezzlement. Glencoe. IL: Free Press

Ge J, Ye F, Feng X et al (2013) Economic interpretation of financial accounting definition. Account Res (06):3–9+95

Ge J, Gao J (2013) On the object, function and objective of accounting. J Xiamen Univ (Philos Soc Sci) 02:30–37

Ge J (2012) Accounting, information and culture. Account Res (08):3–7+96

Gepp A, Kumar K, Bhattacharya S (2021) Lifting the numbers game: identifying key input variables and a best-performing model to detect financial statement fraud. Account Finance 61(3):4601–4638

Hasan I, Noth F, Tonzer L (2023) Cultural norms and corporate fraud: evidence from the Volkswagen scandal. J Corpor Finance 82:102443

Hong H, Hu H, Guo C (2012) Research on financial reporting fraud identification of listed companies based on GONE theory. Account Res (08):84–90+97

Horwarth C (2010) IIA practice guide: fraud and internal audit. In: Western regional conference, pp 1–49

Jin X, Xu L, Xin Y (2023) Enterprise digitalization and reliability of performance forecasts. Account Res 02:52–64

Li J, Wu Y, Lei Y, Huang Y (2020) Effective early warning indicators and artificial intelligence models for listed companies' violations based on deferred tax changes. J Financ Res 08:149–168

Lin CC, Chiu AA, Huang SY, Yen DC (2015) Detecting the financial statement fraud: the analysis of the differences between data mining techniques and experts' judgments. Knowl-Based Syst 89:459–470

Liu J, Stambaugh RF, Yuan Y (2019) Size and value in China. J Financ Econ 134(1):48–69

Lou Q (2004) The four-factor hypothesis of financial reporting fraud. Finance Account Commun 13:63

Perols JL, Bowen RM, Zimmermann C, Samba B (2017) Finding needles in a haystack: using data analytics to improve fraud prediction. Account Rev 92(2):221–245

Povel P, Singh R, Winton A (2007) Booms, busts, and fraud. Rev Financ Stud 20(4):1219–1254

Ran M, Yu L, Wang J (2023) Can CSRC's comprehensive inspection of accounting firms improve audit quality? A quasi-natural experiment based on "double random, one public." Audit Res 06:35–47
Savage LJ (1972) The foundations of statistics. Courier Corporation
Shang X (2020) Accounting information comparability and corporate inefficient investment [Doctoral dissertation]. Zhongnan University of Economics and Law
Shen Y, Gao D, Bu D, Yan L (2019) CEO hometown ties and tax avoidance-evidence from China's listed firms. Acc Financ 58(5): 1549-1580
Song X, Hu J, Li S (2017) Corporate social responsibility information disclosure and stock price crash risk: path analysis based on information effect and reputation insurance effect. J Financ Res 04:161–175
Vousinas GL (2019) Advancing theory of fraud: the SCORE model. J Financ Crime 26(1):372–381
Wolfe DT, Hermanson DR (2004) The fraud diamond: considering the four elements of fraud. CPA J 74: 38–42
Xu X, He K (2021) Deficiency and improvement of internal control elements: from the perspective of internal control and risk management integration. Account Res 11:149–159
Yan DW (1984) Analysis of accounting is an information system: In commemoration of the 35th anniversary of the founding of PRC. Account Res (05): 17-21
Yang S, Liu T, Shi Q (2022) Empirical accounting research: origin, development and reflection. Account Res 05:3–16
Ye Q, Ye F, Huang S (2022) Construction of financial fraud identification framework: based on accounting information system theory and big data perspective. Account Res 03:3–16
Yuan X, Liu H, Zhou Y, Yan C, Feng C, Li X, Li B, Guo T, Qian G, Zeng T (2020) Big data random search algorithm and application for fund correlation feature extraction. Manag Sci 33(06):41–53
Zeng X (2020) Double-entry bookkeeping under blockchain distributed ledger technology: basic concepts, operating mechanism and application prospects. Friends Account 16:155–160
Zhang X, Du Q, Zhang Z (2022) A theory-driven machine learning system for financial disinformation detection. Prod Oper Manag 31(8):3160–3179

Chapter 5
Financial Fraud Litigation and Forensic Accounting

5.1 The U.S. Financial Fraud Litigation and Enforcement System

In the United States' dual enforcement system for financial fraud, both public and private enforcement play critical roles in regulation. At the public enforcement level, the U.S. Securities and Exchange Commission (SEC) holds significant administrative powers and is authorized to sue for fraud in the court under Section 10b of the Securities Exchange Act of 1934 and Section 17a of the Securities Act of 1933. However, due to limitations in budget and personnel, the SEC typically investigates companies that are most likely to have committed financial fraud, often focusing on smaller firms (Ren et al. 2021). Meanwhile, subject to the confidentiality principle, only 19% of cases are disclosed during the early stages of an SEC investigation, which may create opportunities for insider trading (Blackburne et al. 2021).

As a complement to public enforcements, private enforcements are also effective anti-fraud instruments in the U.S. under Rule 10b-5, and the amount of private litigation often exceeds the amount of enforcement by the SEC. Choi and Pritchard (2016) argue that securities class actions (SCAs) exerts greater regulation on violations compared to public enforcement. This private civil right of actions are broad and comprehensive, covering a wide range of fraudulent activities including misrepresentation, fraudulent listings, insider trading and any other fraudulent behaviors. To reduce litigation costs and expand the scope of claims and the intensity of punishment, private litigation is usually initiated as a class action, with institutional investors—who usually suffer the largest financial losses—acting as the main plaintiffs. Through class action, intermediaries such as accounting firms deal with higher damages risk, but this mechanism helps to effectively compensate investors for their losses to some extent.

Joseph Grundfest, a former SEC commissioner, argued that SCAs, whether settled or judged, have negative social effects. They primarily increase the political influence of plaintiff lawyers, but do not fundamentally facilitate the stability of capital

X. Ma and D. Wu, *Financial Fraud Detection Using Machine Learning*, AI for Risks,
https://doi.org/10.1007/978-981-95-0840-2_5

markets. He emphasized that SEC public enforcement has a stronger deterrent effect on financial fraud (Grundfest 1995). In response to concerns over SCAs, the Private Securities Litigation Reform Act (PSLRA) passed by the U.S. Congress in 1995 made restrictions on the scope of defendants, litigation procedures, solicitors, and maximum damages in SCAs and also introduced external auditor oversight as an alternative mechanism to Make up for the erosion of private litigation.

However, the implementation of the PSLRA increases litigation costs while restricting compensation for investors, thereby diminishing the deterrence of private litigation. This contributed to major fraud scandals such as Enron and WorldCom, which compelled Congress quickly passed the Sarbanes–Oxley Act (SOX) in 2002 to enhance SEC public enforcement. The SOX Act enhanced disclosure requirements, intensified internal and external auditing, and increased the accountability and penalties for fraud, raising compliance and litigation risks for publicly listed companies while effectively protecting the interests of small and medium investors. Following the enactment of the SOX Act, the importance of public enforcement was further emphasized, with the SEC's scale expanding by approximately two-thirds.

However, the effectiveness of law enforcement against fraud remains a subject of considerable debate. According to Dyck et al. (2024), financial fraud in U.S. listed companies has caused a market value loss of 1.6%, which, based on the 2021 market value, amounts to approximately $830 billion. Yet, the total settlement fees for securities fraud class actions annually amount to around $10 million, a fraction of the economic losses incurred in the market, with only 28% of the victims receiving settlement compensation (Amiram et al. 2018). Moreover, companies accused of fraud do not necessarily engage in fraudulent behavior, as evidenced by the fact that 85% of securities fraud class actions settled in the U.S. were not subject to administrative penalties (Cox et al. 2003). For the companies involved, litigation is also a costly resolution. In the early stages of litigation, companies must allocate resources to handle the legal process, while also facing the immense financial burden of a potential loss, which increases liquidity risks. Additionally, being entangled in litigation investigations damages a company's reputation, leading to an irreversible market value reduction of 15–25%, severely impacting daily operations (Barko et al. 2023).

Furthermore, the accused companies' performance in operational, liquidity, market, and risk indicators is adversely affected during the investigation period. These companies often resort to fraudulent activities such as forging bank documents and falsifying business vouchers, creating a vicious cycle. Ten percent of the accused companies enter bankruptcy proceedings within three years of the litigation or settlement process (Ren et al. 2021). At the same time, accused companies tend to settle by compensating monetary losses, which further encourages fraud perpetrators to conduct a cost–benefit analysis.

Scholars have argued that private and public enforcement methods should complement each other, drawing on the strengths of both approaches. This includes filtering private lawsuits through the SEC while increasing the amount of SEC enforcement actions. According to the SEC's 2022 Fiscal Year Enforcement Report, the SEC's enforcement activities resulted in a record of $6.4 billion in fines, experiencing a 67%

increase from the previous year. Additionally, companies involved in financial fraud face a minimum fine of $5 million and at least 10 years of imprisonment once the SEC takes enforcement action, reflecting firm commitment to stringent regulation in the U.S. capital market.

5.2 The Chinese Financial Fraud Litigation and Enforcement System

In China, financial fraud enforcements are also divided into private and public enforcements. Public enforcement is primarily carried out by the China Securities Regulatory Commission (CSRC), the People's Bank of China, and public security departments. Hasan et al. (2023) and Li and Ling (2023) have found that a stringent legal system significantly affects the quality of corporate information disclosure and plays a governance role in curbing corporate fraud. The 2019 revised Securities Law imposes stricter information disclosure standards for listed companies, clearly stating that entities violating these standards must bear corresponding civil, criminal, and administrative responsibilities, with civil and administrative liabilities taking precedence.

In terms of civil responsibility, penalties primarily focus on compensating losses, with listed companies bearing the compensation responsibility, while major shareholders, actual controllers, board members, supervisors, senior executives, and intermediary agencies bear joint and several liabilities. Due to the complexities of real-world situations, the legal provisions only set general principles that can be adjusted based on specific cases instead of specifying clear criteria for determining responsible parties, distinguishing between primary and secondary liabilities, or defining prosecution conditions. What is more, administrative responsibilities mainly include measures such as rectification orders, regulatory interviews, issuing warning letters, market bans, and fines. Criminal liability applies only to "individuals," with the responsible person potentially facing up to 10 years of imprisonment and substantial fines. In addition, laws such as the "Regulations on the Management of Information Disclosure by Listed Companies," the "Company Law of the People's Republic of China," the "Accounting Law of the People's Republic of China," and the "Criminal Law of the People's Republic of China" provide strict penalties for financial fraud and related parties, including intermediaries who assist or participate in fraudulent activities, with most of these offenses subject to criminal prosecution.

Unlike the prevalent issues of "frivolous litigation" and "abusive lawsuits" in the United States, which necessitate legislative action to limit private lawsuits, China currently encourages the domestic development of private litigation as an effective supplement to public enforcement. In 2020, the CSRC introduced new disclosure requirements related to "representative securities disputes," making litigation a focal point of regulatory review (Cao et al. 2023). Then, the Supreme People's

Court issued the "Regulations on Several Issues Concerning Representative Securities Disputes" which significantly lowered the litigation threshold and reduced the cost of safeguarding investor rights. Investors can file ordinary or special representative lawsuits against companies. In ordinary representative lawsuits, the representative is the investor, who explicitly joins the litigation, resulting in a longer litigation cycle. In special representative lawsuits, the representative is a securities investment organization entrusted by more than 50 investors, with investors implicitly joining and explicitly opting out, resulting in a shorter litigation cycle.

The 2021 case of Feilo Acoustics' false statements was the first ordinary representative lawsuit following the enactment of this regulations, resulting in compensation of 123 million yuan to 315 investors, with each investor receiving an average of 390,000 yuan. The 2021 Kangmei Pharmaceutical false statements case was the first special representative class action involving over 50,000 investors and compensation totaling 2.459 billion yuan, which marked a significant step forward in the development of China's unique litigation system, further curbing financial fraud and improving the overall ecosystem of the financial market.

5.3 Theories of Forensic Accounting

The essence of forensic accounting is using accounting knowledge to solve legal problems, referring to providing expert advice on legal issues related to financial accounting matters during litigation (Wang 2019). The scope of forensic accounting services includes litigation support, economic loss measurement, financial fraud detection, corporate fraud investigations, and asset valuation, with clients ranging from courts, government agencies, and regulatory bodies to listed companies. It serves as an important tool for preventing economic crime, financial fraud, and corporate violations. Its origins trace back to the "South Sea Bubble" accounting fraud case in the UK in 1720, where accountant Charles Snell reviewed the accounting books of the defendant, the South Sea Company, confirming accounting distortion and financial fraud, and assisted the judge in making the ruling (Wang 2019). Distinct from traditional audit assurance, forensic accounting provides judicial expert reports rather than audit reports.

The term "Forensic Accounting" first appeared in 1946 when the U.S. Internal Revenue Service (IRS) agent Frank Wilson provided assessments of taxable income during the trial of Al Capone, offering evidence for the tax evasion conviction (Feng et al. 2003). After the 1980s, the U.S. significantly promoted the development of forensic accounting in fraud investigations. During the 2002 WorldCom and Enron scandals, forensic accounting assisted the SEC in gathering evidence of accounting fraud and calculating the damage amounts, providing strong litigation support.

Forensic accounting still under exploration in China to take into account the unique characteristics of China's judicial environment and develop the suitable application mode adapted to the situation of economic development. The Chinese certified public accountants (CPAs) originally emerged during World War I falls under the scope of forensic accounting, driven by the needs of national capitalists to resolve economic disputes and litigation. In the 1980s, with the rise of economic crime cases in China, public security, prosecution, and judicial bodies established internal technical departments to conduct accounting audits and judicial appraisals. Under the "Decision on Issues Concerning Judicial Appraisal Management," issued in 2005, the responsibilities of forensic accounting gradually shifted from judicial enforcement agencies to social intermediary institutions such as accounting firms, with its scope of services extending beyond judicial appraisals to include fraud investigations, economic case inquiries, and other areas (Wang 2019).

In 2015, a notice on the implementation of the Certified Forensic Accountant (CFA) program released by the China Association of Chief Accountants is the first initiative to integrate accounting with law for cultivating forensic accountants with both accounting knowledge and legal understanding, promoting the application of forensic accounting in economic case trials and financial fraud investigations. After this notice, CPAs became the primary providers of forensic accounting services. In 2016, the 13th Five-Year Plan for Accounting Reform and Development issued by the Ministry of Finance further identified the development of forensic accounting as one of the key directions for the CPAs.

In recent years, the number of securities civil litigation cases arising from false accounting information has been increasing annually. Although the current Securities Law explicitly stipulates that individuals responsible for false statements must bear civil compensation liabilities, issues such as the inadequacy of legal frameworks, delayed adjustments to accounting standards, and the complexity of the investment market often lead to insufficient support from relevant legal provisions in actual litigation. This not only increases the cost of case handling but also, to some extent, affects the objectivity and fairness of judgments. In this context, forensic accounting experts play an active role in addressing such issues by using accounting knowledge and judicial tools to significantly improve the ability to identify fraudulent activities within enterprises (Jin and Li 2007; Wang 2019). With the gradual establishment and improvement of China's private litigation system, the litigation support function of forensic accounting will become increasingly prominent.

5.4 Summary

This chapter presents a comprehensive overview of the litigation and enforcement systems regarding financial fraud in both China and the U.S., comparing their unique features. With the collective development of private and public enforcement, both systems differ in their approach to financial fraud, with private class actions being more powerful due to their relative flexibility and universality. Meanwhile, forensic accounting, as a component of CPAs in China, has become an effective complement, as it combines accounting with law to resolve litigation, contributing more expertise to the detection of financial fraud both in practice and theory.

References

Amiram D, Bozanic Z, Cox JD, Dupont Q (2018) Financial reporting fraud and other forms of misconduct: a multidisciplinary review of the literature. Rev Account Stud 23:732–783

Barko T, Renneboog L, Zhang H (2023) Corporate fraud and the consequences of securities class action litigation. European Corporate Governance Institute (925)

Blackburne T, Kepler JD, Quinn PJ, Taylor DJ (2021) Undisclosed SEC investigations. Manag Sci 67(6):3403–3418

Cao Y, Zhang Z, Peng K, Zhou Y (2023) The establishment of circuit courts and corporate fraud. Emerg Markets Finance Trade 59:2600–2616

Choi SJ, Pritchard AC (2016) SEC investigations and securities class actions: an empirical comparison. J Empir Leg Stud 13(1):27–49

Cox JD, Thomas RS, Kiku D (2003) SEC enforcement heuristics: an empirical inquiry. Duke LJ 53:737

Dyck A, Morse A, Zingales L (2024) How pervasive is corporate fraud? Rev Account Stud 29(1): 736-769

Feng M, Li R, Jiang W et al (2003) Litigation support of forensic accounting in the United States: evidence from Enron case. Account Res 01:15–20

Grundfest JA (1995) Why disimply? Harv Law Rev 108(3):727–747

Hasan I, Noth F, Tonzer L (2023) Cultural norms and corporate fraud: evidence from the Volkswagen scandal. J Corp Finan 82:102443

Jin Y, Li R (2007) The role of forensic accounting experts in securities civil litigation of false statement: international experience and implications. Account Res (04):19–26+95

Li Z, Ling Z (2023) Does internal control "more words less action" affect audit risk identification? Audit Res 03:148–160

Ren L, Zhong X, Wan L (2021) Missing analyst forecasts and corporate fraud: evidence from China. J Bus Ethics 181(1):171–194

Wang Y (2019) The past and present of forensic accounting: discussion on career prospects of forensic accounting. Friends Account 05:24–27

Chapter 6
Resampling Techniques and Feature Selection

6.1 Resampling Techniques

Financial fraud research commonly employs data resampling techniques to address class imbalance issues in fraud data, improving model performance. These techniques can be categorized into traditional resampling and intelligent hybrid resampling methods. Traditional resampling techniques include RUS (Random Under-Sampling) and ROS (Random Over-Sampling), while intelligent resampling techniques primarily consist of SMOTE (Synthetic Minority Over-sampling Technique) and its variants, such as SMOTE-ENN (SMOTE-Edited Nearest Neighbor), SMOTE-Tomek (SMOTE-Tomek Links), Borderline-SMOTE, and SVM-SMOTE (Support Vector Machine SMOTE). Additional intelligent methods include ADASYN (Adaptive Synthetic Sampling) and Cluster Centroids. While the optimal combination of resampling methods and classification models remains undetermined, most studies suggest that over-sampling techniques generally outperform under-sampling techniques, and hybrid sampling techniques show superior performance compared to traditional sampling methods. This section provides a brief overview of these resampling techniques and their empirical applications.

6.1.1 Under-Sampling Techniques

The core idea of undersampling is to reduce the number of majority class samples to make it comparable or close to a preset ratio with minority class samples. Among various under-sampling techniques, RUS randomly removes some majority class samples, whose randomness may cause serious information loss and underfitting. Tomek Links, proposed by Ivan Tomek in 1976, achieves data balance by removing boundary samples or noise samples from the majority class, which is suitable for situations where the minority class has a relatively large amount of data. Cluster

X. Ma and D. Wu, *Financial Fraud Detection Using Machine Learning*, AI for Risks,
https://doi.org/10.1007/978-981-95-0840-2_6

Centroids, a clustering-based undersampling algorithm, clusters the majority class samples and uses cluster centers to represent samples of that class. ENN removes samples that are inconsistent with the majority class of their k nearest neighbors. While undersampling techniques significantly reduce computational resource requirements, offer short training times, facilitate sample collection and maintain low model complexity, they may also cause information distortion, change the original data distribution, and potentially perform poorly on small datasets. Simple implementations of each undersampling method are shown below.

```
import numpy as np
from collections import Counter
from sklearn.neighbors import NearestNeighbors
from sklearn.cluster import KMeans
from sklearn.datasets import make_classification

# 1. Random Under-Sampling (RUS)
class RandomUnderSampler:
    def __init__(self, ratio=1.0, random_state=None):
        self.ratio = ratio
        self.random_state = random_state
    def fit_resample(self, X, y):
        np.random.seed(self.random_state)
        # Get indices for each class
        majority_idx = np.where(y == 0)[0]
        minority_idx = np.where(y == 1)[0]
        # Random selection from majority class
        n_minority = len(minority_idx)
        n_majority = int(n_minority / self.ratio)
        selected_majority = np.random.choice(majority_idx,
size=n_majority, replace=False)
        # Combine samples
        selected_idx = np.concatenate([selected_majority,
minority_idx])
        return X[selected_idx], y[selected_idx]
```

```
    # 2. Tomek Links
class TomekLinks:
    def __init__(self):
        self.nn = NearestNeighbors(n_neighbors=2)
    def fit_resample(self, X, y):
        self.nn.fit(X)
        distances, indices = self.nn.kneighbors(X)
        # Find Tomek links
        links = []
        for i in range(len(X)):
            if y[i] == 0:  # majority class
                nn_idx = indices[i, 1]
                if y[nn_idx] == 1:  # minority class
                    nn_of_nn = indices[nn_idx, 1]
                    if nn_of_nn == i:
                        links.append(i)
                        # Remove links
        mask = np.ones(len(X), dtype=bool)
        mask[links] = False
        return X[mask], y[mask]

    # 3. Cluster Centroids
class ClusterCentroids:
    def __init__(self, ratio=1.0, random_state=None):
        self.ratio = ratio
        self.random_state = random_state
    def fit_resample(self, X, y):
        # Split classes
        X_maj = X[y == 0]
        X_min = X[y == 1]
        # Apply clustering
        n_clusters = int(len(X_min) / self.ratio)
        kmeans            =            KMeans(n_clusters=n_clusters,
random_state=self.random_state)
        kmeans.fit(X_maj)
        # Get new samples
        X_new = np.vstack([kmeans.cluster_centers_, X_min])
        y_new            =            np.hstack([np.zeros(n_clusters),
np.ones(len(X_min))])
        return X_new, y_new

    # 4. Edited Nearest Neighbors (ENN)
class EditedNearestNeighbors:
    def __init__(self, n_neighbors=3):
        self.n_neighbors = n_neighbors
        self.nn = NearestNeighbors(n_neighbors=n_neighbors + 1)
```

```
    def fit_resample(self, X, y):
        self.nn.fit(X)
        distances, indices = self.nn.kneighbors(X)
        # Select samples
        keep = []
        for i in range(len(X)):
            if y[i] == 0:  # majority class
                neighbor_labels = y[indices[i, 1:]]
                if np.sum(neighbor_labels == 0) >= self.n_neighbors
/ 2:
                    keep.append(i)
            else:  # keep all minority samples
                keep.append(i)
        return X[keep], y[keep]
```

Paired sampling, which can be considered an under-sampling strategy, is a common approach to address the rarity of fraud samples. This method originated from Beasley (1996) and involves matching fraudulent and non-fraudulent companies based on attributes such as stock exchange listing, industry, year, listing duration, and size, typically using either a 1:1 ratio or ratios approximating actual fraud rate (Beaver 1966; Beasley 1996; Chen et al. 2006; Lin et al. 2015; Hass et al. 2016; Barboza et al. 2017; Liu et al. 2023).For instance, Chen et al. (2006) matched 169 pairs of fraudulent and non-fraudulent companies from 1999 to 2003 to study the impact of ownership structure and board characteristics on corporate fraud, using stock exchange, industry, year, and listing duration as matching criteria. Ravisankar et al. (2011) created a dataset of 101 paired samples to evaluate the effectiveness of data mining techniques in detecting financial statement fraud. Hong et al. (2012) explored the relationship between GONE fraud factors and financial statement fraud using matched companies penalized for financial fraud based on industry and size during 2006–2009.

Hass et al. (2016) matched 2618 pairs of fraudulent and non-fraudulent samples based on company size and industry to investigate the impact of equity incentives on fraud frequency in Chinese companies. Wei et al. (2011) examined the role of social media in corporate fraud detection using 64 matched pairs of companies, with matching criteria including fraud year, company size, and industry. Gepp et al. (2021) implemented stringent matching criteria based on year, industry, size, age, and stock exchange to construct 464 matched pairs from 1998 to 2007, thereby expanding the sample size for training, optimizing, and comparing data mining models. Although paired-sampling techniques have demonstrated good classification performance in previous studies, it has notable limitations. This technique often introduce choice-based sample bias with only limited numbers of samples meeting the matching criteria, potentially compromising the generalization ability of the classification model. Overall, undersampling can be combined with other sampling methods for better results. Meanwhile, we can use cross-validation to find the optimal undersampling ratios.

6.1.2 Over-Sampling Techniques

The core idea of oversampling is to balance samples by increasing minority class samples. However, overemphasizing minority samples may lead to overfitting and poor model generalization. Among most commonly-used over-sampling techniques, ROS is simple and efficient through randomly duplicating minority class samples. Based on ROS, SMOTE is explored by generating new synthetic samples through artificial interpolation of minority class samples, which reduces overfitting risk and improves noise resistance. While the high computational cost and the high sensitivity to outliers also restrict its application. Borderline-SMOTE is an enhanced version of SMOTE that only oversamples minority class samples in boundary regions to effectively improve classification accuracy. But it may ignore important non-boundary samples and is sensitive to parameters setting. SMOTE-ENN combines SMOTE and ENN, generating new minority samples in local regions through KNN, which also helps reduce overfitting risk. Additionally, using density distribution as a criterion, ADASYN generates more synthetic samples in regions with lower sample density and fewer or no samples in regions with higher density. Simple implementations of each oversampling method are shown below.

```
import numpy as np
from collections import Counter
from sklearn.neighbors import NearestNeighbors
from sklearn.datasets import make_classification

# 1. Random Over-Sampling (ROS)
class RandomOverSampler:
    def __init__(self, ratio=1.0, random_state=None):
        self.ratio = ratio
        self.random_state = random_state
    def fit_resample(self, X, y):
        if self.random_state is not None:
            np.random.seed(self.random_state)
```

```
            # Get minority samples
        minority_idx = np.where(y == 1)[0]
        majority_idx = np.where(y == 0)[0]
        # Calculate number of samples needed
        n_majority = len(majority_idx)
        n_sample = int(n_majority * self.ratio) - len(minority_idx)
        # Random sampling with replacement
        resampled_idx          =          np.random.choice(minority_idx,
size=n_sample, replace=True)
        # Combine samples
        X_new = np.vstack([X, X[resampled_idx]])
        y_new = np.hstack([y, y[resampled_idx]])
        return X_new, y_new

    # 2. SMOTE
class SMOTE:
    def __init__(self, k_neighbors=5, ratio=1.0, random_state=None):
        self.k = k_neighbors
        self.ratio = ratio
        self.random_state = random_state
    def fit_resample(self, X, y):
        if self.random_state is not None:
            np.random.seed(self.random_state)
            # Get minority samples
        minority_X = X[y == 1]
        majority_X = X[y == 0]
        # Find k nearest neighbors
        nn = NearestNeighbors(n_neighbors=self.k)
        nn.fit(minority_X)
        distances, indices = nn.kneighbors(minority_X)
        # Calculate synthetic samples needed
        n_majority = len(majority_X)
        n_synthetic = int(n_majority * self.ratio) - len(minority_X)
        # Generate synthetic samples
        synthetic_samples = []
        for _ in range(n_synthetic):
            idx = np.random.randint(0, len(minority_X))
            nn_idx = np.random.choice(indices[idx, 1:])
            # Get the two points
            point = minority_X[idx]
            nn_point = minority_X[nn_idx]
            # Generate synthetic sample
            alpha = np.random.random()
```

```
            synthetic_sample = point + alpha * (nn_point - point)
            synthetic_samples.append(synthetic_sample)
            # Combine all samples
        X_new = np.vstack([X, synthetic_samples])
        y_new = np.hstack([y, np.ones(len(synthetic_samples))])
        return X_new, y_new

    # 3. Borderline-SMOTE
class BorderlineSMOTE:
    def __init__(self, k_neighbors=5, m_neighbors=10, ratio=1.0,
random_state=None):
        self.k = k_neighbors
        self.m = m_neighbors
        self.ratio = ratio
        self.random_state = random_state
    def fit_resample(self, X, y):
        if self.random_state is not None:
            np.random.seed(self.random_state)
            # Find borderline samples
        nn = NearestNeighbors(n_neighbors=self.m)
        nn.fit(X)
        minority_idx = np.where(y == 1)[0]
        majority_idx = np.where(y == 0)[0]
        # Identify danger samples
        danger_idx = []
        for idx in minority_idx:
            distances, indices = nn.kneighbors(X[idx].reshape(1, -
1))
            n_majority = sum(y[indices[0][1:]] == 0)
            if self.m / 2 <= n_majority < self.m:
                danger_idx.append(idx)
                # Apply SMOTE to danger samples
        danger_X = X[danger_idx]
        nn = NearestNeighbors(n_neighbors=self.k)
        nn.fit(X[minority_idx])
        # Generate synthetic samples
        n_synthetic = int(len(majority_idx) * self.ratio) -
len(minority_idx)
        synthetic_samples = []
        for _ in range(n_synthetic):
            idx = np.random.randint(0, len(danger_X))
            distances, indices =
nn.kneighbors(danger_X[idx].reshape(1, -1))
```

```
            nn_idx = np.random.choice(indices[0][1:])
            # Generate synthetic sample
            alpha = np.random.random()
            synthetic_sample    =    danger_X[idx]    +    alpha    *
(X[minority_idx[nn_idx]] - danger_X[idx])
            synthetic_samples.append(synthetic_sample)
            # Combine samples
        X_new = np.vstack([X, synthetic_samples])
        y_new = np.hstack([y, np.ones(len(synthetic_samples))])
        return X_new, y_new

    # 4. ADASYN
class ADASYN:
    def __init__(self, k_neighbors=5, ratio=1.0, random_state=None):
        self.k = k_neighbors
        self.ratio = ratio
        self.random_state = random_state
    def fit_resample(self, X, y):
        if self.random_state is not None:
            np.random.seed(self.random_state)
            # Calculate density ratio for each minority sample
        nn = NearestNeighbors(n_neighbors=self.k + 1)
        nn.fit(X)
        minority_idx = np.where(y == 1)[0]
        majority_idx = np.where(y == 0)[0]
        density_ratio = []
        for idx in minority_idx:
            distances,  indices  =  nn.kneighbors(X[idx].reshape(1,  -
1))
            ratio = sum(y[indices[0][1:]] == 0) / self.k
            density_ratio.append(ratio)
            # Normalize density ratios
        density_ratio = np.array(density_ratio)
        if density_ratio.sum() > 0:
            density_ratio = density_ratio / density_ratio.sum()
            # Calculate number of synthetic samples for each minority
sample
        n_synthetic   =   int(len(majority_idx)   *   self.ratio)   -
len(minority_idx)
        n_samples = np.rint(density_ratio * n_synthetic).astype(int)
        # Generate synthetic samples
        synthetic_samples = []
        nn.fit(X[minority_idx])
```

```
        for idx, n in enumerate(n_samples):
            if n == 0:
                continue
            distances,                    indices                    =
nn.kneighbors(X[minority_idx[idx]].reshape(1, -1))
            for _ in range(n):
                nn_idx = np.random.choice(indices[0][1:])
                alpha = np.random.random()
                synthetic_sample = (X[minority_idx[idx]] +
                                    alpha                            *
(X[minority_idx[nn_idx]] - X[minority_idx[idx]]))
                synthetic_samples.append(synthetic_sample)
                # Combine samples
        if synthetic_samples:
            X_new = np.vstack([X, synthetic_samples])
            y_new = np.hstack([y, np.ones(len(synthetic_samples))])
        else:
            X_new, y_new = X, y
        return X_new, y_new
```

6.1.3 Application of Resampling Techniques

Contemporary research predominantly integrates resampling techniques with ensemble algorithms to construct imbalanced ensemble learning classifiers to improve model classification performance (Rahman and Zhu 2023). Chawla et al. (2003) first proposed the SMOTEBoost algorithm, combining SMOTE with the Boosting process on imbalanced datasets, improving F1 scores. Subsequently, Seiffert et al. (2009) combined RUS with AdaBoost to develop a more concise and efficient hybrid machine learning algorithm named as RUSBoost. Faris et al. (2020) combined ensemble algorithms (AdaBoost, Bagging, and RF) with oversampling techniques (ROS, SMOTE, ADASYN, and SMOTE-Borderline) to build imbalanced classifiers that achieved reliable performance in bankruptcy prediction. The imbalanced ensemble learning model built with AdaBoost and SMOTE again demonstrated optimal detection performance, with overall accuracy, Type I error rate, Type II error rate, and G-means of 98.3%, 0.006, 0.45, and 0.73 respectively. Esenogho et al. (2022) achieved sensitivity and specificity of 0.996 and 0.998 by training an LSTM-AdaBoost ensemble classifier with SMOTE-ENN resampling.

Following the researches of Dechow et al. (2011) and Cecchini et al. (2010), Rahman and Zhu (2023) used financial ratios and numbers to investigate machine learning models for predicting accounting fraud in Chinese listed companies, further verifying that ensemble learning classifiers could more effectively detect accounting fraud, particularly imbalanced ensemble learning classifiers like RUSBoost outperforming traditional ensemble learning models such as AdaBoost and XGBoost. What is more, Perols et al. (2017) improved fraud prediction performance by approximately 10% through undersampling observations. Xiao et al. (2021) compared ten resampling methods and nine classification models under credit scoring problems, finding that LR and AdaBoost algorithms outperformed other classifiers, while RUS and SMOTE-ENN resampling methods surpassed other sampling techniques, with RUS-based ensemble learning models showing the best classification performance. Ghorbani and Ghousi (2020) found that SVM-SMOTE performed better compared to Borderline-SMOTE, ROS, SMOTE, SMOTE-ENN, and SMOTE-Tomek resampling methods since after resampling with SVM-SMOTE, the RF algorithm achieved optimal prediction results.

In summary, although some scholars question the reliability of resampling techniques in generating or eliminating certain samples, this technique still remains the most widely applicable and operationally simple data preprocessing technique. Imbalanced machine learning classifiers adjusted by resampling techniques demonstrate remarkable classification performance on fraud datasets.

6.2 Feature Selection Methods

Feature selection represents a crucial preprocessing step in developing financial fraud detection models (Tang and Allen 2021). Financial fraud detection studies typically employ large-scale, complex datasets with numerous available features, where feature selection methods have demonstrated positive impacts on both dimensionality reduction and detection performance (Dhal and Azad 2022). The multifaceted nature of financial fraud, coupled with the inherent multicollinearity among variables, presents significant high-dimensional data challenges. The primary objectives of feature selection encompass the elimination of irrelevant or redundant information, reduction of feature dimensionality, and minimization of computational burden, while ensuring that the retained features adequately represent the information content of the original dataset. Effective feature selection methodologies not only reduce model classification costs but also substantially enhance model interpretability. However, the identification of critical discriminative variables exhibits considerable variation across studies, influenced by multiple factors including sample selection, methodological approaches, and market characteristics (Amiram et al. 2018).

Feature selection process comprises two fundamental steps including feature evaluation and optimal feature combination search, ultimately identifying the optimal feature subset that represents the original dataset. In a study on predicting Small and Medium Enterprise (SME) bankruptcy, Kou et al. (2021) conceptualized feature selection as a two-stage multi-objective optimization problem. The first stage employs Feature Relevance analysis and the Optimum-Seeking Method to eliminate redundant features, while the second stage utilizes a Multiobjective Wrapper-based feature selection approach to further optimize the feature set dimensionality in pursuit of the optimal feature subset. Experimental results demonstrate that this two-stage multi-objective feature selection methodology achieves comparable model classification performance while optimizing feature quantity.

Specifically, feature evaluation methodologies encompass three primary categories: Filter methods, Wrapper methods, and Embedded methods (Guyon and Elisseeff 2003), with the selection of an appropriate methodology contingent upon the specific research context (Cai et al. 2018). Filter methods compute correlation scores between individual features and core data attributes, eliminating low-scoring features before evaluating performance across various learning algorithms. These methods incorporate Best First, Greedy, Exhaustive, and genetic algorithm-based approaches. Common techniques for measuring feature-label correlations include Chi-squared Test, Relief algorithm, enhanced ReliefF algorithm, Information Gain (IG), and Gain Ratio (Kou et al. 2021). Wrapper methods employ iterative learning through specific algorithms, systematically adding or removing features during each iteration while evaluating the fitness of new feature subsets to determine the optimal configuration. Embedded methods integrate both filter and wrapper approaches, optimizing performance through specific data mining algorithms. While wrapper-based methods produce feature subsets dependent on the employed learning algorithm, filter methods operate independently of the learning algorithm, offering lower computational complexity and faster execution times, occasionally outperforming wrapper-based approaches in certain scenarios (Yildirim 2015).

This section systematically reviews feature selection methods employed in financial fraud detection literature, encompassing expert judgment, basic statistical approaches, and machine learning techniques. Firstly, a substantial body of financial fraud detection research continues to rely on fundamental theories and expert judgement for feature selection, including double-entry bookkeeping and accounting information systems theory (Ye et al. 2022), fraud triangle theory (Lin et al. 2015; Gepp et al. 2021), and the four-factor fraud theory (Hong et al. 2012; Xu et al. 2023). Kaminski et al. (2004) evaluated the fraud detection capability of financial ratios using expert experience and accounting reconciliation relationships.

Secondly, simple statistical models have also been extensively employed in feature screening processes. Beaver's 1966 study pioneered feature selection through variable mean comparison. Piramuthu (2003) introduced a Hausdorff Distance-based feature selection methodology. Kirkos et al. (2007) demonstrated that Analysis of Variance (ANOVA) selected features features outperformed expert-selected features in distinguishing between fraudulent and non-fraudulent groups. Benesty et al. (2008) utilized Pearson Correlation Coefficient (PCC) to reduce noise interference. Xu and Zhang (2009) integrated Altman Z-score, Ohlson O-score, and option pricing models for feature selection. Chen and Liginlal (2008) developed a maximum entropy-based feature selection technique. Building upon feature sets from Green and Choi (1997), Beneish M-score (1999), and Dechow F-score (2009), Cecchini et al. (2010) constructed datasets by eliminating features with over 25% missing values. Ravisankar et al. (2011) employed t-statistics for feature differentiation, creating subsets of top 10 and 18 features to compare data mining performance. Kim and Upneja (2014) utilized Mann–Whitney U Test to validate significant differences between financial distress and non-distress groups. Qian and Luo (2015) developed the C-score fraud detection model for Chinese markets using backward elimination on M-score and F-score predictive variables. Li and Chi (2021) innovatively employed indicator discrimination and redundancy analysis for feature selection, establishing a default assessment framework with strong discriminative capability. Perols et al. (2017) improved fraud prediction performance by approximately 10% through feature subset division based on specific fraud types. Principal Component Analysis (PCA) has emerged as a prominent dimensionality reduction method, particularly in ensemble learning applications (Qian et al. 2022). Kumaraswamy et al. (2022) demonstrated the effectiveness of PCA by reducing 176 features to 15 principal components while preserving 85% of the original variance.

In recent years, machine learning approaches have gained increasing prominence in financial fraud detection research for feature selection. These methods evaluate feature importance by measuring classification error variations upon feature removal, thereby assessing each feature's impact on model classification performance. Furthermore, hybrid approaches combining machine learning models with basic statistical methods and expert knowledge have demonstrated promising results. Zhou et al. (2024) conducted a comparative analysis of data mining techniques and Domain Knowledge as feature selection methods for financial distress prediction. Their findings revealed that the integration of domain knowledge with genetic algorithms maximized the Area Under the Curve (AUC) of the Receiver Operating Characteristic (ROC) curve. Mu et al. (2018) developed a hybrid approach combining Pearson correlation coefficients with decision trees, utilizing correlation coefficients to determine optimal splitting attributes in decision trees, thereby reducing computational time. Yuan et al. (2022) employed Gibbs Sampling within the Markov Chain Monte Carlo (MCMC) framework to extract eight financial fraud risk factors from 183 features, subsequently developing a financial fraud risk early warning model. Additionally, they proposed a two-stage feature selection methodology integrating Gibbs random sampling with CART decision trees, specifically designed for identifying features characterizing rural household poverty status.

What is more, Li et al. (2018) introduced a composite Random Forest model combining dimensionality reduction and classification (Principal Component Analysis and Random Forest with Potential Nearest Neighbor, PCARF-PNN). This model optimizes the Random Forest algorithm through PCA and Potential Nearest Neighbor (PNN) algorithms, effectively enhancing insurance fraud detection accuracy. Omuya et al. (2021) proposed a hybrid feature selection model integrating PCA and Information Gain (PCA-IG), demonstrating improved performance metrics—including precision, recall, accuracy, and computational efficiency—across Decision Tree (DT), Support Vector Machine (SVM), and Gaussian Naive Bayes (GaussianNB) models. Tang and Allen (2021) developed an Integrated Principal Component Analysis (iPCA) methodology, extending traditional PCA for key feature extraction in disease diagnosis. Rao et al. (2019) introduced an Artificial Bee Colony Optimization with Decision Tree (ABCoDT) algorithm, which significantly enhanced both the efficiency and quality of feature selection processes. Ileberi et al. (2022) integrated genetic algorithm-based feature selection with multiple machine learning algorithms—including GaussianNB, DT, Logistic Regression (LR), SVM, and Random Forest (RF)—for credit card fraud detection. This integration demonstrated improved performance across all base machine learning algorithms, with the genetic algorithm-enhanced Random Forest model achieving a remarkable 99.98% overall accuracy. Qian et al. (2022) employed Permutation Importance (PIMP) to correct measurement bias in feature importance evaluation, revealing that the PIMP-XGBoost algorithm, which combines PIMP with XGBoost, exhibits superior predictive capability and interpretability.

6.3 Summary

This chapter reviews prevalent data preprocessing and feature selection methodologies employed in financial fraud detection research, addressing both class imbalance issues and the 'curse of dimensionality.' Given the multifaceted nature of financial fraud determinants, diversity of feature selection approaches, and scarcity of fraudulent instances, empirical research necessitates comprehensive consideration of data sampling methods, feature selection techniques, and machine learning algorithm selection. Innovation across data processing, indicator selection, and model algorithms is essential for developing more efficient financial fraud detection tools, aiming to enhance financial fraud detection accuracy while validating core indicators crucial to financial fraud detection, thereby expanding both the depth and breadth of financial fraud research.

References

Amiram D, Bozanic Z, Cox JD, Dupont Q (2018) Financial reporting fraud and other forms of misconduct: a multidisciplinary review of the literature. Rev Account Stud 23:732–783

Barboza F, Kimura H, Altman E (2017) Machine learning models and bankruptcy prediction. Expert Syst Appl 83:405–417

Beasley MS (1996) An empirical analysis of the relation between the board of director composition and financial statement fraud. Account Rev 71:443–465

Beaver WH (1966) Financial ratios as predictors of failure. J Account Res 4:71–111

Beneish MD (1999) The detection of earnings manipulation. Financ Anal J 55(5):24–36

Benesty J, Chen J, Huang Y (2008) On the importance of the Pearson correlation coefficient in noise reduction. IEEE Trans Audio Speech Lang Process 16(4):757–765

Cai J, Luo J, Wang S, Yang S (2018) Feature selection in machine learning: a new perspective. Neurocomputing 300:70–79

Cecchini M, Aytug H, Koehler GJ, Pathak P (2010) Detecting management fraud in public companies. Manag Sci 56(7):1146–1160

Chawla NV, Lazarevic A, Hall LO, Bowyer KW (2003) SMOTEBoost: Improving prediction of the minority class in boosting. Knowl Discov Databases PKDD 2003:107–119

Chen Y, Liginlal D (2008) A maximum entropy approach to feature selection in knowledge-based authentication. Decis Support Syst 46(1):388–398

Chen G, Firth M, Gao DN, Rui OM (2006) Ownership structure, corporate governance, and fraud: evidence from China. J Corp Finan 12(3):424–448
Dechow PM, Shakespear C (2009) Do managers time securitization transactions to obtain accounting benefits? Account Rev 84(1):99–132
Dechow PM, Ge W, Larson CR, Sloan RG (2011) Predicting material accounting misstatements. Contemp Account Res 28(1):17–82
Dhal P, Azad C (2022) A comprehensive survey on feature selection in the various fields of machine learning. Appl Intell 52:4543–4581
Esenogho E, Mienye ID, Swart TG, Maleka AM (2022) A neural network ensemble with feature engineering for improved credit card fraud detection. IEEE Access 10:16400–16407
Faris H, Abukhurma R, Almanaseer W, Saadeh M, Mora AM, Castillo PA, Aljarah I (2020) Improving financial bankruptcy prediction in a highly imbalanced class distribution using oversampling and ensemble learning: a case from the Spanish market. Prog Artif Intell 9:31–53
Gepp A, Kumar K, Bhattacharya S (2021) Lifting the numbers game: identifying key input variables and a best-performing model to detect financial statement fraud. Account Finance 61(3):4601–4638
Ghorbani R, Ghousi R (2020) Comparing different resampling methods in predicting students' performance using machine learning techniques. IEEE Access 8:67899–67911
Green BP, Choi JH (1997) Assessing the risk of management fraud through neural network technology. Auditing 16:14–28
Guyon I, Elisseeff A (2003) An introduction to variable and feature selection. J Mach Learn Res 3(Mar):1157–1182
Hass LH, Tarsalewska M, Zhan F (2016) Equity incentives and corporate fraud in China. J Bus Ethics 138:723–742
Hong H, Hu H, Guo C (2012) Research on financial reporting fraud identification of listed companies based on GONE theory. Account Res (08):84–90+97
Ileberi E, Sun Y, Wang Z (2022) A machine learning based credit card fraud detection using the GA algorithm for feature selection. J Big Data 9(1):1–17
Kaminski KA, Sterling Wetzel T, Guan L (2004) Can financial ratios detect fraudulent financial reporting? Manag Audit J 19(1):15–28
Kim SY, Upneja A (2014) Predicting restaurant financial distress using decision tree and AdaBoosted decision tree models. Econ Model 36:354–362
Kirkos E, Spathis C, Manolopoulos Y (2007) Data mining techniques for the detection of fraudulent financial statements. Expert Syst Appl 32(4):995–1003
Kou G, Xu Y, Peng Y, Shen F, Chen Y, Chang K, Kou S (2021) Bankruptcy prediction for SMEs using transactional data and two-stage multiobjective feature selection. Decis Support Syst 140:113429
Kumaraswamy N, Markey MK, Barner JC, Brown CM (2022) Feature engineering to detect fraud using healthcare claims data. Expert Syst Appl 210:118433
Li Z, Chi G (2021) Research on credit risk of listed companies based on maximum index discrimination and optimal relative membership. Chin J Manag Sci 29(04):1–15
Li Y, Yan C, Liu W, Li M (2018) A principle component analysis-based random forest with the potential nearest neighbor method for automobile insurance fraud identification. Appl Soft Comput 70:1000–1009
Lin CC, Chiu AA, Huang SY, Yen DC (2015) Detecting the financial statement fraud: The analysis of the differences between data mining techniques and experts' judgments. Knowl-Based Syst 89:459–470
Liu R, Huang J, Zhang Z (2023) Tracking disclosure change trajectories for financial fraud detection. Prod Oper Manag 32(2):584–602
Mu Y, Liu X, Wang L (2018) A Pearson's correlation coefficient based decision tree and its parallel implementation. Inf Sci 435:40–58
Omuya EO, Okeyo GO, Kimwele MW (2021) Feature selection for classification using principal component analysis and information gain. Expert Syst Appl 174:114765

Perols JL, Bowen RM, Zimmermann C, Samba B (2017) Finding needles in a haystack: using data analytics to improve fraud prediction. Account Rev 92(2):221–245

Piramuthu S (2003) On learning to predict web traffic. Decis Support Syst 35(2):213–229

Qian H, Wang B, Yuan M, Li J (2022) Financial distress prediction using a corrected feature selection measure and gradient boosted decision tree. Expert Syst Appl 190:116202

Qian P, Luo M (2015) Financial fraud prediction model for Chinese listed companies. Account Res (07):18–25+96

Rahman MJ, Zhu H (2023) Predicting accounting fraud using imbalanced ensemble learning classifiers–evidence from China. Account Finance 63(3):3455–3486

Rao H, Shi X, Rodrigue AK, Feng J (2019) Feature selection based on artificial bee colony and gradient boosting decision tree. Appl Soft Comput 74:634–642

Ravisankar P, Ravi V, Rao GR, Bose I (2011) Detection of financial statement fraud and feature selection using data mining techniques. Decis Support Syst 50(2):491–500

Seiffert C, Khoshgoftaar TM, Van Hulse J, Napolitano A (2009) RUSBoost: a hybrid approach to alleviating class imbalance. IEEE Trans Syst Man Cybern Part A Syst Hum 40(1):185–197

Tang TM, Allen GI (2021) Integrated principal components analysis. J Mach Learn Res 22(1):8953–9023

Wei L, Xu L, Liu J (2011) Identification of financial reporting fraud in listed companies: an empirical study based on triangle theory. Audit Res 02:98–106

Xiao J, Wang Y, Chen J, Li X (2021) Impact of resampling methods and classification models on the imbalanced credit scoring problems. Inf Sci 569:508–526

Xu M, Zhang C (2009) Bankruptcy prediction: the case of Japanese listed companies. Rev Account Stud 14(4):534–558

Xu X, Xiong F, An Z (2023) Using machine learning to predict corporate fraud: evidence based on the gone framework. J Bus Ethics 186(1):137–158

Ye Q, Ye F, Huang S (2022) Construction of financial fraud identification framework: based on accounting information system theory and big data perspective. Account Res 03:3–16

Yildirim P (2015) Filter based feature selection methods for prediction of risks in hepatitis disease. Int J Mach Learn Comput 5(4):258

Yuan X, Zhou Y, Yan C, Liu H, Qian G, Wang F, Wei L, Li Z, Li B, Li X, Zeng T (2022) Establishment and application of financial fraud risk characteristic screening framework. Chin J Manag Sci 30(03):43–54

Zhou Y, Fan J, Xue L (2024) How much can machines learn finance from Chinese text data? Manag Sci 70(12):8962–8987

Chapter 7
Detection Models and Applications

This chapter briefly introduces the evolution of financial fraud detection methods from traditional statistical regression through conventional machine learning algorithms to ensemble learning and deep learning algorithms, along with their specific applications in financial fraud research. Al-Hashedi and Magalingam (2021) reviewed 75 fraud studies using big data mining techniques between 2009 and 2019, finding that applications of big data mining techniques in financial statement fraud remained relatively limited, and most related researches (61 articles, 81.33%) focused on bank and insurance fraud detection. As Beneish and Vorst (2022) noted, fraud detection models based on big data technologies may be too costly to implement in accounting audit practice.

Currently, financial fraud detection research demonstrates two parallel trends: innovation in complex algorithms such as deep learning and knowledge graphs, and extensive research utilizing established machine learning methods within accounting domain knowledge frameworks, both yielding remarkable research results. Although deep learning anomaly detection techniques have increasingly been applied to financial fraud detection in recent years, traditional non-deep models such as MLP, SVM, LR, and DT remain common and mature detection models in the field of financial statement fraud detection (De Bock et al. 2020). Al-Hashedi and Magalingam (2021) summarized that SVM was one of the most widely used data mining techniques among for fraud identification, accounting for approximately 23% of all 34 studies, followed by Naive Bayes and RF at 15% each. Similarly, Zhu et al. (2021) examined 33 prominent articles in intelligent financial fraud detection, finding that 39.4% (13 articles) employed non-deep learning methods, including traditional machine learning algorithms such as Bayesian, LR, RF, and SVM, achieving favorable classification results and interpretability.

However, financial fraud detection studies vary significantly in specific contexts, utilizing different databases, fraud definitions, indicator systems, and model algorithms, leading to variations in classification results. While the best accuracy rates generally maintain above 80%, there is no consensus in academia regarding the

X. Ma and D. Wu, *Financial Fraud Detection Using Machine Learning*, AI for Risks,
https://doi.org/10.1007/978-981-95-0840-2_7

optimal financial fraud detection model. Meanwhile, the classification results based on data mining models should serve as complementary tools to expert opinions, rather than replacing them (Lin et al. 2015; Gepp et al. 2021). Additionally, emerging fraud detection tools such as text and voice analysis remain underutilized in financial fraud detection research, suggesting significant potential for future development (Zhou et al. 2024).

In its early stages, financial fraud detection primarily relied on statistical regression models, including Linear Discriminant Analysis (LDA), binary Probit regression, and Logit regression (Su and Lin 2010; Hong et al. 2012; Qian and Luo 2015; Yao and Zhao 2016; Li et al. 2020). Some of these models evolved into fraud indices such as Mscore, Fscore, and Cscore to measure the occurrence likelihood of financial fraud. As data mining techniques continue to evolve, machine learning algorithms are increasingly superseding traditional statistical analysis methods. In this section, we conduct a comprehensive analysis comparing traditional machine learning algorithms with deep learning approaches in the context of financial fraud detection. Each algorithm is thoroughly examined through an analysis of its underlying mathematical principles and implementation details. The mathematical foundations are presented alongside corresponding code implementations to provide a comprehensive understanding of each method.

7.1 Traditional Machine Learning Algorithms

Scholars have integrated machine learning algorithms into statistical regression methods for classification, regression, clustering, prediction, and anomaly detection (Ravisankar et al. 2011; Gepp et al. 2018; Craja et al. 2020). Traditional machine learning classification algorithms include linear regression model, logisctic regression (LR) model (Bertomeu et al. 2021), decision tree (DT) model (Li et al. 2020; Gepp et al. 2021), support vector machine (SVM) model and its derivatives (Cecchini et al. 2010; Ravisankar et al. 2011; Purda and Skillicorn 2015; Gepp et al. 2021), bayesian model, regularization, neural networks (Lin et al. 2015; Gepp et al. 2018) and their ensembles. This section briefly introduces mathematical principles of seven traditional machine learning models, including LR, SVM, Gaussian Naive Bayes (GaussianNB), the random forest (RF), Adaptive Boosting (AdaBoost), and Gradient Boosting Decision Tree (GBDT).

Machine learning algorithms have been successfully integrated into statistical regression methods, enabling various analytical tasks including classification, regression, clustering, prediction, and anomaly detection (Ravisankar et al. 2011; Gepp et al. 2018; Craja et al. 2020). Traditional machine learning encompasses several key classification algorithms: logistic regression (LR) (Bertomeu et al. 2021), decision trees (DT) (Li et al. 2020; Gepp et al. 2021), support vector machines (SVM) and their derivatives (Cecchini et al. 2010; Ravisankar et al. 2011; Purda and Skillicorn 2015; Gepp et al. 2021), Bayesian models, regularization techniques, neural networks (Lin et al. 2015; Gepp et al. 2018), and their ensemble variants. This section examines the mathematical principles underlying seven prominent machine learning models: LR, SVM, Gaussian Naive Bayes (GaussianNB), Random Forest (RF), Adaptive Boosting (AdaBoost), and Gradient Boosting Decision Tree (GBDT). Among them, SVM and GaussianNB are derived from statistical learning theory, and LR is a traditional statistical analysis technique, while the RF, AdaBoost, and GBDT belong to ensemble learning techniques which commonly employ the DT model as a base learner. These machine learning algorithms are capable of analyzing the same problem from multiple perspectives based on different mathematical principles. Each algorithm approaches problem-solving from a unique mathematical perspective, offering diverse analytical capabilities.

7.1.1 Logistic Regression

The logistic regression model transforms continuous input values into probability estimates through the Sigmoid function, which maps values from (-∞, + ∞) to the interval (0, 1). This probabilistic output quantifies the likelihood of specific events, such as corporate financial fraud or loan default. The model implements classification decisions through a threshold mechanism – typically set at 0.5 – where observations exceeding this threshold are classified as positive cases (e.g., fraudulent companies). The mathematical framework incorporates a feature vector X and a parameter vector β, with $P(Y = 1)$ denoting the probability of the positive class, which can be expressed as below.

$$P(Y = 1) = \frac{1}{1 + e^{-X\beta}}$$

In binary classification problems, the target variable Y takes values of either 0 or 1. The conditional probability of Y, given feature vector X and parameter vector β, can be expressed as:

$$P(Y|X, \beta) = \left(\frac{1}{1 + e^{-X\beta}}\right)^{Y} \left(1 - \frac{1}{1 + e^{-X\beta}}\right)^{1-Y}$$

The logistic regression model estimates its parameters β through maximum likelihood estimation, optimizing the likelihood function $L(\beta)$. The optimal parameter estimates are obtained when $L(\beta)$ reaches its maximum value. Several optimization algorithms can be employed for this purpose, including Gradient Descent, Newton's method, Quasi-Newton methods, Stochastic Gradient Descent, and Least Angle Regression. These methods iteratively adjust the values of β to maximize the likelihood function.

$$L(\beta) = \prod_{i=1}^{n} P(Y_i|X_i, \beta) = \prod_{i=1}^{n} \left(\frac{1}{1 + e^{-X_i\beta}}\right)^{Y_i} \left(1 - \frac{1}{1 + e^{-X_i\beta}}\right)^{1-Y_i}$$

This implementation encompasses data preprocessing, model training, performance evaluation, visualization of results, and probability analysis. The code provides a foundation for binary classification tasks using logistic regression.

```
import numpy as np
import pandas as pd
import matplotlib.pyplot as plt
from sklearn.model_selection import train_test_split
from sklearn.linear_model import LogisticRegression
from sklearn.preprocessing import StandardScaler
from sklearn.metrics import accuracy_score, classification_report,
confusion_matrix
import seaborn as sns

# Assuming X and Y have benn input, split them into training and testing sets
# Data Preprocessing
X_train, X_test, y_train, y_test = train_test_split(X, Y, test_size=0.2,
random_state=42)
scaler = StandardScaler()
X_train_scaled = scaler.fit_transform(X_train)
X_test_scaled = scaler.transform(X_test)

# Model Training and Evaluation
model = LogisticRegression(random_state=42, max_iter=1000)
model.fit(X_train_scaled, y_train)
y_pred = model.predict(X_test_scaled)
y_pred_prob = model.predict_proba(X_test_scaled)[:, 1]

# Performance Metrics
print(f"Accuracy: {accuracy_score(y_test, y_pred):.4f}")
print("\nClassification Report:")
print(classification_report(y_test, y_pred))

# Visualization
plt.figure(figsize=(15, 5))
# Feature importance plot
plt.subplot(131)
feature_importance = pd.DataFrame({
```

```
    'Feature': [f'Feature {i+1}' for i in range(X.shape[1])],
    'Coefficient': model.coef_[0]
})
sns.barplot(data=feature_importance, x='Feature', y='Coefficient')

# Confusion matrix
plt.subplot(132)
cm = confusion_matrix(y_test, y_pred)
sns.heatmap(cm, annot=True, fmt='d', cmap='Blues')

# ROC curve
plt.subplot(133)
fpr, tpr, _ = roc_curve(y_test, y_pred_prob)
roc_auc = auc(fpr, tpr)
plt.plot(fpr, tpr, label=f'ROC curve (AUC = {roc_auc:.2f})')
plt.plot([0, 1], [0, 1], linestyle='—')

# Probability Analysis
probability = model.predict_proba(X_test_scaled[0:1])[0]
print(f"Class probabilities: {probability}")
```

To implement a more advanced logistic regression, optimizations are needed in several aspects including model training and optimization, cross-validation, feature selection, model diagnostics, and confidence intervals, which will enhance the robustness, interpretability, reliability, and practicality of this model. Here are several sophisticated enhancements we can add to make the logistic regression more comprehensive and advanced.

(1) Model Training & Optimization includes custom gradient descent implementation, L1 and L2 regularization, Learning rate optimization and convergence monitoring.

```
import numpy as np
from sklearn.preprocessing import StandardScaler
from sklearn.model_selection import train_test_split

class AdvancedLogisticRegression:
    def __init__(self, learning_rate=0.01, max_iter=1000,
                 tolerance=1e-6, lambda_l1=0.1, lambda_l2=0.1):
        self.learning_rate = learning_rate
        self.max_iter = max_iter
        self.tolerance = tolerance
        self.lambda_l1 = lambda_l1
        self.lambda_l2 = lambda_l2
        self.weights = None
        self.intercept = None
        self.training_loss = []

    def sigmoid(self, z):
        """Sigmoid activation function"""
        return 1 / (1 + np.exp(-np.clip(z, -250, 250)))

    def fit(self, X_train, y_train):
        """Train the model"""
        n_samples, n_features = X_train.shape
        # Initialize parameters
        self.weights = np.zeros(n_features)
        self.intercept = 0
        for iteration in range(self.max_iter):
            # Forward propagation
            z = np.dot(X_train, self.weights) + self.intercept
            predictions = self.sigmoid(z)
            # Calculate loss
            loss = self._compute_loss(y_train, predictions)
            self.training_loss.append(loss)
            # Calculate gradients
            d_weights, d_intercept = self._compute_gradients(
                X_train, y_train, predictions, n_samples)
            # Update parameters
            weights_old = self.weights.copy()
            self.weights -= self.learning_rate * d_weights
            self.intercept -= self.learning_rate * d_intercept
```

```
            # Check convergence
            if np.all(np.abs(self.weights - weights_old) < self.tolerance):
                print(f"Converged at iteration {iteration}")
                break
        return self

    def _compute_loss(self, y_true, y_pred):
        """Compute loss function (including regularization)"""
        # Cross-entropy loss
        eps = 1e-15
        cross_entropy = -np.mean(
            y_true * np.log(y_pred + eps) +
            (1 - y_true) * np.log(1 - y_pred + eps)
        )

        # Regularization terms
        l1_reg = self.lambda_l1 * np.sum(np.abs(self.weights))
        l2_reg = self.lambda_l2 * np.sum(self.weights ** 2)

        return cross_entropy + l1_reg + l2_reg

    def _compute_gradients(self, X, y_true, y_pred, n_samples):
        """Compute gradients (including regularization)"""
        # Base gradients
        d_weights = (1 / n_samples) * np.dot(X.T, (y_pred - y_true))
        d_intercept = np.mean(y_pred - y_true)

        # Add regularization gradients
        d_weights += (self.lambda_l1 * np.sign(self.weights) +
                      2 * self.lambda_l2 * self.weights)
        return d_weights, d_intercept

    def predict_proba(self, X):
        """Predict probabilities"""
        z = np.dot(X, self.weights) + self.intercept
        return self.sigmoid(z)

    def predict(self, X, threshold=0.5):
        """Predict classes"""
        return (self.predict_proba(X) >= threshold).astype(int)
```

(2) Comprehensive Cross-Validation includes four key factors including k-fold cross-validation, multiple evaluation metrics, training–testing performance comparison and model stability assessment.

```python
from sklearn.model_selection import KFold, cross_validate
from sklearn.metrics import make_scorer, accuracy_score, precision_score
from sklearn.metrics import recall_score, f1_score, roc_auc_score
import numpy as np
import pandas as pd

class AdvancedCrossValidation:
    def __init__(self, n_splits=5, random_state=42):
        self.n_splits = n_splits
        self.random_state = random_state
        self.cv_results = None

    def get_scoring_metrics(self):
        """Define multiple evaluation metrics"""
        return {
            'accuracy': make_scorer(accuracy_score),
            'precision': make_scorer(precision_score),
            'recall': make_scorer(recall_score),
            'f1': make_scorer(f1_score),
            'roc_auc': make_scorer(roc_auc_score)
        }

    def perform_cv(self, model, X_train, y_train):
        """Perform cross-validation with multiple metrics"""
        # Initialize K-Fold
        kf = KFold(
            n_splits=self.n_splits,
            shuffle=True,
            random_state=self.random_state
        )
        # Get scoring metrics
        scoring = self.get_scoring_metrics()
        # Perform cross-validation
        self.cv_results = cross_validate(
            estimator=model,
            X=X_train,
            y=y_train,
            cv=kf,
            scoring=scoring,
            return_train_score=True,
            n_jobs=-1
        )
```

```
        return self.cv_results

    def analyze_cv_results(self):
        """Analyze cross-validation results"""
        if self.cv_results is None:
            raise ValueError("No CV results available. Run perform_cv first.")

            # Calculate mean and std for each metric
        analysis = {}
        for metric in self.get_scoring_metrics().keys():
            test_scores = self.cv_results[f'test_{metric}']
            train_scores = self.cv_results[f'train_{metric}']
            analysis[metric] = {
                'test_mean': np.mean(test_scores),
                'test_std': np.std(test_scores),
                'train_mean': np.mean(train_scores),
                'train_std': np.std(train_scores),
                'overfitting_gap': np.mean(train_scores) - np.mean(test_scores)
            }
        return pd.DataFrame(analysis).round(4)
```

(3) Feature selection encompasses automated feature selection, dimensionality reduction, feature importance analysis and interaction terms creation.

```
import numpy as np
import pandas as pd
from sklearn.preprocessing import StandardScaler, RobustScaler
from sklearn.feature_selection import SelectKBest, RFE, SelectFromModel
from sklearn.decomposition import PCA
from sklearn.ensemble import RandomForestClassifier
from sklearn.linear_model import Lasso

class AdvancedFeatureProcessor:
    def __init__(self):
        # Data preprocessing
        self.scaler = StandardScaler()
        self.robust_scaler = RobustScaler()
        # Feature selection components
        self.selector_k_best = SelectKBest(k=10)
```

```
        self.selector_rfe = RFE(
            estimator=RandomForestClassifier(random_state=42),
            n_features_to_select=10
        )
        self.selector_l1 = SelectFromModel(
            Lasso(alpha=0.01, random_state=42)
        )
        # Dimensionality reduction
        self.pca = PCA(n_components=0.95)  # Preserve 95% variance
        # Store feature names
        self.feature_names = None
        self.selected_features = None

    def feature_engineering(self, X):
        """Create new features"""
        if isinstance(X, pd.DataFrame):
            X = X.copy()
            # Numerical feature interactions
            num_cols = X.select_dtypes(include=['float64', 'int64']).columns
            for i in range(len(num_cols)):
                for j in range(i + 1, len(num_cols)):
                    col1, col2 = num_cols[i], num_cols[j]
                    X[f'{col1}_mult_{col2}'] = X[col1] * X[col2]
                    X[f'{col1}_div_{col2}'] = X[col1] / (X[col2] + 1e-8)
                    # Polynomial features
            for col in num_cols:
                X[f'{col}_squared'] = X[col] ** 2
                X[f'{col}_cubed'] = X[col] ** 3
            return X
        else:
            raise ValueError("Input data must be pandas DataFrame")

    def feature_selection(self, X, y):
        """Comprehensive feature selection"""
        # Calculate importance scores
        importance_scores = {}
        # K-Best selection
        self.selector_k_best.fit(X, y)
        importance_scores['k_best'] = self.selector_k_best.scores_
        # RFE selection
        self.selector_rfe.fit(X, y)
        importance_scores['rfe'] = self.selector_rfe.ranking_
        # L1 selection
        self.selector_l1.fit(X, y)
```

```
        importance_scores['l1'] = self.selector_l1.feature_importances_
        return importance_scores

    def fit_transform(self, X_train, y_train):
        """Complete feature processing pipeline"""
        # Save feature names
        self.feature_names = (X_train.columns
                              if isinstance(X_train, pd.DataFrame)
                              else None)

        # 1. Feature engineering
        X_train_engineered = self.feature_engineering(X_train)
        # 2. Standardization
        X_train_scaled = self.scaler.fit_transform(X_train_engineered)
        X_train_scaled = pd.DataFrame(
            X_train_scaled,
            columns=X_train_engineered.columns
        )
        # 3. Feature selection
        importance_scores = self.feature_selection(X_train_scaled, y_train)
        # 4. Combine scores to select final features
        final_scores = np.zeros(X_train_scaled.shape[1])
        for scores in importance_scores.values():
            final_scores += (scores - np.min(scores)) / (np.max(scores)
np.min(scores))
            # Select top scoring features
        top_features = np.argsort(final_scores)[-10:]  # Select top 10 features
        self.selected_features = X_train_scaled.columns[top_features]

        # 5. Dimensionality reduction (optional)
        X_train_selected = X_train_scaled[self.selected_features]
        X_train_pca = self.pca.fit_transform(X_train_selected)
        return X_train_pca, importance_scores

    def transform(self, X_test):
        """Transform test data"""
        # 1. Feature engineering
        X_test_engineered = self.feature_engineering(X_test)
        # 2. Standardization
        X_test_scaled = self.scaler.transform(X_test_engineered)
        X_test_scaled = pd.DataFrame(
            X_test_scaled,
            columns=X_test_engineered.columns
        )
        # 3. Feature selection
        X_test_selected = X_test_scaled[self.selected_features]
        # 4. Dimensionality reduction
        X_test_pca = self.pca.transform(X_test_selected)
        return X_test_pca
```

(4) Model diagnostics includes influence point analysis, multicollinearity checks, residual analysis and model stability tests.

```python
import numpy as np
import pandas as pd
import matplotlib.pyplot as plt
import seaborn as sns
from sklearn.metrics import roc_curve, precision_recall_curve
from sklearn.inspection import permutation_importance
from scipy import stats


class AdvancedModelDiagnostics:
    def __init__(self, model):
        self.model = model
        self.diagnostics_results = {}
    def analyze_prediction_distribution(self, X, y_true):
        """Analyze distribution of model prediction probabilities"""
        y_pred_proba = self.model.predict_proba(X)[:, 1]
        plt.figure(figsize=(10, 6))
        sns.histplot(data=pd.DataFrame({
            'Positive Probability': y_pred_proba,
            'Actual Class': y_true
        }), x='Positive Probability', hue='Actual Class', bins=50)
        plt.title('Prediction Probability Distribution')
        plt.show()
        return {
            'mean_prediction_prob': np.mean(y_pred_proba),
            'std_prediction_prob': np.std(y_pred_proba),
            'prediction_quantiles': np.percentile(y_pred_proba, [25, 50, 75])
        }
    def analyze_decision_boundary(self, X, y, feature_names=None):
        """Analyze samples near decision boundary"""
        y_pred_proba = self.model.predict_proba(X)[:, 1]

        # Find samples near decision boundary (probability close to 0.5)
        boundary_samples = np.abs(y_pred_proba - 0.5) < 0.1
        boundary_X = X[boundary_samples]
```

```
        if feature_names is None:
            feature_names = [f'Feature_{i}' for i in range(X.shape[1])]
            # Analyze feature distribution of boundary samples
        boundary_analysis = pd.DataFrame(
            boundary_X,
            columns=feature_names
        ).describe()
        return {
            'boundary_sample_count': len(boundary_X),
            'boundary_sample_ratio': len(boundary_X) / len(X),
            'boundary_analysis': boundary_analysis
        }
    def analyze_prediction_errors(self, X, y_true):
        """Analyze patterns in prediction errors"""
        y_pred = self.model.predict(X)
        y_pred_proba = self.model.predict_proba(X)[:, 1]
        errors = (y_true != y_pred)
        error_probs = y_pred_proba[errors]
        return {
            'error_rate': np.mean(errors),
            'high_confidence_errors': np.sum((y_pred_proba > 0.9) & errors),
            'low_confidence_errors': np.sum((y_pred_proba < 0.6) & errors),
            'error_prob_distribution': {
                'mean': np.mean(error_probs),
                'std': np.std(error_probs),
                'quantiles': np.percentile(error_probs, [25, 50, 75])
            }
        }

    def analyze_feature_importance_stability(self, X, y, n_repeats=10):
        """Analyze stability of feature importance"""
        # Use permutation importance
        result = permutation_importance(
            self.model, X, y,
            n_repeats=n_repeats,
            random_state=42
        )
        importance_stats = pd.DataFrame({
            'mean_importance': result.importances_mean,
            'importance_std': result.importances_std
        })
        return {
            'importance_statistics': importance_stats,
            'stability_score': np.mean(
```

```
                result.importances_std / (result.importances_mean + 1e-10)
            )
        }

    def analyze_model_calibration(self, X, y_true, n_bins=10):
        """Analyze model probability calibration"""
        y_pred_proba = self.model.predict_proba(X)[:, 1]
        # Create probability bins
        bins = np.linspace(0, 1, n_bins + 1)
        bin_indices = np.digitize(y_pred_proba, bins) - 1
        # Calculate actual positive rate for each bin
        calibration_data = []
        for i in range(n_bins):
            mask = (bin_indices == i)
            if np.sum(mask) > 0:
                actual_prob = np.mean(y_true[mask])
                pred_prob = np.mean(y_pred_proba[mask])
                calibration_data.append({
                    'predicted_prob': pred_prob,
                    'actual_prob': actual_prob,
                    'sample_count': np.sum(mask)
                })
        return pd.DataFrame(calibration_data)

    def run_complete_diagnostics(self, X_train, X_test, y_train, y_test):
        """Run complete model diagnostics"""
        self.diagnostics_results = {
            'train': {
                'prediction_dist': self.analyze_prediction_distribution(X_train,
y_train),
                'decision_boundary': self.analyze_decision_boundary(X_train,
y_train),
                'prediction_errors': self.analyze_prediction_errors(X_train,
y_train),
                'feature_importance':
self.analyze_feature_importance_stability(X_train, y_train),
                'calibration': self.analyze_model_calibration(X_train, y_train)
            },
            'test': {
                'prediction_dist': self.analyze_prediction_distribution(X_test,
y_test),
                'decision_boundary': self.analyze_decision_boundary(X_test,
y_test),
                'prediction_errors': self.analyze_prediction_errors(X_test,
y_test),
                'feature_importance':
self.analyze_feature_importance_stability(X_test, y_test),
                'calibration': self.analyze_model_calibration(X_test, y_test)
            }
        }
        return self.diagnostics_results
```

(5) Confidence intervals includes bootstrap estimation, parameter uncertainty quantification, prediction intervals and model reliability assessment.

```
import numpy as np
import pandas as pd
from scipy import stats
from sklearn.utils import resample
from sklearn.metrics import accuracy_score, precision_score, recall_score
import matplotlib.pyplot as plt
from tqdm import tqdm

class AdvancedConfidenceIntervals:
    def __init__(self, model, confidence_level=0.95):
        self.model = model
        self.confidence_level = confidence_level
        self.bootstrap_results = None
    def bootstrap_predictions(self, X, y_true, n_iterations=1000):
        """Calculate prediction confidence intervals using Bootstrap method"""
        n_samples = len(X)
        predictions = []
        metrics = {
            'accuracy': [],
            'precision': [],
            'recall': []
        }
        for _ in tqdm(range(n_iterations), desc="Bootstrap Progress"):
            # Random sampling with replacement
            indices = resample(range(n_samples), n_samples=n_samples)
            X_bootstrap = X[indices]
            y_bootstrap = y_true[indices]

            # Get prediction probabilities
            y_pred_proba = self.model.predict_proba(X_bootstrap)
            y_pred = self.model.predict(X_bootstrap)
            # Store prediction results
            predictions.append(y_pred_proba)
            # Calculate performance metrics
```

```
            metrics['accuracy'].append(accuracy_score(y_bootstrap, y_pred))
            metrics['precision'].append(precision_score(y_bootstrap, y_pred))
            metrics['recall'].append(recall_score(y_bootstrap, y_pred))
        return np.array(predictions), metrics

    def calculate_prediction_intervals(self, X, alpha=0.05):
        """Calculate confidence intervals for individual predictions"""
        predictions = self.model.predict_proba(X)
        # Calculate confidence intervals using Beta distribution
        n_samples = len(X)
        intervals = []
        for i in range(n_samples):
            p = predictions[i, 1]  # Positive class probability
            # Beta distribution parameters
            a = p * 100
            b = (1 - p) * 100
            lower = stats.beta.ppf(alpha / 2, a, b)
            upper = stats.beta.ppf(1 - alpha / 2, a, b)
            intervals.append([lower, upper])
        return np.array(intervals)

    def bayesian_confidence_interval(self, X, y_true, n_samples=1000):
        """Calculate confidence intervals using Bayesian method"""
        n_instances = len(X)
        predictions = self.model.predict_proba(X)[:, 1]
        # Use Beta prior
        alpha_prior = 1
        beta_prior = 1
        # Posterior distribution parameters
        alpha_post = alpha_prior + predictions * n_instances
        beta_post = beta_prior + (1 - predictions) * n_instances
        # Sample from posterior distribution
        posterior_samples = np.random.beta(alpha_post, beta_post,
                                          size=(n_samples, n_instances))
        # Calculate confidence intervals
        lower = np.percentile(posterior_samples, 2.5, axis=0)
        upper = np.percentile(posterior_samples, 97.5, axis=0)
        return np.column_stack([lower, upper])

    def calibrated_confidence_interval(self, X, y_true, n_bins=10):
        """Calculate calibrated confidence intervals"""
        predictions = self.model.predict_proba(X)[:, 1]
        # Create probability bins
        bins = np.linspace(0, 1, n_bins + 1)
```

```
        bin_indices = np.digitize(predictions, bins) - 1
        calibrated_intervals = []
        for i in range(len(predictions)):
            bin_idx = bin_indices[i]
            bin_mask = bin_indices == bin_idx
            if np.sum(bin_mask) > 1:
                # Calculate empirical probability in this bin
                emp_prob = np.mean(y_true[bin_mask])
                # Calculate standard error
                std_error = np.sqrt(emp_prob * (1 - emp_prob) / np.sum(bin_mask))
                # Calculate confidence interval
                z_score = stats.norm.ppf(1 - (1 - self.confidence_level) / 2)
                margin = z_score * std_error
                lower = max(0, emp_prob - margin)
                upper = min(1, emp_prob + margin)
            else:
                # If too few samples in bin, use original prediction
                lower = predictions[i] - 0.1
                upper = predictions[i] + 0.1
            calibrated_intervals.append([lower, upper])
        return np.array(calibrated_intervals)

    def analyze_confidence_intervals(self, X, y_true):
        """Comprehensive analysis of different confidence interval methods"""
        # 1. Bootstrap confidence intervals
        bootstrap_preds,    bootstrap_metrics    =    self.bootstrap_predictions(X,
y_true)
        # 2. Prediction confidence intervals
        pred_intervals = self.calculate_prediction_intervals(X)
        # 3. Bayesian confidence intervals
        bayes_intervals = self.bayesian_confidence_interval(X, y_true)
        # 4. Calibrated confidence intervals
        calibrated_intervals = self.calibrated_confidence_interval(X, y_true)
        return {
            'bootstrap': {
                'predictions': bootstrap_preds,
                'metrics': bootstrap_metrics
            },
            'prediction_intervals': pred_intervals,
            'bayesian_intervals': bayes_intervals,
            'calibrated_intervals': calibrated_intervals
        }
```

7.1.2 Support Vector Machine

Support Vector Machine (SVM) operates on a dataset of n samples, where each sample consists of p input features X $= \left(x_1, x_2, \ldots, x_p\right)$ and a binary output label y that takes values of either 1 or -1. This algorithm seeks to construct an optimal hyperplane $W^T X + b = 0$ in the feature space that maximizes the margin between two classes of samples. Here, W represents the weight vector, b denotes the bias term, and X represents the sample points.

$$W = (w_1, w_2, \ldots, w_p)^T$$

$$X_i = \left(x_{i1}, x_{i2}, \ldots, x_{ip}\right)^T, i = 1,2, \ldots n$$

The key principle of SVM lies in its focus on boundary points, known as support vectors, which alone determine the position of the maximum-margin hyperplane. These support vectors, located on the boundaries between classes, play a crucial role in defining the optimal decision boundary. The algorithm finds this boundary by maximizing the geometric margin d —the Euclidean distance from support vectors to the hyperplane. The optimization process involves solving for parameters W and b through equation shown in below, where $\|W\|$ represents the Euclidean norm of the weight vector.

$$\mathrm{d} = \frac{\left|W^T X + b\right|}{\|W\|}$$

The SVM classifier mitigates the "curse of dimensionality" by basing its decisions solely on support vectors, thereby effectively reducing the risk of overfitting. Additionally, this approach makes SVM particularly robust in handling binary classification problems with small sample sizes, nonlinear relationships, and high-dimensional data. Meanwhile, it employs kernel functions and slack variables to transform the linearly non-separable samples into a higher-dimensional feature space where it can identify an optimal hyperplane by maximizing the geometric margin between classes. The introduction of kernel functions enables SVM to efficiently process complex nonlinear classification tasks without explicitly computing the high-dimensional feature mappings.

The implementation of SVM using scikit-learn encompasses several key components, including data preprocessing, model training and evaluation, visualization techniques, and advanced analysis. We chose the Radial Basis Function (RBF) kernel function as the default, which typically offers good performance across different datasets, and includes probability prediction support for classification tasks. For visualization, the implementation provides decision boundary plotting for two-dimensional data, support vector visualization, and ROC curve analysis to evaluate model performance. The advanced analysis section comprises comprehensive support vector analysis, kernel function parameter examination, cross-validation for model robustness assessment, and hyperparameter tuning through grid search optimization. This implementation provides flexibility in parameter adjustment and visualization settings to accommodate various classification tasks, while the included analysis tools enable thorough model evaluation and optimization.

```
import numpy as np
import pandas as pd
import matplotlib.pyplot as plt
from sklearn.model_selection import train_test_split
from sklearn.svm import SVC
from sklearn.preprocessing import StandardScaler
from sklearn.metrics import accuracy_score, classification_report,
confusion_matrix
from sklearn.metrics import roc_curve, auc
import seaborn as sns

# Data Preprocessing
X_train, X_test, y_train, y_test = train_test_split(X, y, test_size=0.2,
random_state=42)
scaler = StandardScaler()
X_train_scaled = scaler.fit_transform(X_train)
X_test_scaled = scaler.transform(X_test)

# Model Training and Evaluation
# Using RBF kernel which is generally a good default choice
model = SVC(kernel='rbf', probability=True, random_state=42)
model.fit(X_train_scaled, y_train)
y_pred = model.predict(X_test_scaled)
y_pred_prob = model.predict_proba(X_test_scaled)[:, 1]
```

```
# Performance Metrics
print(f"Accuracy: {accuracy_score(y_test, y_pred):.4f}")
print("\nClassification Report:")
print(classification_report(y_test, y_pred))

# Visualization
plt.figure(figsize=(15, 5))
# Support Vector Analysis
plt.subplot(131)
if X.shape[1] == 2:  # Only for 2D data
    x_min, x_max = X_train_scaled[:, 0].min() - 1, X_train_scaled[:, 0].max() + 1
    y_min, y_max = X_train_scaled[:, 1].min() - 1, X_train_scaled[:, 1].max() + 1
    xx, yy = np.meshgrid(np.arange(x_min, x_max, 0.02),
                         np.arange(y_min, y_max, 0.02))
    Z = model.predict(np.c_[xx.ravel(), yy.ravel()])
    Z = Z.reshape(xx.shape)
    plt.contourf(xx, yy, Z, alpha=0.4)
    plt.scatter(X_train_scaled[:, 0], X_train_scaled[:, 1], c=y_train, alpha=0.8)
    plt.scatter(model.support_vectors_[:, 0], model.support_vectors_[:, 1],
               color='red', marker='x', s=100, linewidth=2, label='Support
Vectors')
    plt.title('Decision Boundary and Support Vectors')
    plt.legend()
else:
    # For high-dimensional data, show number of support vectors per class
    n_support = model.n_support_
    classes = np.unique(y_train)
    support_vectors_data = pd.DataFrame({
        'Class': [f'Class {c}' for c in classes],
        'Number of Support Vectors': n_support
    })
    sns.barplot(data=support_vectors_data, x='Class', y='Number of Support
Vectors')
    plt.title('Support Vectors per Class')

# Confusion Matrix
plt.subplot(132)
cm = confusion_matrix(y_test, y_pred)
sns.heatmap(cm, annot=True, fmt='d', cmap='Blues')
plt.title('Confusion Matrix')

# ROC Curve
plt.subplot(133)
fpr, tpr, _ = roc_curve(y_test, y_pred_prob)
```

```
roc_auc = auc(fpr, tpr)
plt.plot(fpr, tpr, label=f'ROC curve (AUC = {roc_auc:.2f})')
plt.plot([0, 1], [0, 1], linestyle='--')
plt.xlabel('False Positive Rate')
plt.ylabel('True Positive Rate')
plt.title('ROC Curve')
plt.legend()
plt.tight_layout()
plt.show()

# Additional Analysis
print("\nModel Details:")
print(f"Number of Support Vectors: {model.n_support_}")
print(f"Support Vector Indices: {model.support_}")

# Kernel Parameters
if model.kernel == 'rbf':
    print(f"Gamma parameter: {model.gamma}")
print(f"C parameter: {model.C}")

# Probability Analysis for a single sample
probability = model.predict_proba(X_test_scaled[0:1])[0]
print(f"\nClass probabilities for first test sample: {probability}")

# Cross-validation score (optional)
from sklearn.model_selection import cross_val_score
cv_scores = cross_val_score(model, X_train_scaled, y_train, cv=5)
print(f"\nCross-validation scores: {cv_scores}")
print(f"Average CV score: {cv_scores.mean():.4f} (+/- {cv_scores.std() * 2:.4f})")

# Hyperparameter tuning (optional)
from sklearn.model_selection import GridSearchCV
param_grid = {
    'C': [0.1, 1, 10],
    'gamma': ['scale', 'auto', 0.1, 1],
    'kernel': ['rbf', 'linear']
}
grid_search = GridSearchCV(SVC(probability=True), param_grid, cv=5)
grid_search.fit(X_train_scaled, y_train)
print("\nBest parameters:", grid_search.best_params_)
print("Best cross-validation score:", grid_search.best_score_)
```

7.1.3 Random Forest

The Random Forest (RF) algorithm is based on Bootstrap Aggregating (Bagging), utilizing Classification and Regression Tree (CART) as weak learners to enhance classification performance through the integration of multiple decision trees (Oztekin 2016). As illustrated in Fig. 7.1, under both single-set and ten-set ten-fold cross-validation, the RF algorithm significantly outperforms individual decision trees. This algorithm introduces randomness by incorporating random selection of training samples and features during the training process, thereby improving generalization performance (Li and Wu 2022).

Figure 7.2 demonstrates the training process of RF algorithm. Let D_{train} denote the original training set, comprising independent variables $X = \{X_1, X_2, X_3, \ldots, X_n\}$ and dependent variable $Y = \{y_1, y_2, y_3, \ldots, y_n\}$. The fundamental concept of the RF classification algorithm involves using Bootstrap sampling to randomly extract M subsamples D_{sub} from D_{train} for decision tree modeling. During each decision tree node split, a candidate feature subset X_{cand} is randomly selected from all features to determine the optimal splitting feature. This process results in M independent decision trees, each producing a classification result $h_i(x)$, with the final classification determined through averaging or voting methods, aa shown in the equation below, where H (x) represents the final classification result of the ensemble model, $h_i(x)$ is the classification result of the i-th decision tree (i = 1,2,3,...M), Y denotes the output class, and I() is the indicator function which equals 1 when $h_i(x) = Y$ and 0 otherwise.

$$H(x) = arg\max_{Y} \sum_{i=1}^{M} I(h_i(x) = Y)$$

The RF algorithm achieves superior performance with robust characteristics and demonstrates enhanced stability on testing sets, despite its slower training speed compared to single decision trees due to its ensemble nature. It exhibits remarkable resilience, being largely unaffected by outliers, noise, missing values, imbalanced samples, and multicollinearity among features, while imposing no restrictions on the number of input variables. Additionally, it effectively addresses overfitting concerns. During training, this algorithm evaluates feature interactions and quantifies their contributions to classification outcomes, providing valuable insights for feature selection through importance metrics. RF has found widespread application across diverse domains, including social media analytics, medical image processing, ecosystem modeling, environmental monitoring, and stock market prediction (Speiser et al. 2019). A notable advantage is its ability to achieve high prediction accuracy even without extensive hyperparameter tuning, maintaining computational efficiency and making it particularly suitable for large-scale data analysis tasks.

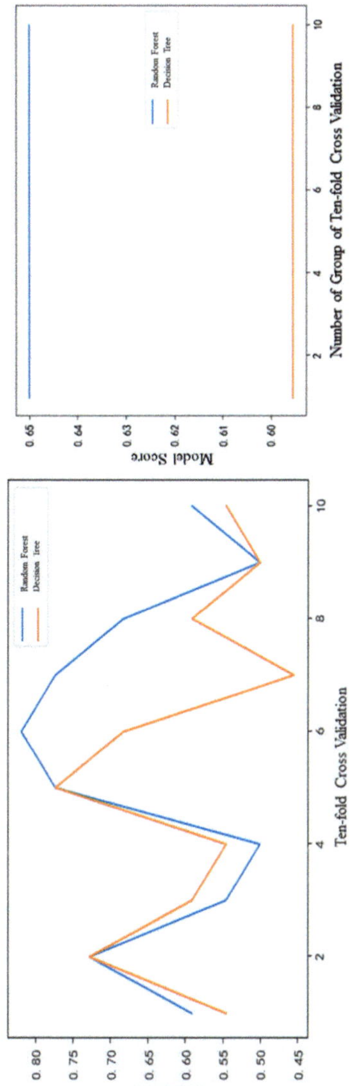

Fig. 7.1 DT and RF model performance under one and ten sets of ten-fold cross validation

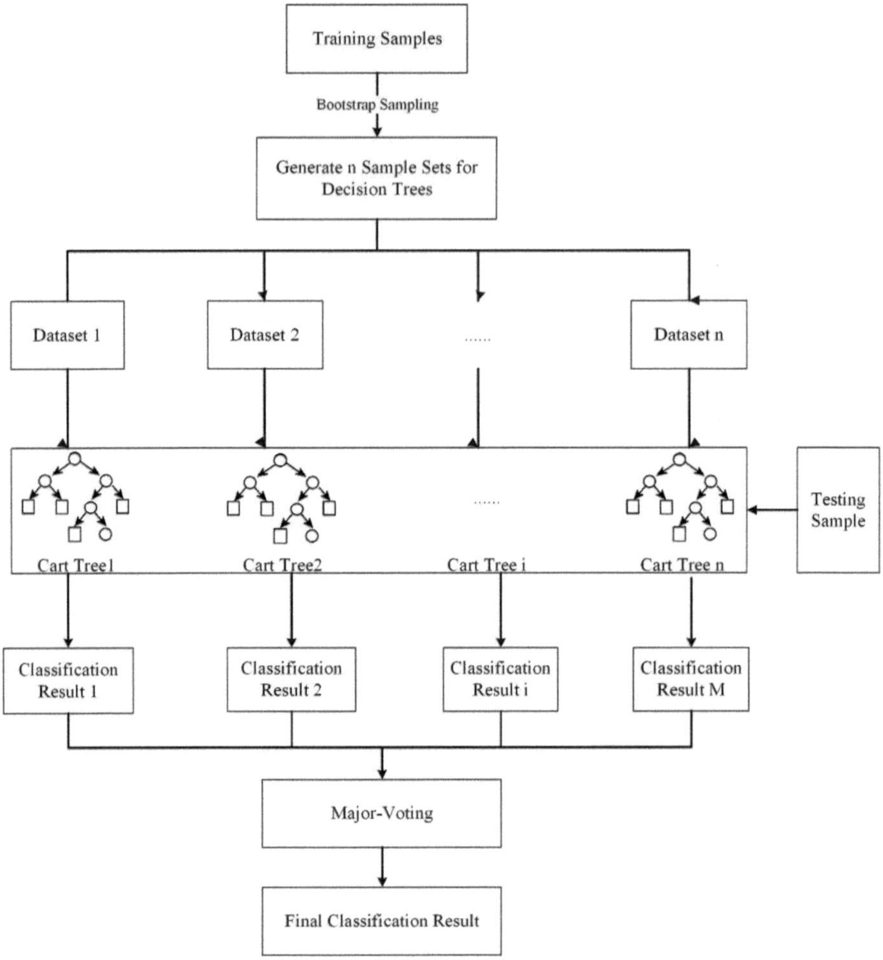

Fig. 7.2 The decision process of the random forest algorithm

7.1.4 Gaussian Naive Bayes

The Gaussian Naive Bayes (GaussianNB) algorithm performs classification based on Bayes' theorem and is used for handling continuous data. It assumes that each feature follows a Gaussian distribution and all features are mutually independent. Assuming the i-th feature x_i follows a Gaussian distribution under class C, its conditional probability $p(x_i|C)$ can be expressed as below, where μ_C^i represents the mean of the i-th feature under class C; σ_C^i represents the standard deviation of the i-th feature under class C; and x_i represents the value of the i-th feature.

$$\mathrm{p}(x_i|\mathrm{C}) = \frac{1}{\sigma_C^i\sqrt{2\pi}}exp\left(-\frac{\left(x_i-\mu_C^i\right)^2}{2\left(\sigma_C^i\right)^2}\right)$$

Due to the assumption of mutual independence between features, for all D features, the conditional probability for class C can be expressed as below, where x $= (x_1, x_2, \ldots, x_D)$ is the feature vector of the sample.

$$\mathrm{p}(\mathrm{x}|\mathrm{C}) = \prod_{d=1}^{D} p(x_d|C) = \prod_{d=1}^{D} \frac{1}{\sigma_c^d\sqrt{2\pi}}exp\left[-\frac{\left(x_i-\mu_c^d\right)^2}{2\left(\sigma_c^d\right)^2}\right]$$

According to Bayes' theorem, the relationship between the posterior probability $p(C|\mathrm{x})$, the conditional probability $p(\mathrm{x}|C)$, and the prior probability $p(C)$ is:

$$p(\mathrm{C}|\mathrm{x}) = \frac{p(\mathrm{x}|C)p(C)}{p(\mathrm{x})}$$

Since $p(\mathrm{x})$ is a constant in classification tasks, we only need to maximize $\mathrm{p}(\mathrm{x}|C)p(C)$ to obtain the final classification result.

$$\mathrm{C} = \underset{c}{\mathrm{argmax}}\left[p(C)\prod_{d=1}^{D} p(x_d|C)\right]$$

The logarithm of the posterior probability is typically taken in practical computation.

$$\mathrm{log}p(C|\mathrm{x}) \propto logp(C) + \sum_{d=1}^{D} logp(x_d|C)$$

The following is a simple implementation code of GaussianNB, which shows the specific parameters of this model and feature importance is calculated based on variance.

```
import numpy as np
import pandas as pd
import matplotlib.pyplot as plt
from sklearn.model_selection import train_test_split
from sklearn.naive_bayes import GaussianNB
from sklearn.preprocessing import StandardScaler
from    sklearn.metrics    import    accuracy_score,    classification_report,
confusion_matrix, roc_curve, auc
import seaborn as sns

# Assuming X and Y have been input, split them into training and testing sets
# Data Preprocessing
X_train,  X_test,  y_train,  y_test  =  train_test_split(X,  Y,  test_size=0.2,
random_state=42)
scaler = StandardScaler()
X_train_scaled = scaler.fit_transform(X_train)
X_test_scaled = scaler.transform(X_test)

# Model Training and Evaluation
model = GaussianNB()
model.fit(X_train_scaled, y_train)
y_pred = model.predict(X_test_scaled)
y_pred_prob = model.predict_proba(X_test_scaled)[:, 1]

# Performance Metrics
print(f"Accuracy: {accuracy_score(y_test, y_pred):.4f}")
print("\nClassification Report:")
print(classification_report(y_test, y_pred))

# Visualization
plt.figure(figsize=(15, 5))

# Feature importance plot (using variance as importance measure)
plt.subplot(131)
feature_importance = pd.DataFrame({
```

```
    'Feature': [f'Feature {i+1}' for i in range(X.shape[1])],
    'Variance': np.var(X_train_scaled, axis=0)
})
sns.barplot(data=feature_importance, x='Feature', y='Variance')
plt.title('Feature Variance')

# Confusion matrix
plt.subplot(132)
cm = confusion_matrix(y_test, y_pred)
sns.heatmap(cm, annot=True, fmt='d', cmap='Blues')
plt.title('Confusion Matrix')

# ROC curve
plt.subplot(133)
fpr, tpr, _ = roc_curve(y_test, y_pred_prob)
roc_auc = auc(fpr, tpr)
plt.plot(fpr, tpr, label=f'ROC curve (AUC = {roc_auc:.2f})')
plt.plot([0, 1], [0, 1], linestyle='--')
plt.title('ROC Curve')
plt.legend()
plt.tight_layout()
plt.show()

# Probability Analysis
probability = model.predict_proba(X_test_scaled[0:1])[0]
print(f"Class probabilities: {probability}")

# Additional Gaussian NB specific information
print("\nGaussian NB Parameters:")
print(f"Class priors: {model.class_prior_}")
print(f"Class count: {model.class_count_}")
print(f"Feature means per class:\n{model.theta_}")
print(f"Feature variances per class:\n{model.var_}")
```

7.1.5 Gradient Boosting Decision Tree

Gradient Boosting Decision Tree (GBDT) algorithm is an ensemble learning algorithm based on the Boosting framework. It serially trains multiple base classifiers (typically CART decision trees), where base classifier of each layer is trained based on the classification results of the previous layer. It assigns higher weights to misclassified samples in the previous round to reduce the residual of model in the previous layer. Finally, it accumulates the prediction results of all tree models to obtain the overall prediction output. GBDT uses an additive model and gradient descent method to fit the objective function. In each iteration, it gradually optimizes the loss function by introducing the first-order derivative of the objective function. The splitting method of leaf nodes is based on the Gini coefficient (Khan et al. 2020). During the optimization process, the parameter updating equation for gradient descent is as follows, where θ^t represents the parameter value at the t-th iteration, $-\eta\frac{\partial J}{\partial\theta^{t-1}}$ is the increment at the t-th iteration, and the weaker the classifier, the smaller the weight η.

$$\theta^t = \theta^{t-1} - \eta\frac{\partial J}{\partial\theta^{t-1}}$$

The final parameter θ can be approximated as the cumulative sum of T iterations of increments, which can be expressed as:

$$\theta = \sum_{t=0}^{T}\left(-\eta\frac{\partial J}{\partial\theta^{t-1}}\right)$$

When extended to the function space of gradient boosting trees, the updated formula for the t-th iteration model is:

$$F^t(x) = F^{t-1}(x) + f_t(x)$$

The increment at the t-th iteration is:

$$f_t(x) = -\eta\frac{\partial L}{\partial F^{t-1}(x)}$$

The final model is obtained by accumulating all increments:

$$F(x) = \sum_{t=0}^{T} f_t(x)$$

The following is a simple implementation code of the GBDT model including its performance metrics, feature importance, training progression and the specific parameters.

```
import numpy as np
import pandas as pd
import matplotlib.pyplot as plt
from sklearn.model_selection import train_test_split
from sklearn.ensemble import GradientBoostingClassifier
from sklearn.preprocessing import StandardScaler
from sklearn.metrics import accuracy_score, classification_report,
confusion_matrix, roc_curve, auc
import seaborn as sns

# Data Preprocessing
X_train, X_test, y_train, y_test = train_test_split(X, Y, test_size=0.2,
random_state=42)
scaler = StandardScaler()
X_train_scaled = scaler.fit_transform(X_train)
X_test_scaled = scaler.transform(X_test)

# Model Training and Evaluation
model = GradientBoostingClassifier(
    n_estimators=100,  # number of boosting stages
    learning_rate=0.1,  # shrinks the contribution of each tree
    max_depth=3,        # maximum depth of individual trees
    random_state=42
)
model.fit(X_train_scaled, y_train)
y_pred = model.predict(X_test_scaled)
y_pred_prob = model.predict_proba(X_test_scaled)[:, 1]

# Performance Metrics
print(f"Accuracy: {accuracy_score(y_test, y_pred):.4f}")
```

```
print("\nClassification Report:")
print(classification_report(y_test, y_pred))

# Visualization
plt.figure(figsize=(15, 5))

# Feature importance plot
plt.subplot(131)
feature_importance = pd.DataFrame({
    'Feature': [f'Feature {i+1}' for i in range(X.shape[1])],
    'Importance': model.feature_importances_
})
sns.barplot(data=feature_importance, x='Feature', y='Importance')
plt.title('Feature Importance')
plt.xticks(rotation=45)

# Confusion matrix
plt.subplot(132)
cm = confusion_matrix(y_test, y_pred)
sns.heatmap(cm, annot=True, fmt='d', cmap='Blues')
plt.title('Confusion Matrix')

# ROC curve
plt.subplot(133)
fpr, tpr, _ = roc_curve(y_test, y_pred_prob)
roc_auc = auc(fpr, tpr)
plt.plot(fpr, tpr, label=f'ROC curve (AUC = {roc_auc:.2f})')
plt.plot([0, 1], [0, 1], linestyle='--')
plt.title('ROC Curve')
plt.xlabel('False Positive Rate')
plt.ylabel('True Positive Rate')
plt.legend()
plt.tight_layout()
plt.show()

# Additional Model-Specific Information
print("\nGBDT Specific Parameters:")
print(f"Number of estimators: {model.n_estimators}")
print(f"Learning rate: {model.learning_rate}")
print(f"Maximum depth: {model.max_depth}")

# Training Score Over Iterations
train_score = model.train_score_
plt.figure(figsize=(8, 4))
```

```
plt.plot(range(1, len(train_score) + 1), train_score, label='Training Score')
plt.xlabel('Boosting Iterations')
plt.ylabel('Score')
plt.title('Training Score vs Boosting Iterations')
plt.legend()
plt.show()

# Probability Analysis
probability = model.predict_proba(X_test_scaled[0:1])[0]
print(f"\nClass probabilities for first test sample: {probability}")
```

7.1.6 Adaptive Boosting

Adaptive Boosting (AdaBoost) is also a Boosting-based ensemble learning algorithm which serially trains weak learners on the same training dataset and adjusts sample weights in each iteration based on classification results to focus more on misclassified samples, thereby improving the classification accuracy of weak learners. It is commonly used to enhance the performance of individual weak classifiers (Yao et al. 2023; Wang and Shen 2023). For example, Yao et al. (2023) used neural networks as weak learners and improved the performance of individual neural networks through the AdaBoost algorithm. Wang et al. (2023) used SVM with linear kernel as weak classifiers to construct an Adaboost-SVM model, achieving a prediction accuracy of 95.80% on positive samples. Taherkhani et al. (2020) integrated AdaBoost with Convolutional Neural Networks (CNN), achieving an accuracy of 94.08% on imbalanced datasets. Wang and Sun (2021) constructed an enhanced AdaBoost algorithm by adjusting the weighted voting parameters of decision trees as base classifiers, achieving an F1-score of up to 0.94, surpassing AdaBoost models based on SVM base classifiers with linear kernel or RBF kernel. Zhou et al. (2020) introduced AUC into the boosting process of AdaBoost and used different decision strategies in order to accurately detect network intrusion behaviors.

In principle, AdaBoost can use any model as a weak learner. While for classification, we usually set CART decision trees as the base learners in AdaBoost. Assuming the number of weak classifiers $G_m(x)$ in AdaBoost is M, through M iterations of training, a strong classifier $G(x)$ will be produced, where $M = 1,2,3,\ldots,m$. The specific process is specified as follow.

Firstly, in the first iteration, the weights of the training samples are initialized by setting equal weight for each training sample. The weight distribution of training samples in the first iteration is D_1. During each iteration, the weights of correctly classified samples are decreased while the weights of misclassified samples are increased, resulting in an updated weight distribution training dataset D_m for the next iteration, where $w_{1i} = \frac{1}{N}$, $i = 1, 2, 3, \ldots, N$, and N is the number of training samples.

$$D_1 = (w_{11}, w_{12}, w_{13}, \ldots, w_{1N})$$

The classification error e_m of each weak learner $G_m(x)$ on the training set is the sum of weights of samples misclassified by that weak learner, calculated as shown in the equation, where y_i is the true label of the sample.

$$e_m = P(G_m(x_i) \neq y_i) = \sum_{i=1}^{N} w_{mi} I(G_m(x_i) \neq y_i)$$

The weights of M weak classifiers, that is, α_m in the final strong classifier is adjusted according to the classification error e_m of each weak classifier. When $e_m \leq 0.5$ and $\alpha_m \geq 0$, α_m increases as e_m decreases, representing that the weights of weak classifiers with smaller classification errors are increased; and conversely, the weights of weak classifiers with larger classification errors are reduced.

$$\alpha_m = \frac{1}{2}\ln\frac{1-e_m}{e_m}$$

Sample weights are updated in the next iteration based on the classification results, as shown in this equation, where Z_m is the normalization factor, ensuring that $\sum_{i=1}^{N} w_{(m+1)i} = 1$.

$$w_{(m+1)i} = \frac{w_{mi}\exp(-\alpha_m y_i G_m(x_i))}{Z_m}$$

After M iterations, all weak learners are weighted and combined into a strong classifier $G(x)$ as shown in equation, where *sign*() is the sign function used for final classification decisions.

$$G(x) = sign\left(\sum_{m=1}^{M} \alpha_m G_m(x)\right)$$

This AdaBoost implementation comprises four core components. First, there is a custom AdaBoost class that implements its essential functionalities incluidng initialization of sample weights, iterative training of weak classifiers, weight updating, and prediction methods capable of outputting probability estimates. The other three components include data preprocessing, visualization and evaluation. These four components collectively form a complete machine learning workflow, enabling users to train, evaluate, and understand the behavior of the AdaBoost model. The corresponding coding is shown in below:

```
import numpy as np
import pandas as pd
import matplotlib.pyplot as plt
from sklearn.model_selection import train_test_split
from sklearn.tree import DecisionTreeClassifier
from sklearn.preprocessing import StandardScaler
from sklearn.metrics import accuracy_score, classification_report,
confusion_matrix, roc_curve, auc
import seaborn as sns


class AdaBoost:
    def __init__(self, n_estimators=50, learning_rate=1.0):
        self.n_estimators = n_estimators
        self.learning_rate = learning_rate
        self.weak_classifiers = []
        self.classifier_weights = []

    def fit(self, X, y):
        n_samples = X.shape[0]
        # Initialize weights uniformly
        sample_weights = np.ones(n_samples) / n_samples
        for _ in range(self.n_estimators):
            # Train weak classifier
            clf = DecisionTreeClassifier(max_depth=1)
            clf.fit(X, y, sample_weight=sample_weights)
            self.weak_classifiers.append(clf)
            # Make predictions
            predictions = clf.predict(X)
            # Calculate error and classifier weight
            incorrect = predictions != y
            error = np.sum(sample_weights * incorrect) / np.sum(sample_weights)
            # Calculate classifier weight
            classifier_weight = self.learning_rate * np.log((1 - error) /
max(error, 1e-10))
            self.classifier_weights.append(classifier_weight)
```

```
            # Update sample weights
            sample_weights *= np.exp(classifier_weight * incorrect)
            sample_weights /= np.sum(sample_weights)  # Normalize

    def predict(self, X):
        predictions = np.zeros(X.shape[0])
        for clf, weight in zip(self.weak_classifiers, self.classifier_weights):
            predictions += weight * clf.predict(X)
        return np.sign(predictions)

    def predict_proba(self, X):
        predictions = np.zeros(X.shape[0])
        for clf, weight in zip(self.weak_classifiers, self.classifier_weights):
            predictions += weight * clf.predict(X)
        probabilities = 1 / (1 + np.exp(-predictions))
        return np.vstack([1 - probabilities, probabilities]).T

    # Assuming X and Y have been input, split them into training and testing sets

X_train, X_test, y_train, y_test = train_test_split(X, Y, test_size=0.2,
random_state=42)
# Data Preprocessing
scaler = StandardScaler()
X_train_scaled = scaler.fit_transform(X_train)
X_test_scaled = scaler.transform(X_test)

# Model Training and Evaluation
model = AdaBoost(n_estimators=50, learning_rate=1.0)
model.fit(X_train_scaled, y_train)
y_pred = model.predict(X_test_scaled)
y_pred_prob = model.predict_proba(X_test_scaled)[:, 1]

# Performance Metrics
print(f"Accuracy: {accuracy_score(y_test, y_pred):.4f}")
print("\nClassification Report:")
print(classification_report(y_test, y_pred))
```

```
# Visualization
plt.figure(figsize=(15, 5))

# Feature importance plot using the first weak classifier
plt.subplot(131)
first_clf = model.weak_classifiers[0]
feature_importance = pd.DataFrame({
    'Feature': [f'Feature {i + 1}' for i in range(X.shape[1])],
    'Importance': first_clf.feature_importances_
})
sns.barplot(data=feature_importance, x='Feature', y='Importance')
plt.title('Feature Importance (First Weak Classifier)')

# Confusion matrix
plt.subplot(132)
cm = confusion_matrix(y_test, y_pred)
sns.heatmap(cm, annot=True, fmt='d', cmap='Blues')
plt.title('Confusion Matrix')

# ROC curve
plt.subplot(133)
fpr, tpr, _ = roc_curve(y_test, y_pred_prob)
roc_auc = auc(fpr, tpr)
plt.plot(fpr, tpr, label=f'ROC curve (AUC = {roc_auc:.2f})')
plt.plot([0, 1], [0, 1], linestyle='--')
plt.title('ROC Curve')
plt.legend()
plt.tight_layout()
plt.show()

# Probability Analysis
probability = model.predict_proba(X_test_scaled[0:1])[0]
print(f"Class probabilities: {probability}")
```

7.2 Deep Learning Algorithms

Deep learning represents an advanced machine learning approach that leverages multi-layer neural networks to automatically extract complex features and patterns from data. This approach excels at processing high-dimensional and unstructured data through various architectures, including Backpropagation Neural Network

(BPNN), Feedforward Neural Networks (FNN), Convolutional Neural Networks (CNN), Recurrent Neural Networks (RNN), Generative Adversarial Networks (GAN), Graph Neural Networks (GNN), Deep Reinforcement Learning (DRL), attention mechanisms and Transformers (such as Bidirectional Encoder Representations from Transformers, BERT), Bayesian Belief Neural Network (BBNN), and Long Short-Term Memory Network (LSTM). These architectures have been extensively studied in financial fraud detection (Kirkos et al. 2007; Karpoff et al. 2017; Gepp et al. 2021). A notable advancement in this field comes from Bochkay et al. (2023), who developed FinBERT, a specialized model for financial text analysis. Their model demonstrates superior performance compared to standard BERT, consistently maintaining accuracy above 80% while reducing computational costs, regardless of training sample size. This section provides an in-depth analysis of the mathematical foundations and implementation details for two cornerstone architectures in deep learning: the Multilayer Perceptron Neural Network and the Convolutional Neural Network. We elucidate both the theoretical underpinnings and practical coding considerations.

7.2.1 Multilayer Perceptron Neural Network

Artificial neural network (ANN), simulating the neuron system of the human brain, is applicable for machine learning, artificial intelligence, data mining, and other fields. The most basic type of ANN is Multilayer Perceptron Neural Network (MLPNN) where data enters the input layer, the hidden layer, and the output layer in turn, to finally get the output value, that is, the prediction result (Gepp et al. 2021). During the process, the hidden layer activates the output layer by judging the influence degree (weighted value) of the input value. This network constantly learns by adjusting the weighted value until there is no deviation between the output result and the actual result and the training process is completed. The weights of the initial training and testing set will affect the training results. When the training data is large, overfitting may occur. The basic structure of MLPNN is shown in Fig. 7.3. Next we provide a detailed mathematical foundation of MLPNN, including its network structure, activation functions, loss function, forward propagation, backpropagation, and optimization techniques.

As illustrated in the architectural diagram, the MLPNN demonstrates complete inter-layer connectivity, wherein each neuron establishes connections with all neurons in the subsequent layer. The network's input layer receives an n-dimensional feature vector denoted as vector X, where each element corresponds to a distinct input neuron.

$$\mathrm{X} = [x_1, x_2, \ldots, x_n]^T$$

This fully connected architecture enables comprehensive information flow and feature extraction across the network's layers. Due to the full connectivity between the

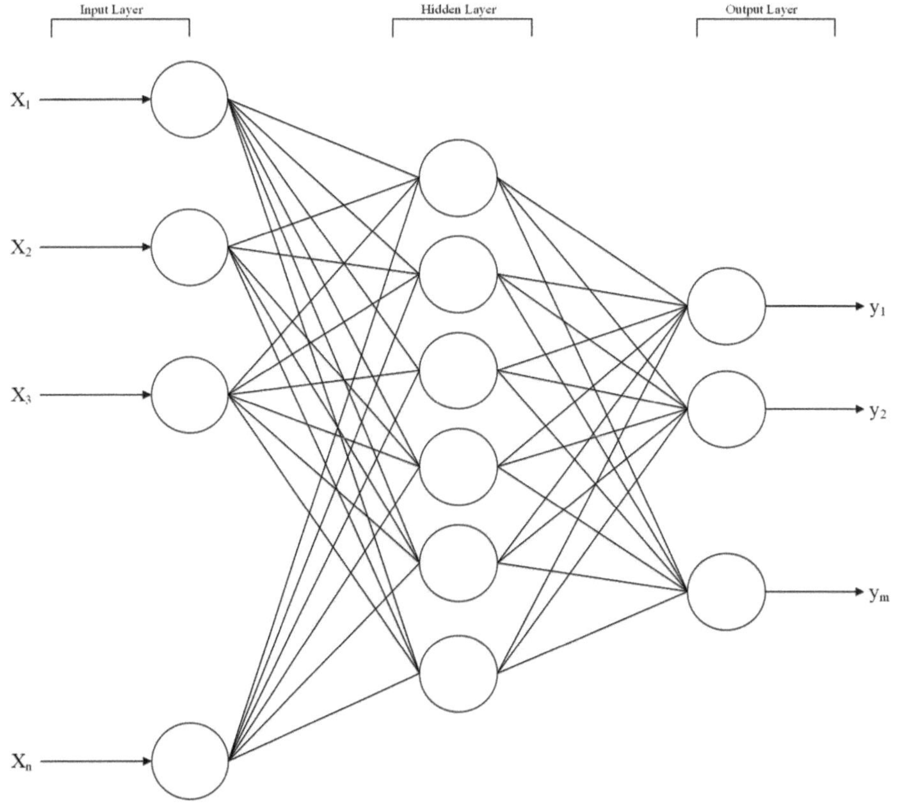

Fig. 7.3 The basic structure of multilayer perceptron neural network

hidden layer and the input layer, the output of the hidden layer can be mathematically expressed as $\mathrm{f}\left(W^l + b^l\right)$, where W^l represents the weights (also known as connection coefficients), b^l represents the bias and the activation function f() introduces non-linearity into the network, commonly implemented as either a Sigmoid, Rectified Linear Unit (ReLU) or Hyperbolic Tangent (Tanh) functions.

$$g(x) = Tanh(z) = \frac{e^z - e^{-z}}{e^z + e^{-z}}$$

$$g(x) = Sigmoid(z) = 1/(1 + e^{-z})$$

$$g(x) = ReLU(z) = \max(0, z)$$

where z is the linear combination of inputs,. $g()$ is the activation function.

Therefore, the parameters of an MLPNN consist of the connection weights and biases between all layers, including W^l and b^l. The optimization problem involves finding the optimal values for these parameters. Finally, the output layer produces the final output $y = [y_1, y_2, \ldots, y_m]^T$. The mathematical representation of the whole network is as follows.

$$W^l = W^l a^{l-1} + b^l, a^l = g(z^l)$$

where W^l is the weight matrix for layer, b^l is the bias vector for layer and a^l is the activation output. The parameters of W^l and b^l are usually updated using gradient descent.

$$W^l = W^l - \alpha \frac{\partial \mathrm{L}}{\partial W^l}, b^l = b^l - \alpha \frac{\partial L}{\partial b^l}$$

where α represents the learning rate and l denotes the total number of layers.

Additionally, the performance of the network is quantified through a loss function L, which measures the discrepancy between the predicted output $\hat{y}$ and the ground truth y. For classification tasks, the Cross-Entropy Loss is predominantly employed, defined as below, where N represents the number of training samples, m denotes the number of classes, y_{ij} is the true label (0 or 1) for sample i in class j and $\hat{y}_{ij}$ represents the predicted probability for sample i belonging to class j.

$$L(y, \hat{y}) = -\frac{1}{N} \sum_{i=1}^{N} \sum_{j=1}^{m} y_{ij} log(\hat{y}_{ij})$$

For binary classification scenarios:

$$L(y, \hat{y}) = -\frac{1}{N} \sum_{i=1}^{N} [y_i log(\hat{y}_i) + (1 - y_i) log(1 - \hat{y}_i)]$$

The forward propagation process sequentially computes the output of the network layer by layer, which can be formally expressed as below.

$$z^l = W^l a^{l-1} + b^l, a^l = g(z^l)$$

The choice of activation function for the output layer is determined by the specific task requirements. For classification tasks, the Softmax function is predominantly employed, transforming the raw outputs of network into a probability distribution across classes.

$$\hat{y}_i = \frac{e^{z_i}}{\sum_j e^{z_j}}$$

Backpropagation, a gradient-based optimization algorithm, computes the partial derivatives of the loss function with respect to the network parameters by systematically applying the chain rule of calculus. The process proceeds through the following sequential steps:

First is the error computation at output layer. For the output layer L, the error term δ^l is computed as below.

$$\delta^l = \frac{\partial \mathrm{L}}{\partial \mathrm{z}^l} = \frac{\partial \mathrm{L}}{\partial \mathrm{z}^l} \odot g\prime(z^l)$$

Second is the error propagation through hidden layers. For each hidden layer, the error term is recursively computed:

$$\delta^l = \left(W^{l+1}\right)^T \delta^{l+1} \odot g\prime(z^l)$$

Finally the parameter gradients with respect to weights and biases are calculated.

$$\frac{\partial \mathrm{L}}{\partial W^l} = \delta^l \left(a^{l-1}\right)^T, \frac{\partial \mathrm{L}}{\partial b^l} = \delta^l$$

To mitigate overfitting and enhance model generalization, regularization techniques are incorporated into the training process. L2 regularization (also known as weight decay or Tikhonov regularization) is particularly prevalent.

$$\mathrm{L}_{reg} = L + \frac{\lambda}{2} \sum_l \|W^l\|^2$$

Here is a complete implementation of a MLP using PyTorch, showing the model architecture, training features and regularization techniques in detail.

```
import torch
import torch.nn as nn
import torch.optim as optim
from torch.utils.data import DataLoader, TensorDataset
import numpy as np
from sklearn.model_selection import train_test_split
```

```
from sklearn.preprocessing import StandardScaler

# 1. Define MLP Model
class MLP(nn.Module):
    def __init__(self, input_size, hidden_sizes, output_size, dropout_rate=0.2):
        super(MLP, self).__init__()

        # Build multi-layer network
        layers = []
        prev_size = input_size
        # Add hidden layers
        for hidden_size in hidden_sizes:
            layers.extend([
                nn.Linear(prev_size, hidden_size),
                nn.ReLU(),
                nn.BatchNorm1d(hidden_size),
                nn.Dropout(dropout_rate)
            ])
            prev_size = hidden_size
            # Add output layer
        layers.append(nn.Linear(prev_size, output_size))
        # Add Softmax for classification
        layers.append(nn.Softmax(dim=1))
        self.model = nn.Sequential(*layers)

    def forward(self, x):
        return self.model(x)

    # 2. Training Function
def train_model(model, train_loader, val_loader, criterion, optimizer, num_epochs,
device):
    model.to(device)
    best_val_loss = float('inf')

    for epoch in range(num_epochs):
        # Training phase
        model.train()
        train_loss = 0.0
        for inputs, labels in train_loader:
            inputs, labels = inputs.to(device), labels.to(device)
            # Zero the gradients
            optimizer.zero_grad()
            # Forward pass
            outputs = model(inputs)
```

```
            loss = criterion(outputs, labels)
            # Backward pass and optimization
            loss.backward()
            optimizer.step()
            train_loss += loss.item()
            # Validation phase
        model.eval()
        val_loss = 0.0
        correct = 0
        total = 0
        with torch.no_grad():
            for inputs, labels in val_loader:
                inputs, labels = inputs.to(device), labels.to(device)
                outputs = model(inputs)
                loss = criterion(outputs, labels)
                val_loss += loss.item()
                _, predicted = torch.max(outputs.data, 1)
                total += labels.size(0)
                correct += (predicted == labels).sum().item()
                # Calculate average loss and accuracy
        train_loss = train_loss / len(train_loader)
        val_loss = val_loss / len(val_loader)
        accuracy = 100 * correct / total
        print(f'Epoch [{epoch + 1}/{num_epochs}]')
        print(f'Train Loss: {train_loss:.4f}, Val Loss: {val_loss:.4f}')
        print(f'Validation Accuracy: {accuracy:.2f}%')
        # Save best model
        if val_loss < best_val_loss:
            best_val_loss = val_loss
            torch.save(model.state_dict(), 'best_model.pth')

        # 3. Data Preparation

def prepare_data(X, y, batch_size=32):
    # Standardize features
    scaler = StandardScaler()
    X_scaled = scaler.fit_transform(X)
    # Split into train and validation sets
    X_train, X_val, y_train, y_val = train_test_split(
        X_scaled, y, test_size=0.2, random_state=42
    )
    # Convert to PyTorch tensors
    X_train = torch.FloatTensor(X_train)
    y_train = torch.LongTensor(y_train)
```

```
    X_val = torch.FloatTensor(X_val)
    y_val = torch.LongTensor(y_val)
    # Create data loaders
    train_dataset = TensorDataset(X_train, y_train)
    train_loader = DataLoader(train_dataset, batch_size=batch_size, shuffle=True)
    val_dataset = TensorDataset(X_val, y_val)
    val_loader = DataLoader(val_dataset, batch_size=batch_size)
    return train_loader, val_loader

def main():
    # Generate sample data for demonstration
    np.random.seed(42)
    X = np.random.randn(1000, 20)  # 1000 samples, 20 features
    y = np.random.randint(0, 3, 1000)  # 3 classes
    # Prepare data
    train_loader, val_loader = prepare_data(X, y, batch_size=32)
    # Initialize model
    input_size = 20
    hidden_sizes = [128, 64]  # Two hidden layers
    output_size = 3  # Three classes
    model = MLP(input_size, hidden_sizes, output_size)
    # Define loss function and optimizer
    criterion = nn.CrossEntropyLoss()
    optimizer = optim.Adam(model.parameters(), lr=0.001, weight_decay=1e-5)  # L2
regularization
    # Train model
    device = torch.device("cuda" if torch.cuda.is_available() else "cpu")
    train_model(
        model=model,
        train_loader=train_loader,
        val_loader=val_loader,
        criterion=criterion,
        optimizer=optimizer,
        num_epochs=50,
        device=device
    )

if __name__ == "__main__":
    main()
```

7.2.2 *Convolutional Neural Network*

Convolutional Neural Networks (CNNs) represent a sophisticated class of deep learning architectures that evolved from traditional artificial neural networks and multi-layer perceptrons. While maintaining the hierarchical structure of conventional neural networks, CNNs introduce specialized layers and novel computational mechanisms that significantly enhance their processing capabilities. Pioneered by distinguished computer scientist Yann LeCun, CNNs have revolutionized the field of computer vision and have become the cornerstone architecture for visual image analysis tasks. The fundamental innovation of CNNs lies in their ability to automatically learn hierarchical feature representations from raw image data, eliminating the need for manual feature engineering that was prevalent in traditional computer vision approaches. This architectural paradigm has proven particularly effective in capturing spatial hierarchies and local patterns inherent in visual data.

As illustrated in the Fig. 7.4, the architecture of CNNs shares similarities with conventional artificial neural networks, particularly in the final fully connected layers. However, CNNs distinguish themselves through their ability to process multiple feature maps as input, rather than being limited to vector inputs. A typical CNN architecture comprises five fundamental layers: the Input layer, Convolutional (CONV) layer, Activation Layer, Pooling layer, and Fully Connected (FC) layer. Firstly, The Input layer performs essential preprocessing operations on raw image data, including mean subtraction, normalization and PCA dimensionality reduction. Secondly, the Convolutional layer, which constitutes the cornerstone of CNNs, is designed to extract localized features from the input data. The convolution operation employs a sliding window mechanism to perform local weighted summations across the input feature map, generating output feature maps. This operation can be mathematically expressed as:

$$z_{i,j,k} = \sum_{m=1}^{M}\sum_{n=1}^{N}\sum_{c=1}^{C} x_{i+m-1,j+n-1,c} \times w_{m,n,c,k} + b_k$$

where $x_{i,j,k}$ represents the value at position (i, j) in channel c of the input feature map; $w_{m,n,c,k}$ denotes the weight at position (m, n) in channel c of the k-th filter; b_k represents the bias term for the k-th filter; $z_{i,j,k}$ indicates the value at position (i, j) in the k-th output feature map; M, N are the height and width of the convolutional kernel and C represents the number of input channels.

The Activation Layer (or Non-linear Layer) performs non-linear transformations on the output of convolutional layers, enabling CNNs to learn complex feature representations. The Rectified Linear Unit (ReLU) is predominantly employed as the activation function due to its computational efficiency, rapid convergence properties, and ability to mitigate the vanishing gradient problem. The ReLU function is mathematically defined as:

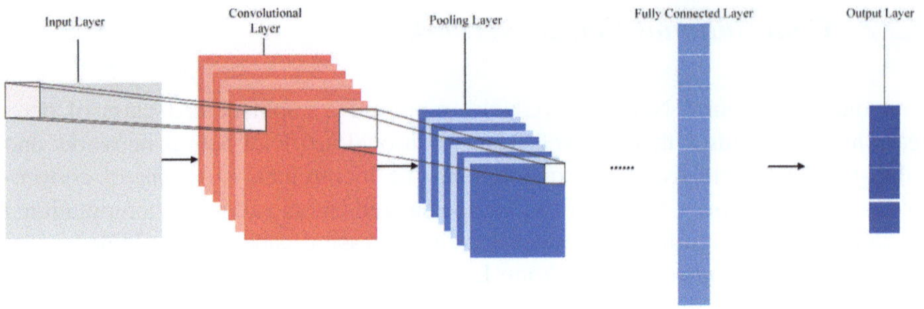

Fig. 7.4 The basic structure of convolutional neural networks

$$f(x) = \max(0, x) = \begin{cases} x, & ifx > 0 \\ 0, & ifx \leq 0 \end{cases}$$

The Pooling Layer, strategically positioned between successive convolutional layers, serves to reduce the dimensionality of feature maps while preserving essential information and mitigating overfitting. Among the various pooling methodologies, Max Pooling and Average Pooling are predominantly employed, with Max Pooling being particularly prevalent. The mathematical formulation for Max Pooling is expressed as:

$$z_{i,j,k} = \max_{m.n} x_{i+m-1,j+n-1,k}$$

where $x_{i,j,k}$ denotes the value at position (i, j) in the k-th input feature map; $z_{i,j,k}$ represents the corresponding value in the output feature map; R_m and R_n define the pooling window dimensions and (m, n) indicates the spatial location within the pooling window. The pooling operation, through the application of local maximum or average operations within defined receptive fields, effectuates a reduction in the spatial dimensions of feature maps. This dimensional reduction serves dual purposes: optimizing computational efficiency and enhancing translational invariance of the model with respect to input data.

Finally, the Fully Connected (FC) layers, typically positioned at the terminal end of convolutional neural networks, perform linear transformations to map high-dimensional features into target class spaces for classification tasks. The mathematical formulation of this transformation can be expressed as:

$$\mathrm{z} = \mathrm{W}x + b$$

where:

- W is the weight matrix with dimensions (n_{out}, n_{in}), where n_{in} is the input feature dimension and n_{out} is the output feature dimension;
- x is the input feature vector;

- b is the bias vector with dimensions (n_{out});
- z is the output vector with dimensions (n_{out}).

CNNs are primarily designed for recognizing two-dimensional patterns with invariance to displacement, scaling, and various forms of distortion. A distinctive advantage of CNNs lies in their ability to learn feature detection layers through training data, eliminating the need for explicit feature extraction in favor of implicit learning from training data. Furthermore, the shared weights among neurons within the same feature map enable parallel learning, representing a significant advantage over fully connected neural networks. CNNs demonstrate unique superiority in speech recognition and image processing applications through their specialized architecture of local weight sharing. Their structure more closely resembles biological neural networks, and the weight sharing mechanism significantly reduces network complexity. Notably, the ability to directly process multidimensional input vectors, particularly images, circumvents the computational complexity associated with data reconstruction during feature extraction and classification processes. This architectural efficiency, combined with their biological plausibility and robust feature learning capabilities, has established CNNs as a cornerstone in modern computer vision applications.

The implementation of a typical CNN model using PyTorch for classifying the CIFAR-10 dataset is shown as below.

```
import torch
import torch.nn as nn
import torch.optim as optim
from torchvision import datasets, transforms
from torch.utils.data import DataLoader

# 1. Define the CNN Model
class CNN(nn.Module):
    def __init__(self):
        super(CNN, self).__init__()
        self.conv1 = nn.Conv2d(in_channels=3, out_channels=32, kernel_size=3,
stride=1, padding=1)
        self.conv2 = nn.Conv2d(in_channels=32, out_channels=64, kernel_size=3,
stride=1, padding=1)
        self.pool = nn.MaxPool2d(kernel_size=2, stride=2)
        self.fc1 = nn.Linear(64 * 8 * 8, 128)
```

```
        self.fc2 = nn.Linear(128, 10)
        self.relu = nn.ReLU()
        self.dropout = nn.Dropout(0.5)
    def forward(self, x):
        x = self.relu(self.conv1(x))  # First convolutional layer + ReLU
        x = self.pool(x)  # Max pooling
        x = self.relu(self.conv2(x))  # Second convolutional layer + ReLU
        x = self.pool(x)  # Max pooling
        x = x.view(x.size(0), -1)  # Flatten the feature map
        x = self.relu(self.fc1(x))  # Fully connected layer 1 + ReLU
        x = self.dropout(x)  # Dropout
        x = self.fc2(x)  # Fully connected layer 2
        return x
    # 2. Data Preprocessing
transform = transforms.Compose([
    transforms.ToTensor(),
    transforms.Normalize((0.5, 0.5, 0.5), (0.5, 0.5, 0.5))
])
train_dataset = datasets.CIFAR10(root='./data', train=True, download=True,
transform=transform)
test_dataset = datasets.CIFAR10(root='./data', train=False, download=True,
transform=transform)
train_loader = DataLoader(train_dataset, batch_size=64, shuffle=True)
test_loader = DataLoader(test_dataset, batch_size=64, shuffle=False)
# 3. Training the Model
def train_model(model, train_loader, criterion, optimizer, num_epochs=10,
device='cpu'):
    model.to(device)
    for epoch in range(num_epochs):
        model.train()
        running_loss = 0.0
        for inputs, labels in train_loader:
            inputs, labels = inputs.to(device), labels.to(device)
            # Forward pass
            outputs = model(inputs)
            loss = criterion(outputs, labels)
            # Backward pass and optimization
            optimizer.zero_grad()
            loss.backward()
            optimizer.step()
            running_loss += loss.item()
        print(f"Epoch [{epoch + 1}/{num_epochs}], Loss: {running_loss /
len(train_loader):.4f}")
```

```
    # 4. Evaluating the Model
def evaluate_model(model, test_loader, device='cpu'):
    model.eval()
    correct = 0
    total = 0
    with torch.no_grad():
        for inputs, labels in test_loader:
            inputs, labels = inputs.to(device), labels.to(device)
            outputs = model(inputs)
            _, predicted = torch.max(outputs, 1)
            total += labels.size(0)
            correct += (predicted == labels).sum().item()
    print(f"Test Accuracy: {100 * correct / total:.2f}%")

# 5. Main Function
device = torch.device("cuda" if torch.cuda.is_available() else "cpu")
model = CNN()
criterion = nn.CrossEntropyLoss()
optimizer = optim.Adam(model.parameters(), lr=0.001)
train_model(model, train_loader, criterion, optimizer, num_epochs=10,
device=device)
evaluate_model(model, test_loader, device=device)
```

7.3 Model Evaluation

Existing research typically treats financial fraud detection as a binary classification task, dividing samples into financial fraud (positive class) and non-financial fraud (negative class). In this book, we introduce seven evaluation metrics: Accuracy, Precision, Recall, False Positive Rate (FPR), F1-score, G-means, and AUC, which will be selected to evaluate the classification results of machine learning models in empirical researches in subsequent chapters. Based on the confusion matrix (Table 7.1), we show each calculation formula composed of four core indicators including True Positive (TP), False Positive (FP), True Negative (TN), and False Negative (FN) 7.1).

$$Recall = \frac{TP}{TP + FN}$$

$$Precision = \frac{TP}{FP + TP}$$

$$Specificity = \frac{TN}{TN + FP}$$

$$FPR = \frac{FP}{TN + FP}$$

$$Accuracy = \frac{TP + TN}{TN + FP + FN + TP}$$

$$F1 - score = \frac{2 \times Recall \times Precision}{Recall + Precision}$$

$$G - means = \sqrt{Recall \times Specificity}$$

To be specific, Accuracy represents the proportion of correctly classified samples out of the total samples. Precision indicates the proportion of actual fraudulent cases among all samples predicted as fraud by the model, evaluating predictive accuracy for fraudulent cases of the model. Specificity measures the ability to identify non-fraudulent samples. Recall, also known as Sensitivity or True Positive Rate (TPR), represents the proportion of correctly identified fraudulent samples among all actual fraudulent samples, serving as a key indicator for evaluating the ability to correctly identify fraud of the model- higher precision and recall indicate lower false positive and false negative errors. F1-score is the harmonic mean of precision and recall, providing a comprehensive measure of model performance while focusing more on fraud detection capability, avoiding the "dilution effect" from the predominant non-fraudulent samples, making it particularly suitable for detection scenarios with severe class imbalance. False Positive Rate (FPR) represents the proportion of actual non-fraudulent samples incorrectly predicted as fraudulent. G-means, calculated as the geometric mean of Sensitivity and Specificity, is sensitive to extreme values in both metrics and considers the classification performance of the model for both positive and negative samples, preventing the optimization of recognition performance for only one class in imbalanced classification problems.

The ROC curve visually demonstrates the discrimination ability between positive and negative samples for a binary classification model, remaining unaffected by changes in class distribution, making it particularly useful for handling imbalanced classification problems. The curve plots the FPR on the x-axis against the TPR on the y-axis, clearly illustrating the trade-off between true positives and false positives. The more the ROC curve bulges toward the upper-left corner, the larger its corresponding area (AUC) becomes, indicating better model performance. AUC is a commonly

Table 7.1 Confusion matrix

Classification result	Real class	
	Non-fraud (0)	Fraud (1)
Non-fraud (0)	True Negative (TN)	False Negative (FN)
Fraud (1)	False Positive (FP)	True Positive (TP)

used evaluation metric for fraud detection model, representing the probability that a randomly chosen fraudulent sample will be predicted as fraudulent with a higher likelihood than a randomly chosen non-fraudulent sample. AUC values range from 0 to 1, with the model only being meaningful when the AUC exceeds 0.5 (better than random guessing), and as the AUC value approaches 1, it indicates stronger classification capability of the model.

Additionally, several other metrics have been employed as important references for measuring model performance, including Matthews Correlation Coefficient (MCC) (Randhawa et al. 2018), Weighted Error Cost (WEC) (Gepp et al. 2021), Expected Cost of Misclassification (ECM) (Perols et al. 2017), Pseudo $- R^2$ and F_β (Bertomeu et al. 2021), and Normalized Discounted Cumulative Gain at rank k (NDCG@k) (Bao et al. 2020). The overall objective of financial fraud detection model is to increase the recall rate of fraud samples minimizing misclassification of non-fraudulent samples, which means keeping the number of (0, 1) combinations in the confusion matrix relatively small.

7.4 Applications of Detection Models

Neural networks, logistic regression, and decision tree models play significant roles in financial statement fraud detection (Ngai et al. 2011). Green and Choi (1997) pioneered the use of revenue indicators to train neural networks, successfully predicting 74.03% of financially distressed companies. Kirkos et al. (2007) demonstrated that Bayesian belief networks outperformed both neural networks and decision trees in detecting fraudulent financial statements. Zhou and Kapoor (2011) developed an adaptive learning model incorporating domain expertise to address evolving financial statement fraud. Lin et al. (2015) conducted a comparative study between expert surveys and data mining methods, revealing that Artificial Neural Networks (ANN) and CART models achieved higher accuracy rates (92.8% and 90.3% respectively) than LR models (88.5%).

Cecchini et al. (2010) introduced an SVM model with a Financial Kernel (SVM-FK) that effectively addressed overfitting issues. This derivate identifies 80% of fraud cases, surpassing the accuracy of classical models explored by Green and Choi (1997), Summers and Sweeney (1998), Beneish (1999), and Dechow (2009). In recent years, West and Bhattacharya (2016) achieved a remarkable 98.1% accuracy using neural networks. Li et al. (2020) demonstrated the superiority of LR in small sample sizes, while the accuracy of SVM and neural networks increases when the number of samples increase and SVM ultimately achieves the highest accuracy at 94.8%. Perols (2011) compared six popular statistical and machine learning models, finding that LR and SVM outperformed complicated models including ANNs, Bagging, C4.5 decision trees, and Stacking.

Recent studies comparing machine learning and deep learning algorithms with traditional regression models reveal that data mining approaches typically outperform statistical regression methods (Xu et al. 2023). This advantage stems from their ability to process data without imposing arbitrary assumptions on input variables. Table 7.2 summarizes the evolving trends of machine learning applications in accounting and finance. Especially, there is a growing body of comparative research on machine learning approaches to financial fraud detection. De Bock et al. (2020) evaluated various methods for predicting corporate financial distress, including discriminant analysis, logistic regression, neural networks, and decision trees, revealing that decision trees and neural networks achieved superior prediction accuracy, with hybrid models demonstrating better performance than individual approaches. Ravisankar et al. (2011) conducted a comprehensive comparison of various data mining techniques, including Logistic Regression (LR), Support Vector Machines (SVM), Multi-Layer Feedforward Neural Network (MLFF), Genetic Programming (GP), Group Method of Data Handling (GMDH), and Probabilistic Neural Network (PNN). Their study revealed that with feature selection implemented, GP and PNN achieved the highest accuracy rates in financial fraud detection at 89.27% and 90.77% respectively. Notably, PNN demonstrated superior performance consistently, outperforming other data mining techniques regardless of whether feature selection was applied. Despite their superior performance, these methods face challenges in model interpretability, making expert auditor involvement essential for result interpretation. (Ran et al. 2023).

Furthermore, researchers are gradually exploring more powerful ensemble machine learning techniques as alternatives to single classifiers by combining two or more classifiers to form a stronger classifier (Gepp et al. 2018). Multiple studies have demonstrated that ensemble learning algorithms outperform traditional machine learning methods in detecting accounting misstatements and fraud (Ravisankar et al. 2011; Perols et al. 2017; Bao et al. 2020; Gepp et al. 2021). Notably, Gepp et al. (2021) conducted the first large-scale comparative analysis of 32 fraud detection models, developing a novel ensemble model, AV5_NoNN, by combining five machine learning approaches: Linear Discriminant Analysis (LDA), Logistic Regression (LR), Decision Trees (DT), Random Forests (RF), and TreeNet (Dynamic Random Gradient Boosting), achieving minimal classification error rates. Bao et al. (2020) further validated the superiority of ensemble learning through RUSBoost, a model combining Adaboost algorithm with RUS undersampling techniques for accounting fraud prediction. Additionally, Dong et al. (2018) constructed an optimal threshold hybrid model based on three submodels of Naive Bayes, Linear Discriminant, and Multivariate Adaptive Regression Splines, achieving high accuracy in default discrimination.

Moreover, Heo and Yang (2014) compared traditional machine learning models (BPNN, SVM, and DT) with the AdaBoost ensemble learning model for predicting bankruptcy among Korean construction companies, finding that AdaBoost achieved the highest overall accuracy at 78.5%. Hajek and Henriques (2017) evaluated machine learning methods for detecting financial statement fraud in mining companies, revealing that ensemble learning methods achieved higher recall rates (true positive rates) in identifying fraudulent firms. Barboza et al. (2017) found that machine learning models (SVM, Bagging, Boosting, and RF) outperformed traditional logistic

Table 7.2 Development of machine learning methods in accounting and finance

Research subject	Models used	Types of models used	Scholars
Fraud Detection	SVM-FK; Logit Regression; RUSBoost	Statistical regression; Basic machine learning; Imbalanced ensemble learning	Bao et al. (2020)
Bankruptcy Prediction	KNN; DT; RF; AdaBoost; Bagging; Rotation Forest; Meta-learner, Naive Bayes, Neural Networks	Imbalanced ensemble learning; Traditional ensemble learning; Basic machine learning	Faris et al. (2020)
Misstatement Detection	GBRT; RF; RUSBoost; KNN; LDA; SVM; DT; Backward Logistic Regression; Naive Bayes	Statistical regression; Traditional ensemble learning; Basic machine learning	Bertomeu et al. (2021)
Fraud Detection	MDA; LR; SVM; DT; Neural Networks; Ensemble Learning	Statistical regression; Basic machine learning; Traditional ensemble learning	Gepp et al. (2021)
Anomaly Detection	DT; RF; Extra Trees; Ensemble Learning	Basic machine learning; Traditional ensemble learning	Zhuang and Zhang (2023)
Fraud Detection	SVM; DT; AdaBoost; LSTM; Neural Networks; LSTM-Adaboost based on SMOTE-ENN	Imbalanced ensemble learning; Basic machine learning; Traditional ensemble learning	Esenogho et al. (2022)
Anomaly Detection	DT; LR; RF; XGBoost; Naive Bayes	Basic machine learning; Traditional ensemble learning	Huang and Gao (2025)
Fraud Prediction	GBDT; RF; LR; SVM; Neural Networks	Basic machine learning; Traditional ensemble learning	Xu et al. (2023)
Fraud Detection	LR; SVM; XGBoost; GAN		
Fraud Detection	Probit Regression	Statistical regression	Chen et al. (2006)
Fraud Detection	DT; Neural Networks; Bayesian Belief Networks	Basic machine learning	Kirkos et al. (2007)
Fraud Detection	SVM-FK	Basic machine learning	Cecchini et al. (2010)

(continued)

Table 7.2 (continued)

Research subject	Models used	Types of models used	Scholars
Fraud Detection	LR; DT; Neural Networks; Bayesian Belief Networks; Adaptive Framework (Based on Response Surface)	Statistical regression; Basic machine learning	Zhou and Kapoor (2011)
Fraud Detection	LR; SVM; Bagging; C4.5 Decision Tree; Stacking; Neural Networks	Basic machine learning; Traditional ensemble learning	Perols (2011)
Fraud Detection	MLFF; SVM; GP; GMDH; LR; PNN	Statistical regression; Basic machine learning	Ravisankar et al. (2011)
Fraud Detection	LR; AdaBoost; XGBoost; CUSBoost; RUSBoost	Imbalanced ensemble learning; Traditional ensemble learning; Basic machine learning	Rahman and Zhu (2023)
Fraud Detection	Logit Regression	Statistical regression	Hong et al. (2012)
Fraud Detection	Logit Regression; CART Decision Tree; Neural Networks	Statistical regression; Basic machine learning	Lin et al. (2015)
Bankruptcy Prediction	KNN; Ripper; SVM; Neural Networks; C4.5 Decision Tree	Statistical regression; Basic machine learning	Zhou et al. (2015)
Fraud Detection	Logit Regression	Statistical regression	Hass et al (2016)
Fraud Detection	LR; SVM; DT; RF; AdaBoost; Neural Networks; Bayesian Belief Networks	Basic machine learning; Traditional ensemble learning	Hajek and Henriques (2017)
Bankruptcy Prediction	MDA; LR; RF; SVM; Boosting; Bagging; Neural Networks	Statistical regression; Basic machine learning; Traditional ensemble learning	Barboza et al. (2017)
Fraud Detection	SVM; DT; LR; Neural Networks	Statistical regression; Basic machine learning	Dong et al. (2018)
Violation Detection	Logit Regression; Probit Regression; XGboost based on Decision Tree	Statistical regression; , Traditional ensemble learning	Li et al. (2020)

Notes: LR = Logistic Regression, KNN = K-Nearest Neighbors Algorithm, DT = Decision Tree Algorithm, RF = Random Forest Algorithm, AdaBoost = Adaptive Boosting Algorithm, LDA = Linear Discriminant Analysis, MDA = Multiple Discriminant Analysis, SVM = Support Vector Machine Algorithm, LSTM = Long Short-Term Memory Network, SVM-FK = Support Vector Machine with Financial Kernel Function, GBRT = Gradient Boosting Regression Trees, RUSBoost = Random Under-Sampling Boosting (Combined model of AdaBoost and random under-sampling technique), XGBoost = eXtreme Gradient Boosting Algorithm, GAN = Generative Adversarial Network, MLFF = Multi-Layer Feed-Forward Neural Networks, GP = Genetic Programming, GMDH = Group Method of Data Handling, Meta-learner = Meta Learning Algorithm, PNN = Probabilistic Neural Networks, CUSBoost = Cluster-based Under-Sampling with Boosting Ensemble Learning Algorithm

regression and discriminant analysis models by an average of 10% in overall accuracy, with RF achieving the highest accuracy at 87%. Similarly, Xu et al. (2023), in predicting Chinese fraudulent enterprises, tested traditional ensemble learning algorithms (RF, GBDT, and RUSBoost) against conventional machine learning models (LR, SVM, and ANN), confirming the superiority of RF in fraud prediction. Bertomeu et al. (2021) further validated the effectiveness of ensemble learning when identifying accounting restatements, comparing ensemble models (RF, RUSBoost, and GBRT) with traditional machine learning methods (LDA, GaussianNB, SVM, DT, and KNN), finding GBRT to be the top performer. Faris et al. (2020) conducted a comprehensive comparison combining various feature selection and sampling techniques, evaluating traditional machine learning algorithms (KNN and DT) against ensemble algorithms (RF, AdaBoost, Bagging, Rotation Forest, and Meta-learner) for bankruptcy prediction, further demonstrating the distinction power of ensemble algorithms with AdaBoost achieving the highest accuracy at 98.3%.

Moreover, text analysis has emerged as a key research focus in financial fraud detection by exploring text mining algorithms for financial statement sentiment analysis, whose effectiveness has been demonstrated in several notable studies (Zhou et al. 2024). For example, Purda and Skillicorn (2015) developed a language-based SVM method that achieved the highest 82% accuracy in fraud detection. Hoberg and Lewis (2017) used automated voice emotion analysis software to analyze Chief Executive Officer (CEO) voice samples from earnings conference calls and identified a positive correlation between voice disturbance and the likelihood of financial restatements, providing an additional tool for fraud detection. Chi and Dong (2022) improved loan default prediction accuracy by extracting sentiment information from loan descriptions. Dong et al. (2018) achieved prediction accuracy of 80% by incorporating linguistic features alongside traditional financial ratios.

Meanwhile, Natural Language Processing (NLP) methods have increasingly been applied in sentiment analysis, similarity detection, readability analysis, and topic detection (Bochkay et al. 2023). These methods transform textual data into numerical inputs through techniques such as Bag of Words (BOW) and word embeddings, then employ NLP models ranging from simple transformations to machine learning and deep learning approaches for efficient input–output mapping. Future research in financial fraud detection will likely leverage a broader range of textual and audio sources, including SEC mandatory disclosure, earnings announcements, conference call transcripts, media articles, social media posts, analyst reports, investor meeting materials and CEO interview, to incorporate more valuable information for detecting financial fraud (Amiram et al. 2018).

7.5 Summary

This chapter examines simple statistical regression models, traditional machine learning models, traditional ensemble learning models and deep learning models, focusing on mathematical principles, implementation coding and applications comparison. In fraud detection practice, model performance is influenced by various factors including application scenarios, data quality, and input indicators. There remains no definitive consensus on either the most cost-effective fraud detection methods or a comprehensive indicator system that captures all essential fraud information (Gepp et al. 2021). Furthermore, financial fraud data is inherently scarce. While existing research employs data preprocessing methods such as resampling techniques and model parameter optimization to enhance the model ability to identify scared positive samples, the effectiveness of these enhancements is difficult to accurately assess and shows poor comparability across different data scenarios. Therefore, this book aims to address theses challenges in financial fraud detection models in subsequent chapters by optimizing their performance and interpretability through three key aspects of model algorithms, feature selection, and imbalanced data processing, thereby advancing empirical research in this field.

References

Al-Hashedi KG, Magalingam P (2021) Financial fraud detection applying data mining techniques: a comprehensive review from 2009 to 2019. Comput Sci Rev 40:100402

Amiram D, Bozanic Z, Cox JD, Dupont Q (2018) Financial reporting fraud and other forms of misconduct: a multidisciplinary review of the literature. Rev Account Stud 23:732–783

Bao Y, Ke B, Li B, Yu YJ, Zhang J (2020) Detecting accounting fraud in publicly traded US firms using a machine learning approach. J Account Res 58(1):199–235

Barboza F, Kimura H, Altman E (2017) Machine learning models and bankruptcy prediction. Expert Syst Appl 83:405–417

Beneish MD (1999) The detection of earnings manipulation. Financ Anal J 55(5):24–36

Beneish MD, Vorst P (2022) The cost of fraud prediction errors. Account Rev 97(6):91–121

Bertomeu J, Cheynel E, Floyd E, Pan W (2021) Using machine learning to detect misstatements. Rev Account Stud 26(2):468–519

Bochkay K, Brown SV, Leone AJ et al (2023) Textual analysis in accounting: what's next? Contemp Account Res 40(2):765–805

Cecchini M, Aytug H, Koehler GJ, Pathak P (2010) Detecting management fraud in public companies. Manag Sci 56(7):1146–1160

Chen G, Firth M, Gao DN, Rui OM (2006) Ownership structure, corporate governance, and fraud: evidence from China. J Corp Finan 12(3):424–448

Chi G, Dong B (2022) Default discrimination research based on loan descriptions. Manag Rev 34(11):261–271

Craja P, Kim A, Lessmann S (2020) Deep learning for detecting financial statement fraud. Decis Support Syst 139:113421

De Bock KW, Coussement K, Lessmann S (2020) Cost-sensitive business failure prediction when misclassification costs are uncertain: a heterogeneous ensemble selection approach. Eur J Oper Res 285(2):612–630

Dechow PM, Shakespear C (2009) Do managers time securitization transactions to obtain accounting benefits? Account Rev 84(1):99–132

Dong W, Liao S, Zhang Z (2018) Leveraging financial social media data for corporate fraud detection. J Manag Inf Syst 35(2):461–487

Esenogho E, Mienye ID, Swart TG, Maleka AM (2022) A neural network ensemble with feature engineering for improved credit card fraud detection. IEEE Access 10:16400–16407

Faris H, Abukhurma R, Almanaseer W, Saadeh M, Mora AM, Castillo PA, Aljarah I (2020) Improving financial bankruptcy prediction in a highly imbalanced class distribution using oversampling and ensemble learning: a case from the Spanish market. Prog Artif Intell 9:31–53
Gepp A, Linnenluecke MK, O'Neill TJ, Smith T (2018) Big data techniques in auditing research and practice: current trends and future opportunities. J Account Lit 40(1):102–115
Gepp A, Kumar K, Bhattacharya S (2021) Lifting the numbers game: identifying key input variables and a best-performing model to detect financial statement fraud. Account Finance 61(3):4601–4638
Green BP, Choi JH (1997) Assessing the risk of management fraud through neural network technology. Auditing 16:14–28
Hajek P, Henriques R (2017) Mining corporate annual reports for intelligent detection of financial statement fraud—a comparative study of machine learning methods. Knowl-Based Syst 128:139–152
Hass LH, Tarsalewska M, Zhan F (2016) Equity incentives and corporate fraud in China. J Bus Ethics 138:723–742
Heo J, Yang JY (2014) AdaBoost based bankruptcy forecasting of Korean construction companies. Appl Soft Comput 24:494–499
Hoberg G, Lewis C (2017) Do fraudulent firms produce abnormal disclosure? J Corp Finance 43:58–85
Hong H, Hu H, Guo C (2012) Research on financial reporting fraud identification of listed companies based on GONE theory. Account Res (08):84–90+97
Huang C, Gao J (2025) Code smell detection method integrating feature selection and multi-model soft voting ensemble learning. Mini-Micro Syst 46(02): 504-512
Karpoff JM, Koester A, Lee DS, Martin GS (2017) Proxies and databases in financial misconduct research. Account Rev 92(6):129–163
Khan WA, Chung SH, Awan MU, Wen X (2020) Machine learning facilitated business intelligence (part II) neural networks optimization techniques and applications. Ind Manag Data Syst 120(1):128–163
Kirkos E, Spathis C, Manolopoulos Y (2007) Data mining techniques for the detection of fraudulent financial statements. Expert Syst Appl 32(4):995–1003
Li J, Wu Y, Lei Y, Huang Y (2020) Effective early warning indicators and artificial intelligence models for listed companies' violations based on deferred tax changes. J Financ Res 8:149–168
Li L, Wu D (2022) Forecasting the risk at infractions: an ensemble comparison of machine learning approach. Ind Manag Data Syst 122(1):1–19
Lin CC, Chiu AA, Huang SY, Yen DC (2015) Detecting the financial statement fraud: the analysis of the differences between data mining techniques and experts' judgments. Knowl-Based Syst 89:459–470
Ngai EWT, Hu Y, Wong YH, Chen Y, Sun X (2011) The application of data mining techniques in financial fraud detection: a classification framework and an academic review of literature. Decis Support Syst 50(3):559–569
Oztekin A (2016) A hybrid data analytic approach to predict college graduation status and its determinative factors. Ind Manag Data Syst 116(8):1678–1699
Perols J (2011) Financial statement fraud detection: an analysis of statistical and machine learning algorithms. Audit J Pract Theory 30(2):19–50
Perols JL, Bowen RM, Zimmermann C, Samba B (2017) Finding needles in a haystack: using data analytics to improve fraud prediction. Account Rev 92(2):221–245
Purda L, Skillicorn D (2015) Accounting variables, deception, and a bag of words: assessing the tools of fraud detection. Contemp Account Res 32(3):1193–1223
Qian P, Luo M (2015) Financial fraud prediction model for Chinese listed companies. Account Res (07):18–25+96
Rahman MJ, Zhu H (2023) Predicting accounting fraud using imbalanced ensemble learning classifiers–evidence from China. Account Finance 63(3):3455–3486

Ran M, Yu L, Wang J (2023) Can CSRC's comprehensive inspection of accounting firms improve audit quality? A quasi-natural experiment based on "double random, one public". Audit Res 6:35–47

Randhawa K, Loo CK, Seera M et al (2018) Credit card fraud detection using AdaBoost and majority voting. IEEE Access 6:14277–14284

Ravisankar P, Ravi V, Rao GR, Bose I (2011) Detection of financial statement fraud and feature selection using data mining techniques. Decis Support Syst 50(2):491–500

Speiser JL, Miller ME, Tooze J, Ip E (2019) A comparison of random forest variable selection methods for classification prediction modeling. Expert Syst Appl 134:93–101

Su D, Lin D (2010) Equity incentives, earnings management and corporate governance. Econ Res J 45(11):88–100

Summers SL, Sweeney JT (1998) Fraudulently misstated financial statements and insider trading: an empirical analysis. Account Rev 73:131–146

Taherkhani A, Cosma G, McGinnity TM (2020) AdaBoost-CNN: an adaptive boosting algorithm for convolutional neural networks to classify multi-class imbalanced datasets using transfer learning. Neurocomputing 404:351–366

Wang W, Sun D (2021) The improved AdaBoost algorithms for imbalanced data classification. Inf Sci 563:358–374

Wang M, Tian Y, Yang E et al (2023) Prediction method of reverse pressure drive effect of oil wells based on AdaBoost-SVM algorithm. Math Pract Theory 53(02):128–135

Wang M, Shen W (2023) Research on artificial intelligence audit system based on BP neural network. Inf Syst Eng 7:130–132

West J, Bhattacharya M (2016) Intelligent financial fraud detection: a comprehensive review. Comput Secur 57:47–66

Xu X, Xiong F, An Z (2023) Using machine learning to predict corporate fraud: evidence based on the gone framework. J Bus Ethics 186(1):137–158

Yao Y, Zhao M (2016) Chinese-style risk disclosure, disclosure level and market reaction. Econ Res J 51(07):158–172

Yao H, Li X, Fang Y (2023) Asset allocation based on AdaBoost ensemble algorithm and Black–Litterman model. Syst Eng Theory Pract 43(11):3182–3196

Zhou W, Kapoor G (2011) Detecting evolutionary financial statement fraud. Decis Support Syst 50(3):570–575

Zhou Y, Mazzuchi TA, Sarkani S (2020) M-AdaBoost-A based ensemble system for network intrusion detection. Expert Syst Appl 162:113864

Zhou Y, Fan J, Xue L (2024) How much can machines learn finance from Chinese text data? Manag Sci 70:8962–8987

Zhu X, Ao X, Qin Z, Chang Y (2021) Intelligent financial fraud detection practices in post-pandemic era. Innovation 2(4):100176

Zhuang R, Zhang H (2023) Anomaly detection based on average feature importance and ensemble learning. Comput Syst Appl 32(06):60–69

Zhou L, Lu D, Fujita H (2015) The performance of corporate financial distress prediction models with features selection guided by domain knowledge and data mining approaches. Knowledge-Based Systems 85: 52-61

Chapter 8
Financial Fraud Detection Based on Litigation and Resampling Methods

This chapter addresses the challenge of increasingly sophisticated financial fraud by integrating external litigation information with traditional financial reporting and internal management data, creating a multi-modal analytical framework. Recent years have witnessed a series of major financial fraud cases characterized by prolonged duration, extensive falsification, and multiple stakeholder involvement, severely undermining capital market integrity. This trend, coupled with escalating fraud risks and their mounting real-world implications for listed companies, necessitates the development of more sophisticated fraud detection models. Within this context, this chapter employs regulatory penalty incidents which exhibit strong correlation with financial fraud, as proxy variables to construct an imbalanced large-sample dataset. The research develops fraud detection models by integrating resampling techniques with machine learning methods, considering scenarios both with and without feature selection. Through comparative performance analysis, we identify optimal combinations of resampling methods and classification models while investigating the 'curse of dimensionality' arising from abundant features but rare fraud samples. Furthermore, this chapter makes an innovative contribution by examining the role of litigation factors in financial fraud detection within immature legal environments, providing a new research perspective for financial fraud detection studies.

8.1 Corporate Litigation and Financial Fraud

The preceding discussion delineates the similarities and differences between Chinese and American financial fraud regulatory enforcement systems, exploring the synergy of private and public enforcement procedures. Especially, the private litigation enforcement system, having undergone adjustments and optimizations across various phases, has progressively evolved into a distinctively deterrent anti-fraud mechanism.

X. Ma and D. Wu, *Financial Fraud Detection Using Machine Learning*, AI for Risks,
https://doi.org/10.1007/978-981-95-0840-2_8

In China, with the emergence of characteristic private litigation system, representative litigation has assumed a crucial governance role in cases involving false statements in capital markets, leading to a continuous increase in both the frequency and monetary value of litigation involvement of listed companies (Wang and Bi 2022). Concurrently, the Ministry of Finance has encouraged CPAs to develop forensic accounting services in order to effectively utilize accounting expertise to address legal issues, which also tightens the relationship between litigation arbitration and financial fraud.

The Securities Law of 2019 further emphasizes that companies must disclose significant litigation and arbitration matters in a timely, accurate, and comprehensive manner, while explicitly delineating legal responsibilities for non-compliant disclosure. Additionally, there has been a year-by-year increase in the number of listed companies facing regulatory penalties for misleading or incomplete litigation disclosure. Meanwhile, the disclosure of significant litigation matters may potentially negatively impact various aspects of corporation operations, including bank loans, bond issuance, trading credit, corporate reputation and finally the sustainable development. Meanwhile, fraudulent behavior itself is intrinsically linked to negative corporate indicators such as performance deterioration, liquidity crises, and financial distress. Therefore, it is reasonable to connect litigation risk with corporate fraud.

Within the economics and management domain in China, litigation-related researches have primarily concentrated on risk management, examining how factors such as internal control quality and delisting pressure influence litigation risk (Mao and Meng 2013) and the impact of litigation risk on audit opinions, audit fees, corporate innovation activities, debt financing costs and other multiple variables (Pan et al. 2015; Zhang et al. 2015; Wang et al. 2016; Wang and Bi 2022). However, most litigation-related researches do not consider connections between litigation risk and financial fraud. To address this research gap, this chapter employs an integrated approach combining resampling techniques with machine learning methods to investigate the relationship between litigation risk and financial fraud. The study utilizes the binary variable 'occurrence of significant litigation and arbitration' from the CSMAR database as a measurement indicator of litigation (Pan et al. 2015) and applies machine learning methodologies to assess the significance of litigation in fraud detection as well as their contribution in identifying fraudulent behavior.

8.2 Research Data and Methods

8.2.1 Research Data and Variables

This study employs general violations as proxy variables for financial fraud and the violation information is extracted from the CSMAR database, encompassing date of punishment, type of violations, time of announcement, methods of sanction, and the specific contents of violation disclosed by the Ministry of Finance, CSRC and Stock Exchanges (such as the Shanghai and Shenzhen Stock Exchanges). There are sixteen types of violations including delayed disclosure, false records (misleading statements), material omissions, fictitious assets, unauthorized changes in fund utilization, and misappropriation of corporate assets, as shown in Table 8.1. Based on severity, methods of punishments are classified into criticism, warning, condemnation, monetary fines, confiscation of illegal gains, revocation of business licenses (mandatory closure), market access prohibition, and other sanctions, as shown in Table 8.2.

In terms of the construction of indicator system, we incorporate litigation information into the framework based on the theoretical foundations of financial fraud discussed in Chap. 4, initially selecting 70 financial fraud identification indicators across seven dimensions of solvency, operational capability, development, profitability, risk level, market indicators, and corporate governance (Beneish 1999; Kirkos et al. 2007; Bhatore et al. 2020). The proxy variable of litigation information is a binary variable named as 'occurrence of significant litigation or arbitration', where 0 indicates no significant litigation or arbitration cases and 1 indicates the occurrence of significant litigation or arbitration cases. After eliminating factors with missing data exceeding 15%, sixty-eight fraud detection indicators are retained. All financial data and non-financial data are obtained from CSMAR and WIND databases.

Given that Reform of non-tradable shares in China implemented in 2007 drove the stock market into a new developmental phase, this study selects the sample period of

Table 8.1 Classification of violation events

Code	Type of Violation	Code	Type of Violation
P2501	Fictitious Profits	P2509	Unauthorized Change in Fund Usage
P2502	Fabricated Assets	P2510	Assets Misappropriation
P2503	Misleading Representations	P2511	Insider Trading
P2504	Delayed Disclosure	P2512	Illegal Stock Trading
P2505	Material Omissions	P2513	Stock Price Manipulation
P2506	False Disclosures	P2514	Irregular Guarantees
P2507	IPO Fraud	P2515	General Accounting Irregularities
P2508	Illegal Contributions	P2599	Other Violations

Table 8.2 Punishment methods of violations

Code	Type of Punishment
P2601	Criticism
P2602	Warning
P2603	Reprimand
P2604	Monetary Fine
P2605	Confiscation of Illegal Gains
P2606	License Revocation (Forced Closure)
P2607	Market Entry Ban
P2699	Other Penalties

2006–2021, considering both data comparability and accessibility. This timeframe encompasses multiple economic cycles and significant global events, including the financial crisis, the U.S.-China trade conflict, and the COVID-19 pandemic, enabling analysis of long-term trends in financial fraud and examination of model stability in detecting fraudulent behavior across varying economic conditions. Following researches of Ren et al. (2021), Yuan et al. (2022), and Xu et al. (2023), we classified firms exhibiting one or more regulatory violations as financial fraud, with the dependent variable, whether there exits financial fraud, coded as Y = 1, and Y = 0 otherwise. The time of violations is the actual implementation year, rather the announcement time. Specifically, if a company commits a violation in year T but is discovered by the CSRC in year T + 2, year T is designated as the year of violation.

In the initial data preprocessing stage, we implemented two primary exclusion criteria: (1) samples where listed companies were not the principal violating entities, and (2) companies operating within the financial sector. To mitigate the potential overestimation of fraud probability in cases of continuous fraud, only the initial fraud year for each company were retained (Cecchini et al. 2010; Hong et al. 2012). For samples where the exact year of financial fraud was unclear, the announcement year of punishment is designated as the fraud year. Additionally, for absolute value variables such as market capitalization and company size, logarithmic transformation is applied. Missing values in quantitative variables were addressed through linear interpolation, followed by Z-score standardization, while observations with missing categorical variables were directly eliminated from the analysis. Finally, we collect 43,062 firm-year observations spanning 2006–2021, with fraudulent cases accounting for 14% (5066 observations) of the total sample, representing a typical imbalanced dataset. Table 8.3 presents the temporal distribution of financial fraud ratios over the period 2006–2021, ranging from its lowest point of 3.73% in 2006 to its peak of 12.39% in 2017, with an average annual fraud ratio of approximately 8.44% throughout the sample period.

Table 8.3 Distribution of fraudulent companies from 2006 to 2021

Year	Fraud	Company	Fraud rate (%)	Year	Fraud	Company	Fraud rate (%)
2006	67	1796	3.73	2014	340	3575	9.51
2007	93	2150	4.33	2015	459	3744	12.26
2008	94	2386	3.94	2016	493	3995	12.34
2009	118	2504	4.71	2017	557	4495	12.39
2010	145	2550	5.69	2018	584	4936	11.83
2011	255	2676	9.53	2019	537	5168	10.39
2012	303	2861	10.59	2020	505	5150	9.81
2013	258	3169	8.14	2021	442	5131	8.61

8.2.2 Research Design and Methods

This study explores hybrid financial fraud detection models by integrating data resampling techniques with machine learning algorithms, while examining the impact of feature selection on model accuracy. Following the research of Liang et al. (2023), we split the original dataset into training and testing sets using a 7:3 ratio for model training and validation respectively. Based on the training set, we implemented two traditional sampling methods (RUS and ROS) and eight intelligent sampling approaches (SMOTE, SMOTE Tomek, SMOTE-ENN, BorderlineSMOTE, SVMSMOTE, Cluster Centroids, TomekLinks, and ADASYN) to address the class distribution imbalance. We then conducted a comprehensive performance comparison by training seven machine learning algorithms on both the resampled datasets and the original dataset. The machine learning models comprised four individual classifiers (SVM, DT, GaussianNB, and LR) and three ensemble models (RF, AdaBoost, and GBDT), with all implementations executed in Python 3.6.

Following Bertomeu et al. (2021), we employed ten-fold cross-validation in conjunction with grid search for hyperparameter optimization, maximizing the average AUC on the training set to obtain more objective comparative results. As illustrated in Fig. 8.1, the ten-fold cross-validation method divides the training data into ten equal groups, with nine groups serving as training data and one as testing data in each iteration. The optimal hyperparameters are determined by averaging the evaluation metrics obtained from ten iterations (Khan et al. 2020). Moreover, in terms of the grid search methodology, it first sets a range for each parameter, then trains models for each parameter combination, ultimately selecting the optimal parameter combination (Xiao et al. 2021). The detailed parameter optimization process based on ten-fold cross-validation and grid search is presented in Fig. 8.2.

Finally, model performance is evaluated on the test samples to mitigate potential bias from random sampling and classification thresholds can be adjusted to achieve optimal classification results. Regarding feature selection, following Ravisankar et al. (2011), we employed the SelectKBest feature selection function to compute F-statistics of each feature, selecting the top 20 highest-scoring features, as shown in Table 8.4 to discuss the influence of feature selection on model accuracy. The complete research framework in this chapter is depicted in Fig. 8.3.

8.3 Empirical Results and Discussion

As previously discussed, this study constructs an imbalanced fraud dataset comprising 42,062 observations and 68 features to examine broadly defined financial fraud among listed companies from 2006 to 2021, with positive cases constituting only 14% of the whole sample. Then, ten distinct resampling techniques including RUS, ROS, SMOTE, SMOTE Tomek, SMOTE-ENN, BorderlineSMOTE, SVMSMOTE, Cluster Centroids, TomekLinks, and ADASYN were applied to

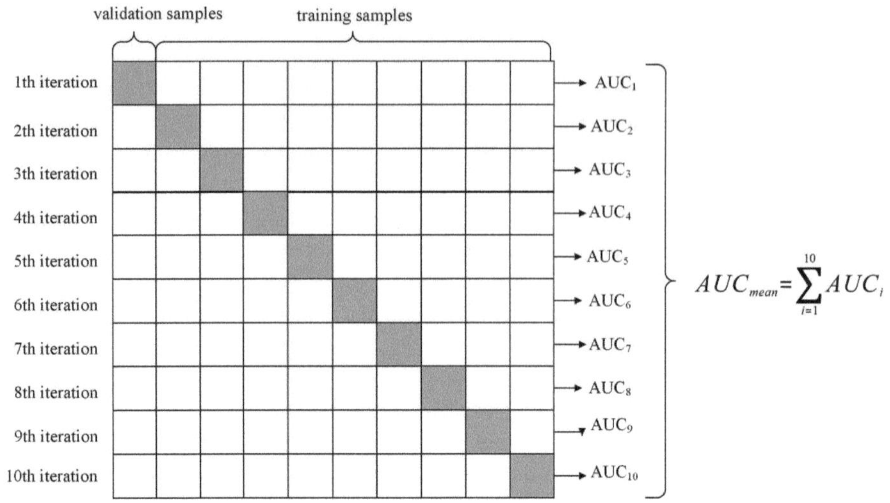

Fig. 8.1 Ten-fold cross validation

generate ten balanced datasets for training various machine learning algorithms, including LR, GaussianNB, RF, GBDT, and AdaBoost. Additionally, we set the weight parameter as "balanced" to impose higher misclassification costs for minority classes, thereby balancing the class weight ratio between majority and minority samples (Zhou and Kapoor 2011).

The training process was conducted three times. First, all initial fraud identification variables were input into models without feature selection and the feature set was named as OrigF. Second, the f_classif method within SelectKBest was employed to compute F-statistics for each feature to select the top 20 highest-scoring features and this feature set is named as Top20F. And finally, we constructed a feature set excluding litigation information (NoLitF) to investigate the role of litigation information during the classification process in each model. All training processes with different features and machine learning models were completed using Python 3.6. Importantly, feature selection and parameter optimization were conducted on the training dataset to preserve the test set as a holdout sample for validation.

8.3.1 Performance of Hybrid Machine Learning Models Based on Resampling Techniques

Table 8.5 presents a comprehensive comparison of machine learning models performance across different combinations of resampling techniques and feature selection methods, with classification results on the original highly imbalanced dataset as

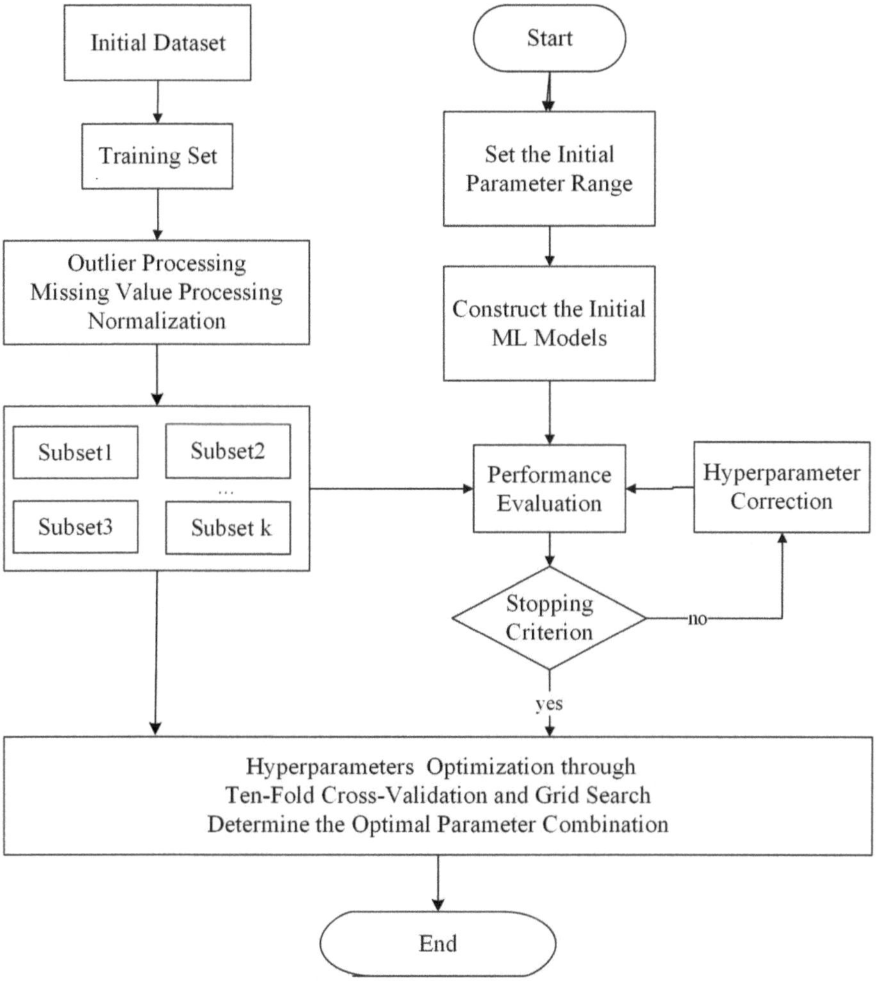

Fig. 8.2 Parameter optimization based on ten-fold cross validation and grid searching

benchmark. The empirical result shows that models trained on the original imbalanced dataset shows poor performance in recall, precision, and F1-score, while maintaining relatively high accuracy and AUC scores, regardless of feature selection. Machine learning models tend to misclassify minority class samples as majority class samples to result in a high accuracy for majority cases and suboptimal accuracy for minority cases. Especially ensemble classifiers such as GBDT, RF, and AdaBoost exhibited particularly low recall rates of approximately 10%, rendering them impractical for real-world applications.

The introduction of resampling techniques alleviate this situation with machine learning models achieving higher precision, recall, and F1-score while maintaining

Table 8.4 Top 20 features selected by F-test

Rank	Category	Name (Abbreviation)	Description
1	Governance	Audittyp	Type of audit opinion
2	Risk level	IsLoss	Is Loss (NP < 0)
3	Solvency	PBIT/L	Profit before interest and tax/total liabilities
4	Governance	GeneralmeetingNum	Number of shareholder meetings held
5	Market	EPS	Earning per share
6	Governance	BoardmeetingNum	Number of board meetings
7	Governance	ContrshrProportion	Proportion of controlling shareholders (%)
8	Governance	IsCorrection	Is accounting correction
9	Solvency	CashFlowRatio	CashFlowRatio
10	Market	NAPS	Net assets per share
11	Governance	Shrhfd	H index
12	Governance	InsInvestorProp	Proportion of institutional investors (%)
13	Governance	PropertyRightsNature	Nature of property rights
14	Solvency	CurrentRatio	CurrentRatio
15	Profitability	OperatingGrossMargin	Operating gross margin
16	Solvency	QuickRatio	QuickRatio
17	Market	NCFfromOA	NCF per share from OA
18	Risk level	NPtoShareholders	NP to shareholders
19	Governance	IsInvolvedLA	Is a major litigation or arbitration
20	Solvency	CashRatio	CashRatio

acceptable levels of accuracy and AUC. Among these combined models, GaussianNB classifier achieves recall rates of 96.68%, 98.25%, 98.34%, and 99.40% on balanced datasets processed by RUS, BorderlineSMOTE, SMOTE, and Cluster Centroids techniques respectively. Furthermore, top 20 fraud identification factors retained based on F-statistics largely preserved the discriminative capability of each model. Even though comprehensive information can draw a whole picture of financial fraud, the relationship between feature quantity and model performance is not necessarily positively correlated, which align with the finding of Almamy et al. (2016).

Figure 8.4 and Fig. 8.5 illustrate the performance comparison of machine learning models trained on different datasets with feature selection (Top20F). There is an inverse relationship between accuracy and recall rate, indicating that maintaining high recall necessitates a trade-off with overall model accuracy—a phenomenon particularly pronounced in ensemble learning methods such as GBDT, AdaBoost, and RF. From an accuracy perspective, ensemble learning classifiers (GBDT, RF, and AdaBoost) demonstrated obviously superior performance compared to traditional

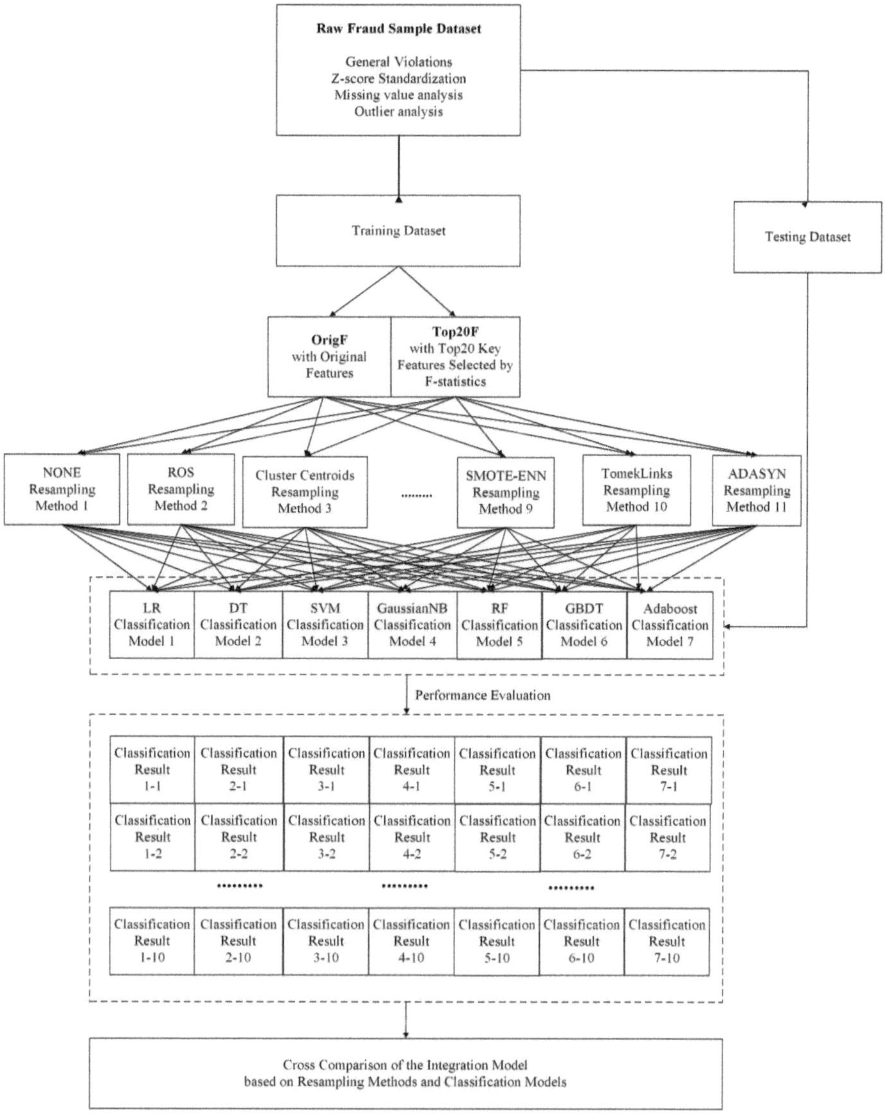

Fig. 8.3 The research framework

machine learning classifiers like LR, SVM, and GaussianNB, aligning with the findings of West and Bhattacharya (2016), Perols et al. (2017), Bao et al. (2020), Gepp et al. (2021), and Xu et al. (2023). Overall, model accuracy fluctuated within the range of 70–90%, with GaussianNB being the notable exception, exhibiting particularly poor accuracy—reaching a mere 27.03% when integrated with the Cluster Centroids

Table 8.5 Performance comparison of machine learning models with and without feature selection

Algorithms	Datasets	Accuracy		Precision		Recall		F1 Score		AUC	
		Top20F	OrigF	Top20F	OrigF	Top20F	OrigF	Top20F	OrigF	Top20F	OrigF
LR	Original	0.7607	0.6947	0.1723	0.1187	0.4476	0.3811	0.2488	0.1811	0.6811	0.5902
	SMOTE	0.7585	0.6537	0.1722	0.1233	0.4537	0.4764	0.2496	0.1959	0.6835	0.6007
	SMOTE-ENN	0.7296	0.8626	0.1610	0.1589	0.4878	0.1285	0.2421	0.1421	0.6800	0.5868
	SMOTETomek	0.7600	0.6518	0.1718	0.1237	0.4476	0.4816	0.2482	0.1968	0.6827	0.6027
	BorderlineSMOTE	0.7648	0.6583	0.1734	0.1210	0.4397	0.4563	0.2488	0.1912	0.6787	0.5956
	SVMSMOTE	0.8189	0.8184	0.1877	0.1506	0.3138	0.2264	0.2349	0.1809	0.6757	0.6014
	ClusterCentroids	0.6944	0.6669	0.1438	0.1095	0.4948	0.3872	0.2228	0.1707	0.6534	0.5699
GaussianNB	Original	0.8176	0.9049	0.1869	0.2069	0.3164	0.0262	0.2350	0.0465	0.6616	0.6004
	SMOTE	0.3428	0.0939	0.1033	0.0878	0.8357	0.9834	0.1838	0.1612	0.6540	0.5835
	SMOTE-ENN	0.3124	0.9043	0.1019	0.1504	0.8663	0.0175	0.1824	0.0313	0.6524	0.5907
	SMOTETomek	0.3425	0.9054	0.1035	0.1803	0.8383	0.0192	0.1842	0.0348	0.6503	0.5854
	BorderlineSMOTE	0.5035	0.0979	0.1192	0.0881	0.7212	0.9825	0.2046	0.1617	0.6579	0.5943
	SVMSMOTE	0.7998	0.4607	0.1784	0.1079	0.3497	0.7002	0.2363	0.1870	0.6607	0.5913
	ClusterCentroids	0.2703	0.0899	0.0991	0.0882	0.8951	0.9939	0.1785	0.1621	0.6460	0.5724
RF	Original	0.8452	0.8666	0.2166	0.2425	0.2858	0.2386	0.2464	0.2405	0.6871	0.6929
	SMOTE	0.8971	0.8898	0.2764	0.2595	0.1005	0.1320	0.1474	0.1750	0.6692	0.6854
	SMOTE-ENN	0.8505	0.8540	0.2167	0.2198	0.2631	0.2544	0.2377	0.2358	0.6837	0.6922
	SMOTETomek	0.8924	0.8937	0.2598	0.2705	0.1163	0.1180	0.1606	0.1643	0.6679	0.6830
	BorderlineSMOTE	0.8830	0.8831	0.2452	0.2630	0.1547	0.1775	0.1897	0.2119	0.6754	0.6959
	SVMSMOTE	0.8892	0.8989	0.2396	0.2725	0.1154	0.0848	0.1558	0.1293	0.6799	0.6977
RF	ClusterCentroids	0.4130	0.2870	0.1113	0.0956	0.8059	0.8339	0.1956	0.1716	0.6475	0.5906

(continued)

Table 8.5 (continued)

Algorithms	Datasets	Accuracy		Precision		Recall		F1 Score		AUC	
		Top20F	OrigF	Top20F	OrigF	Top20F	OrigF	Top20F	OrigF	Top20F	OrigF
AdaBoost	Original	0.9104	0.9091	0.4253	0.3929	0.0323	0.0481	0.0601	0.0857	0.6888	0.6962
	SMOTE	0.8964	0.8986	0.2867	0.2515	0.1145	0.0734	0.1636	0.1137	0.6698	0.6410
	SMOTE-ENN	0.7946	0.7967	0.1801	0.1715	0.3715	0.3383	0.2426	0.2276	0.6782	0.6537
	SMOTETomek	0.8838	0.8998	0.2510	0.2727	0.1573	0.0787	0.1934	0.1221	0.6703	0.6391
	BorderlineSMOTE	0.9074	0.9091	0.3452	0.3465	0.0507	0.0306	0.0884	0.0562	0.6551	0.6655
	SVMSMOTE	0.9032	0.9032	0.2981	0.3094	0.0691	0.0752	0.1121	0.1210	0.6698	0.6817
	ClusterCentroids	0.4239	0.2280	0.1104	0.0907	0.7797	0.8549	0.1933	0.1640	0.6363	0.5610
GBDT	Original	0.9095	0.9094	0.3684	0.3548	0.0306	0.0289	0.0565	0.0534	0.6946	0.7043
	SMOTE	0.9089	0.9096	0.3962	0.3983	0.0551	0.0411	0.0967	0.0745	0.6732	0.6804
	SMOTE-ENN	0.8628	0.8656	0.2268	0.2329	0.2281	0.2255	0.2275	0.2291	0.6904	0.6882
	SMOTETomek	0.9080	0.9097	0.3690	0.3964	0.0542	0.0385	0.0945	0.0701	0.6814	0.6738
	BorderlineSMOTE	0.9106	0.9068	0.4337	0.3315	0.0315	0.0516	0.0587	0.0893	0.6791	0.6703
	SVMSMOTE	0.9086	0.9067	0.3806	0.3152	0.0516	0.0455	0.0908	0.0794	0.6832	0.6934
	ClusterCentroids	0.3900	0.2326	0.1089	0.0918	0.8199	0.8619	0.1923	0.1659	0.6463	0.5697

Notes: This table presents the classification results of machine learning algorithms across different training datasets, comparing classification performance with and without feature selection. Column 1 lists the machine learning models: LR, GaussianNB, RF, GBDT, and AdaBoost. Column 2 shows the training results on datasets processed by six resampling techniques (SMOTE, SMOTE-ENN, SMOTETomek, BorderlineSMOTE, SVMSMOTE, and ClusterCentroids) compared with results on the original imbalanced dataset (Original). Columns 3–12 display five model performance metrics (Accuracy, Precision, Recall, F1-score, and AUC) under two conditions: with feature selection (Top20F) and without feature selection (OrigF). All metrics are reported to four decimal places

resampling technique. Among the resampling methods, SVMSMOTE, BorderlineSMOTE, and ADASYN demonstrated superior accuracy, with BorderlineSMOTE-enhanced GBDT and AdaBoost respectively achieving the highest accuracy rates of 91.06% and 90.74%.

In financial fraud detection research, the recall rate is particularly crucial for performance evaluation since it focuses more on the correct classification of actual fraud cases (positive class). However, considering recall rate, traditional machine learning classifiers such as LR, SVM, and GaussianNB perfomed better than ensemble learning classifiers, with the GaussianNB classifier combined with Cluster Centroids resampling achieving the highest recall rate of 89.51%. We extract GaussianNB algorithm and Cluster Centroids resampling method to observe individual performance and find each has distinct advantages. Specifically, hybrid machine learning models incorporating Cluster Centroids resampling technigue always achieved more notable recll rates of 89.51% with GaussianNB, 80.59%

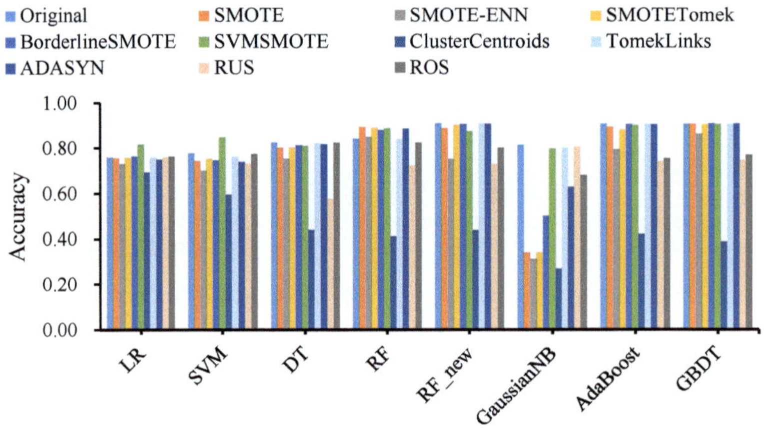

Fig. 8.4 Accuracy of ML methods under balanced and imbalanced samples

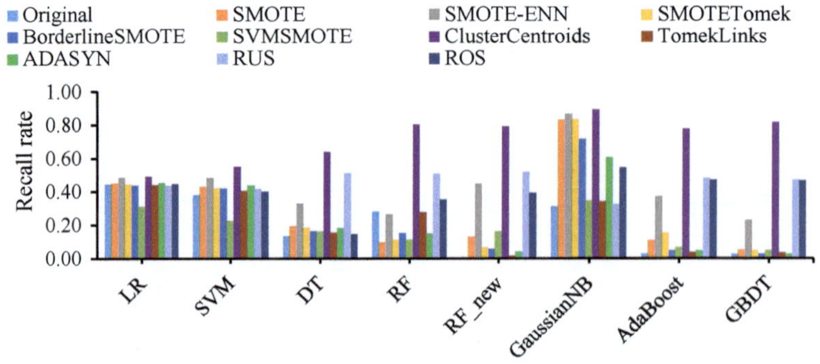

Fig. 8.5 Recall rate of ML methods under balanced and imbalanced samples

with RF, 77.97% with AdaBoost, and 81.99% with GBDT, substantially outperforming models utilizing alternative sampling techniques. Furthermore, the GaussianNB algorithm demonstrated consistently superior performance across various resampling techniques, achieving recall rate of 83.57% with SMOTE, 86.63% with SMOTE-ENN, 83.83% with SMOTETomek, 72.12% with BorderlineSMOTE, and 89.51% with ClusterCentroids, generally surpassing other hybrid machine learning configurations.

As a supplementary analysis, we introduced a Convolutional Neural Network (CNN) model drawing inspiration from Lecun et al. (1998), with each sample reshaped into a 10×6 matrix to meet convolutional layer input requirements. The final output layer comprised a single neuron utilizing a Sigmoid activation function to generate binary classification probabilities. During model training, we employed the Adam optimizer for parameter optimization and utilized binary cross-entropy as the loss function.

Experimental results revealed significant limitations of the CNN approach. On the original imbalanced dataset, despite achieving an 88% accuracy, the model demonstrated zero fraud sample identification, rendering it impractical for real-world applications. After applying the SMOTETomek resampling technique, the CNN model's performance metrics were as follows: accuracy of 0.12, precision of 0.12, recall of 1.0, and F1-score of 0.21. While the model successfully captured all positive class samples, the extensive false positives resulted in low precision and F1-score, further substantiating the inherent limitations of deep learning algorithms for this specific dataset. Consequently, we opted not to pursue deep learning approaches in our primary analysis.

8.3.2 Indicator Analysis Based on Hybrid Machine Learning Models

The comparative analysis of resampling techniques integrated with machine learning algorithms revealed that the GaussianNB algorithm demonstrated the most optimal classification performance on this fraud dataset, while Cluster Centroid and SMOTE Tomek resampling techniques exhibited notable superiority. Consequently, this section further investigates the impact of input features on model classification performance, focusing on two hybrid models: the GaussianNB integrated with Cluster Centroid (GNB_CC) and the GaussianNB integrated with SMOTE Tomek (GNB_SMOTE), with the experimental process illustrated in Fig. 8.6.

Firstly, we used Cluster Centroid and SMOTE Tomek resampling techniques to generate two new datasets named as DS_CC and DS_SMOTE with positive-to-negative sample ratio of 1:1. For each dataset, we then created three feature sets: without feature selection (OrigF), with feature selection (Top20F), and excluding litigation information (NoLitF)., to train the GaussianNB classifier with the "class_weight" parameter set to "balanced" and conducted cross-compared performance

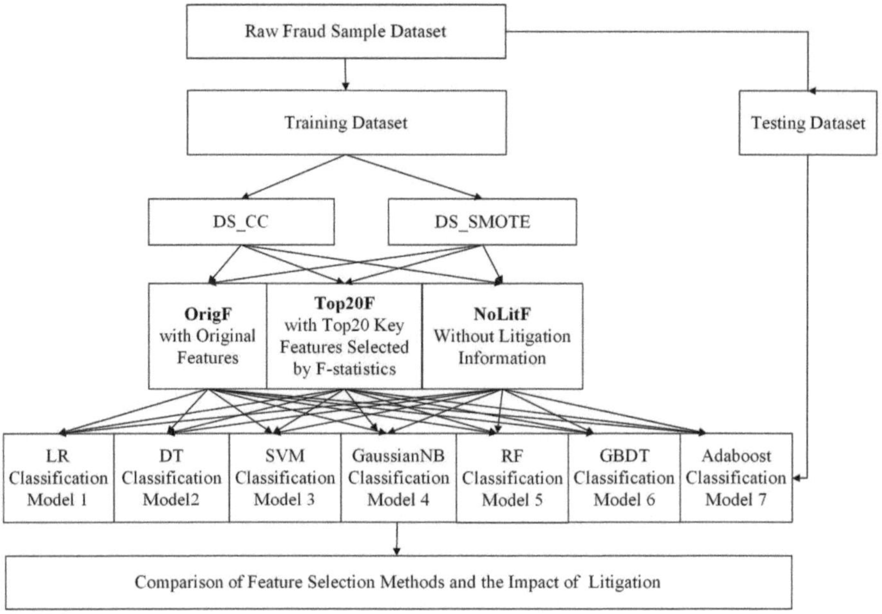

Fig. 8.6 Feature analysis framework based on GaussianNB hybrid model

analysis with other SVM, DT, RF, LR, AdaBoost, and GBDT machine learning models. The Cluster Centroid-integrated models were denoted as SVM_CC, DT_CC, RF_CC, LR_CC, AB_CC, and GBDT_CC, while the SMOTE Tomek-integrated models were labeled as SVM_SMOTE, DT_SMOTE, RF_SMOTE, LR_SMOTE, AB_SMOTE, and GBDT_SMOTE. Experimental results are presented in Table 8.6.

The AUC consistently remained stable between 0.6 and 0.7 across model combinations. Following Craja et al. (2020), we prioritized recall rate as the primary evaluation metric to assess the model performance to detect more real fraud cases. We first compared the fraud detection rate of hybrid machine learning algorithms under without and without feature selection (OrigF and Top20F). After feature selection based on F-statistics (Top20F), the average recall rate across hybrid machine learning algorithms decreased by 3.26%. Among these combined models, SVM_CC, GNB_SMOTE, and DT_CC experienced the most substantial declines, with each recall rate respectively reduced by 13.73%, 13.46%, and 13.37%. Moderate decreases were observed in GNB_CC (9.88%), AB_CC (7.52%), GBDT_CC (4.20%), LR_SMOTE (4.19%), DT_SMOTE (3.32%), and RF_CC (2.80%). Interestingly, LR_CC, SVM_SMOTE, and AB_SMOTE showed slight improvements of 10.76%, 8.30%, and 7.78% in recall rate, though their overall performance remained poor.

Without feature selection (OrigF), the top five hybrid models arranged by recall rate were GNB_CC (99.39%), GNB_SMOTE (97.29%), GBDT_CC (86.19%), AB_CC (85.49%), and RF_CC (83.39%). After feature selection (Top20F), the ranking shifted to GNB_CC (89.51%), GNB_SMOTE (83.83%), GBDT_CC (81.99%), RF_

Table 8.6 Classification results of hybrid machine learning model after feature selection

Hybrid Models	OrigF	Top20F	NoLitF	Hybrid Models	OrigF	Top20F	NoLitF
	Recall				AUC		
LR_CC	0.3872	0.4948	0.0315	LR_CC	0.5699	0.6534	0.5590
SVM_CC	0.6932	0.5559	0.6888	SVM_CC	0.5405	0.6244	0.5440
GNB_CC	0.9939	0.8951	0.9939	GNB_CC	0.5724	0.6460	0.5733
DT_CC	0.7771	0.6434	0.7727	DT_CC	0.5129	0.5331	0.5094
RF_CC	0.8339	0.8059	0.8357	RF_CC	0.5906	0.6475	0.5965
AB_CC	0.8549	0.7797	0.8575	AB_CC	0.5610	0.6363	0.5654
GBDT_CC	0.8619	0.8199	0.8628	GBDT_CC	0.5697	0.6463	0.5689
LR_SMOTE	0.4895	0.4476	0.0341	LR_SMOTE	0.6014	0.6827	0.5952
SVM_SMOTE	0.3427	0.4257	0.3453	SVM_SMOTE	0.6061	0.6688	0.6049
GNB_SMOTE	0.9729	0.8383	0.4108	GNB_SMOTE	0.5816	0.6503	0.5845
DT_SMOTE	0.2220	0.1888	0.2063	DT_SMOTE	0.5431	0.5263	0.5328
RF_SMOTE	0.1250	0.1163	0.1241	RF_SMOTE	0.6810	0.6679	0.6828
AB_SMOTE	0.0795	0.1573	0.0970	AB_SMOTE	0.6249	0.6703	0.6398
GBDT_SMOTE	0.0455	0.0542	0.0428	GBDT_SMOTE	0.6734	0.6814	0.6799

Notes: This table presents the AUC and recall rate of hybrid machine learning models using Cluster Centroid and SMOTE Tomek resampling techniques across three kinds of feature sets. Column 1 & 5 is the abbreviations name of hybrid machine learning model; columns 2–4 and columns 6–8 represent the recall rate and AUC. All numbers are reported to four decimal places. OrigF: Original feature set without selection. Top20F: Top 20 features selected by F-statistics. NoLitF: Feature set excluding litigation information. The SMOTETomek resampling method integrates seven machine learning models—Gaussian Naive Bayes (GNB_SMOTE), Support Vector Machine (SVM_SMOTE), Decision Tree (DT_SMOTE), Random Forest (RF_SMOTE), Logistic Regression (LR_SMOTE), AdaBoost (AB_SMOTE), and Gradient Boosting Decision Tree (GBDT_SMOTE); The Cluster Centroid resampling method integrates seven machine learning models—Gaussian Naive Bayes (GNB_CC), Support Vector Machine (SVM_CC), Decision Tree (DT_CC), Random Forest (RF_CC), Logistic Regression (LR_CC), AdaBoost (AB_CC), and Gradient Boosting Decision Tree (GBDT_CC)

CC (80.59%), and AB_CC (77.97%). Despite the overall recall rate showed obvious reduction after feature selection, GNB_CC, GNB_SMOTE, GBDT_CC, AB_CC, and RF_CC consistently demonstrated superior performance regardless of feature selection. Particularly the GaussianNB-based hybrid algorithms (GNB_CC and GNB_SMOTE) maintained the best power to detect the most actual fraud cases before and after feature selection, significantly outperforming other hybrid models. At same time, the Top20 feature set did retain most of the initial information, resulting in minimal impact on model performance with limited number of factors.

We next compared the recall rate of hybrid machine learning algorithms under without feature selection (OrigF) and excluding litigation information (NoLitF), in order to explore the role of litigation information in financial fraud detection. After eliminating litigation information, the average fraud detection rate across hybrid machine learning algorithms decreased by 9.83%, a more substantial decline compared to the feature selection (Top20F) scenario mentioned before, indicating the significance of litigation indicators during modelling. Notably, the GNB_SMOTE model experienced the most dramatic reduction in recall rate of 56.21%. In other words, incorporating litigation information elevated its accuracy to detect fraud from 41.08% to 97.29%. Similarly, hybrid logistic regression models (LR_SMOTE and LR_CC) respectively experienced substantial performance improvements of 45.54% and 35.57% when litigation indicators were included.

Interestingly, for the GNB_CC hybrid model which exhibited the optimal fraud detection performance in the OrigF scenario, there is no discernible impact on its recall rate when removing litigation information and this ratio still maintains its peak of 99.39%. The inclusion of litigation indicators showed minimal performance variations among other hybrid models. In the NoLitF scenario, the top 5 fraud detection models were exclusively Cluster Centroid-integrated hybrid models, including GNB_CC (99.39%), GBDT_CC (86.28%), AB_CC (85.75%), RF_CC (83.57%), and DT_CC (77.27%). In contrast, the SMOTE Tomek-integrated machine learning models show considerably more dependence on litigation indicators.

To summarize the empirical results related with litigation, litigation indicators significantly influence the capacity of model to detect financial fraud detection through the comparison on performance of hybrid machine learning models with or without litigation information as input. Moreover, from the feature importance analysis, we found that litigation indicators are consistently ranked within the top twenty indicators across different machine learning classification processes under different feature selection methods. Table 8.7 reports the description statistics result of top 20 indicators selected through F-statistics and litigation ranked as the 19th most critical factor to assess corporate financial fraud, which is accordance with the occurracne path of real faud scandals.

We use the Kangde Xin financial fraud case to exemplify the critical relationship between litigation and financial fraud. This company faced a class-action lawsuit in 2019, then in 2020, CSRC formally imposed administrative penalties due to the systematic and continuous financial manipulation from 2015 to 2018 which artificially overstated profits by approximately 11.5 billion yuan through manipulating business revenue, operating costs, and sales expenses. This massive financial fraud triggered a dramatic stock price collapse and subsequent stock suspension, with the class-action lawsuit setting unprecedented records in terms of defendant count, estimated claimant numbers, and potential compensation amounts. Similarly, the Kangmei Pharmaceutical financial fraud case also underscores the intrinsic connection between class-action litigation and financial misconduct. In 2020, it was identified by the CSRC as significant financial reporting irregularities, including artificially inflating monetary funds by 88.6 billion yuan and business revenue by 29.1 billion yuan, causing substantial investor losses. Therefore, investors initiated a class-action lawsuit at the Guangzhou Intermediate People's Court. Overall, since the amendment of the Securities Law in 2019, the class-action litigation system has achieved preliminary success in Chinese capital markets and accordingly, litigation indicators have emerged as a crucial observing factor for financial fraud, which has been further validated in this chapter using hybrid machine learning approaches.

Table 8.7 Descriptive statistics for the top 20 variables

Sign	Name (Abbreviation)	mean	std	min	25%	50%	75%	max
Y	IsFraud	0.12	0.32	0	0	0	0	1
X65	Audittyp	1	1	0	1	1	1	1
X45	IsLoss	0.11	0.32	0	0	0	0	1
X8	PBIT/L	0.31	0.52	−9.98	0.10	0.20	0.39	14.00
X64	GeneralmeetingNum	0	1	−1.83	−0.71	−0.15	0.42	16.74
X31	EPS	0	1	−147.03	−0.01	0	0	115.53
X62	BoardmeetingNum	0	1	−2.36	−0.63	−0.14	0.35	11.96
X56	ContrshrProportion	0.36	0.16	0	0.24	0.34	0.47	1.55
X68	IsCorrection	0.10	0.30	0	0	0	0	1
X9	CashFlowRatio	0.19	0.44	−14.24	0.01	0.11	0.27	17.20
X33	NAPS	0	1	−0.06	−0.01	−0.01	−0.01	140.15
X51	Shrhfd	0.14	0.12	0	0.05	0.10	0.20	0.81
X55	InsInvestorProp	0.45	0.24	0	0.26	0.47	0.64	2.11
X53	PropertyRightsNature	0.38	0.48	0	0	0	1	1
X1	CurrentRatio	2.58	4.01	−5.13	1.08	1.60	2.67	204.74
X29	OperatingGrossMargin	0.28	0.22	−20.83	0.16	0.25	0.38	1.15
X2	QuickRatio	2.08	3.70	−5.13	0.69	1.16	2.11	179.58
X34	NCFfromOA	0	1	−89.61	−0.01	0	0	182.94
X41	NPtoShareholders	0	1	−21.41	−0.13	−0.10	0	54.62
X70	IsInvolvedLA	0.13	0.33	0	0	0	0	1
X3	CashRatio	0.99	2.67	−5.06	0.18	0.38	0.87	167.54

The United States has a well-established class-action litigation system spanning 60 years, extensively applied in domains of securities fraud and other types of fraud and has constructed specialized databases like the Stanford Securities Class Action Clearinghouse (SCAC) to track and collect securities class-action litigation cases. Previous researches have utilized private enforcement cases from Securities Class Actions (SCAs) to proxy accounting fraud samples (Choi and Pritchard et al. 2016; Karpoff et al. 2017; Donelson et al. 2021) and found that litigation matters significantly impact the market value of listed companies (Barko et al. 2023) and provide more precise detection of corporate misconduct (Amiram et al. 2018).However, 10% of sued enterprises will enter bankruptcy proceedings (Ren et al. 2021).

Although China's financial fraud-related litigation system is at the early development stage, our empirical findings preliminarily validate the critical role of litigation-related indicators in financial fraud detection within Chinese capital markets from a machine learning perspective, while the direction and magnitude of this influence show variability across different machine learning models. In the following chapters, we will further employ traditional econometric analysis to clarify the impact of indicators on financial fraud behavior. In future, with the continuous development of litigation databases, we can leverage more advanced data mining techniques like deep learning to comprehensively explore the pivotal role of litigation to enhance the effectiveness of financial fraud detection.

Lastly, as a validation, we selected the most recent financial fraud cases announced in 2023 to assess the performance of the previously identified optimal fraud detection model of GNB_CC. The validation sample included twenty listed companies investigated by the CSRC for financial fraud, such as ST Hongtu (600,122.SH), *ST Pangda (601,258.SH), *ST Kaile (600,260.SH), *ST Hangtong (600,677.SH), and *ST Zixing (688,086.SH). Based on the original dataset comprised by 68 features from 2022 (the year preceding fraud announcement) in the CSMAR database, we applied the GNB_CC model for sample classification. Remarkably, all samples were correctly classified as financial fraud, further validating the effectiveness of the optimal model established to detect financial misconduct in this chapter.

8.4 Summary

The Chinese financial landscape confronts significant challenges in fraud detection, manifested through extended concealment periods, protracted investigation processes, minimal exposure rates, and increasingly sophisticated operational methodologies. These systemic complexities urgently demand the development of a robust financial fraud detection framework to support the sustainable evolution of high-quality capital markets. This chapter employed general regulatory violation events as a proxy for financial fraud, introducing the "occurrence of significant litigation or arbitration" indicator to establish an imbalanced fraud dataset comprising 42,062 samples with 68 features, with fraud rate of only 14%. To address data scarcity and dimensionality disaster of indicators, we integrated resampling techniques with machine learning algorithms to construct hybrid fraud detection models to select the GNB_CC algorithm as the optimal classification approach after rigid cross-comparison. This GNB_CC model can correctly detect 89.51% and 99.40% of real fraud cases with and without feature selection. We also undertook an extensive investigation into the performance implications of feature selection across different machine learning algorithms through training machine learning models using three feature sets: the initial feature set (OrigF), F-statistic-based selected features (Top20F), and features excluding litigation information (NoLitF). Across multiple feature sets and experimental configurations, the GNB_CC hybrid model consistently exhibited superior fraud detection precision, empirically substantiating its methodological robustness and computational reliability.

Statistical feature selection through F-statistic revealed the significance of litigation indicators within the top 20 features. The condensed feature set demonstrated remarkable information retention, exhibiting minimal performance variance compared to the original feature space. The integration of litigation information yielded a transformative impact on the predictive capability of GNB_SMOTE model, dramatically elevating the accuracy to detect financial fraud from a modest 41.08%

to an impressive 97.29%. This methodological approach introduces a pioneering framework for financial fraud identification, strategically bridging quantitative analysis in the following chapters by empirically demonstrating the pivotal classification significance of litigation indicators through advanced machine learning techniques.

Subsequent validation utilizing independent sample datasets comprehensively confirmed the predictive robustness and generalizability of the GNB_CC model across diverse financial fraud detection scenarios. Our innovative research framework presents a versatile methodological approach with significant transferability to domains characterized by data scarcity and high-dimensional complexity. Potential application domains include earnings management analysis, financial accounting restatement investigations, detection of substantial accounting misstatements, corporate bankruptcy prediction, and auditor change assessments. This robust architectural design provides a comprehensive strategy for enhancing anomaly detection model performance across multifaceted analytical scenarios.

References

Almamy J, Aston J, Ngwa LN (2016) An evaluation of Altman's Z-score using cash flow ratio to predict corporate failure amid the recent financial crisis: evidence from the UK. J Corp Finance 36:278–285

Amiram D, Bozanic Z, Cox JD, Dupont Q (2018) Financial reporting fraud and other forms of misconduct: a multidisciplinary review of the literature. Rev Account Stud 23:732–783

Bao Y, Ke B, Li B, Yu YJ, Zhang J (2020) Detecting accounting fraud in publicly traded US firms using a machine learning approach. J Account Res 58(1):199–235

Barko T, Renneboog L, Zhang H (2023) Corporate fraud and the consequences of securities class action litigation. European Corporate Governance Institute (925)

Beneish MD (1999) The detection of earnings manipulation. Financ Anal J 55(5):24–36

Bertomeu J, Cheynel E, Floyd E, Pan W (2021) Using machine learning to detect misstatements. Rev Account Stud 26(2):468–519

Bhatore S, Mohan L, Reddy YR (2020) Machine learning techniques for credit risk evaluation: a systematic literature review. J Bank Financ Technol 4(1):111–138

Cecchini M, Aytug H, Koehler GJ, Pathak P (2010) Detecting management fraud in public companies. Manag Sci 56(7):1146–1160

Choi SJ, Pritchard AC (2016) SEC investigations and securities class actions: an empirical comparison. J Empir Leg Stud 13(1):27–49

Craja P, Kim A, Lessmann S (2020) Deep learning for detecting financial statement fraud. Decis Support Syst 139:113421

Donelson DC, Kartapanis A, McInnis J, Yust CG (2021) Measuring accounting fraud and irregularities using public and private enforcement. Account Rev 96(6):183–213

Gepp A, Kumar K, Bhattacharya S (2021) Lifting the numbers game: identifying key input variables and a best-performing model to detect financial statement fraud. Account Finance 61(3):4601–4638

Hong H, Hu H, Guo C (2012) Research on financial reporting fraud identification of listed companies based on GONE theory. Account Res (08):84–90+97

Karpoff JM, Koester A, Lee DS, Martin GS (2017) Proxies and databases in financial misconduct research. Account Rev 92(6):129–163

Khan WA, Chung SH, Awan MU, Wen X (2020) Machine learning facilitated business intelligence (Part II) neural networks optimization techniques and applications. Ind Manag Data Syst 120(1):128–163

Kirkos E, Spathis C, Manolopoulos Y (2007) Data mining techniques for the detection of fraudulent financial statements. Expert Syst Appl 32(4):995–1003

Lecun Y, Bottou L, Bengio Y, Haffner P (1998) Gradient-based learning applied to document recognition. Proc IEEE 86(11):2278–2324

Liang Q, Wang Z, Guan X, Wang D (2023) Party direct control and corporate fraud: evidence from China. Q Rev Econ Finance 92:274–290

Mao X, Meng J (2013) Internal control and litigation risk. Manag World 11:155–165

Pan Y, Pan J, Dai Y (2015) Corporate litigation risk, judicial local protectionism and enterprise innovation. Econ Res J 50(03):131–145

Perols JL, Bowen RM, Zimmermann C, Samba B (2017) Finding needles in a haystack: using data analytics to improve fraud prediction. Account Rev 92(2):221–245

Ravisankar P, Ravi V, Rao GR, Bose I (2011) Detection of financial statement fraud and feature selection using data mining techniques. Decis Support Syst 50(2):491–500

Ren L, Zhong X, Wan L (2021) Missing analyst forecasts and corporate fraud: evidence from China. J Bus Ethics 181(1):171–194

Wang J, Bi C (2022) How does litigation risk affect corporate cost stickiness? Evidence from Chinese listed companies. Account Res (12):119–137

Wang Y, Jiang G, Xin Q (2016) Litigation risk, legal environment and cost of debt. Account Res (06):30–37+94

West J, Bhattacharya M (2016) Intelligent financial fraud detection: a comprehensive review. Comput Secur 57:47–66

Xiao J, Wang Y, Chen J, Li X (2021) Impact of resampling methods and classification models on the imbalanced credit scoring problems. Inf Sci 569:508–526

Xu X, Xiong F, An Z (2023) Using machine learning to predict corporate fraud: evidence based on the gone framework. J Bus Ethics 186(1):137–158

Yuan X, Zhou Y, Yan C, Liu H, Qian G, Wang F, Wei L, Li Z, Li B, Li X, Zeng T (2022) Establishment and application of financial fraud risk characteristic screening framework. Chin J Manag Sci 30(03):43–54

Zhang J, Liu H, Yang B (2015) Research on the impact of pending litigation on audit fees and audit opinion types. Audit Res 01:67–74

Zhou W, Kapoor G (2011) Detecting evolutionary financial statement fraud. Decis Support Syst 50(3):570–575

Chapter 9
Financial Fraud Detection Based on Feature Selection and the GONE Framework

Chapter 8 conceptualizes financial fraud as violation events, strategically designed to enable proactive risk identification and early warning mechanisms for listed enterprises, finally enhancing corporate governance. However, given the fact that resource constraints in regulatory agencies limit large-scale on-site investigations (Wu et al. 2021), how to develop sophisticated machine learning models capable of precisely classifying significant financial fraud events with heightened computational accuracy is a critical problem requiring resolution. Therefore, we set strict standard for financial fraud to only include major accounting fraud including false records, misleading statements and material omissions which is identified based on violation typologies and penalty magnitude into our analytical framework. Leveraging the GONE (Greed, Opportunity, Need, Exposure) theoretical construct, the research implements an innovative two-stage feature selection methodology integrating Pearson correlation coefficients and average feature importance scores, simultaneously validating theoretical foundations of the GONE theory and optimizing machine learning model performance. This methodological approach not only mitigates multicollinearity and reduces feature dimensionality but also extends boundaries of existing fraud detection research, providing a sophisticated computational framework for regulatory bodies to enhance financial fraud detection precision and systemic risk management capabilities.

The research arrangement of this chapter is as follows. Initially, we rigorously screened sample companies meeting criteria of major accounting fraud, constructing a precisely matched sample set. Leveraging the GONE (Greed, Opportunity, Need, Exposure) theoretical framework, the research categorizes initial indicator systems into four fundamental dimensions of "greed", "opportunity", "need", and "exposure" to construct an initial comprehensive dataset and subsequent train machine learning models. Subsequently, the research conducts extensive model training, meticulously analyzing fraud detection precision and feature importance to determine the optimal financial fraud detection model and primary identification features.

X. Ma and D. Wu, *Financial Fraud Detection Using Machine Learning*, AI for Risks,
https://doi.org/10.1007/978-981-95-0840-2_9

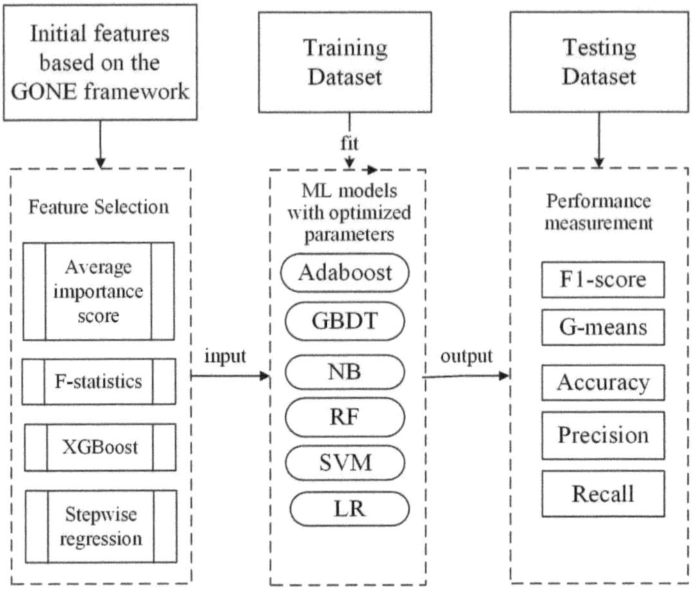

Fig. 9.1 Framework design for financial fraud detection based on machine learning

A novel feature selection methodology is then proposed, integrating average feature importance scores and Pearson correlation coefficients to perform supplementary analytical validation. This approach enables comparative performance assessment of models before and after feature selection, simultaneously enhancing model accuracy and empirically validating the GONE theoretical framework. The overall research design culminates in deriving substantive research conclusions, with the overall research framework illustrated in Fig. 9.1.

9.1 Research Methods and Data

9.1.1 Sample Data

This study presents a distinctive methodological approach to defining major accounting fraud, differentiating itself from prior research by Xu et al. (2023) and Li et al. (2024), who primarily focused on fraudulent assets and profit fabrication. Our framework incorporates the comprehensive fraud definition established by the 2019 New Securities Law, while also considering regulatory penalties as significant indicators of fraud severity (Farrar and King 2023). Specifically, we classify major accounting fraud as encompassing three categories of false statements—false records, misleading statements, and material omissions—that have resulted in regulatory fines imposed by authorities such as the CSRC and designate the year of actual fraudulent activity, rather than the year of regulatory action, as the fraud year. Contemporary input variables are used to detect corporate financial fraud within the same fiscal year, aiming to precisely identify occurred financial fraud incidents. In cases where companies exhibited multiple instances of major accounting fraud across non-consecutive years, we retained only the case with the highest monetary penalty, ultimately identifying 146 major accounting fraud (positive class) cases spanning 2006–2021.

Following the methodologies of Beaver (1966) and Hong et al. (2012), we matched each fraud (positive class) company with a healthy (negative class) company based on characteristics of year, asset size and industry. The matching process selected 146 healthy companies that operated in the same period and industry, with the closest asset size to their fraudulent counterparts, establishing a 1:1 matching ratio. Industry classification adhere to the "Guidelines for Industry Classification of Listed Companies" revised by CSRC in 2012, with total assets serving as the primary metric for corporate scale.

The final dataset construction proceeded from the initial indicator framework established in Chap. 8. After applying a 15% missing value threshold for variable elimination, we developed a balanced small-sample dataset comprising 60 indicator variables and 220 data samples, including 110 companies each from major accounting fraud samples and financially healthy samples. The dependent variable "Fraud" represents "whether major accounting fraud occurred", coded as 1 for yes and 0 for no. Violation data is sourced from the CSMAR Violation Penalty Database, while financial and non-financial data are obtained from CSMAR, CNRDS, and Wind databases. Detailed matching criteria and sample company information are documented in Table 9.1.

9.1.2 The Construction of Indicator System Based on the GONE Theory

The evolutionary trajectory of fraud causation theories, encompassing the GONE (Greed, Opportunity, Need, Exposure) theory, Diamond theory, Pentagon theory, and Hexagon theory, provides the theoretical foundation for constructing indicator variables. Notably, the fraud identification factors in AICPA SAS99 were developed based on the Fraud Triangle theory (Huang et al. 2021). Huang et al. (2017) employed the Fraud Triangle theory to identify and rank the relative importance of financial statement fraud factors and found that motivation/pressure was the most crucial dimension, while rationalization was the least significant, thereby enhancing the efficiency of fraud detection and key indicator assessment. Wei et al. (2011) constructed identification indicators based on the Fraud Triangle theory, achieving a 93.7% accuracy rate using their logistic regression-based fraud detection model.

Table 9.1 Distribution of paired fraud and non-fraud samples (part)

Experimental Group - Fraud Firms				Control Group - Non-fraud Firms			
StockCode	IndustryCode	FraudYear	AssetSize	StockCode	IndustryCode	MatchedYear	AssetSize
000040	G54	2014	2289926214	600834	G54	2014	2057205046
600764	D44	2015	1412346299	600719	D44	2015	1466373685
600180	C38	2013	2232329282	000070	C38	2013	2253466928
600477	K70	2012	3152575071	600159	K70	2012	3246882642
000908	K70	2016	814383677	200160	K70	2016	626756827.3
600822	C18	2011	4368864476	601566	C18	2011	4757782964
600319	C17	2016	3533911926	002327	C17	2016	3528226263
000858	C30	2010	20849090536	600801	C30	2010	17812222066
600145	R86	2018	446518647.1	603721	R86	2018	621410594
600598	I64	2016	18002472210	002624	I64	2016	16297492815
000668	C28	2017	1115379143	600889	C28	2017	1845371129
300268	C26	2011	920220613	600378	C26	2011	926208847.9
000755	C39	2016	5904734903	300408	C39	2016	5883411619
600634	C21	2016	6773665725	002489	C21	2016	6527504172
300028	E50	2011	995841018.9	002542	E50	2011	813764674.8
000760	C15	2016	2429529174	600616	C15	2016	2442817821
300269	A02	2007	2051926161	600189	A02	2007	2418258744
600806	F52	2015	2815121514	601116	F52	2015	2804575146
000518	B06	2016	818082450.2	600714	B06	2016	712251519.8
002164	C13	2012	1833676478	600191	C13	2012	2012055877
600983	A01	2011	8008170156	000860	A01	2011	10332867123

(continued)

Table 9.1 (continued)

Experimental Group - Fraud Firms				Control Group - Non-fraud Firms			
StockCode	IndustryCode	FraudYear	AssetSize	StockCode	IndustryCode	MatchedYear	AssetSize
000636	F51	2014	6588186242	600278	F51	2014	6118146671
002323	C41	2016	782410932.7	603038	C41	2016	768657812.4
002450	C36	2019	12227756592	000957	C36	2019	12070492595
600836	I65	2017	3696462736	300253	I65	2017	3712302568
000806	L72	2014	2886526585	000058	L72	2014	2659717718
002638	N77	2017	7163440004	000035	N77	2017	8130264343
600112	C14	2016	2673396879	002650	C14	2016	2850586123
600807	C37	2017	9414574940	000008	C37	2017	10678315230
002247	C34	2014	4834319258	002266	C34	2014	5049501171
002766	E48	2015	1843660342	002775	E48	2015	1769620661
600532	C29	2018	2715185873	002420	C29	2018	2731142099
002069	C27	2015	4195580674	000766	C27	2015	4155687059
002535	C32	2015	7710653034	600531	C32	2015	7434867569
000802	C22	2013	6472935974	600069	C22	2013	6091292213
002517	M74	2015	6110139817	300284	M74	2015	5445683124
600589	C35	2016	4258479324	300171	C35	2016	4198018568

Note: The table displays the stock code, industry code, fraudulent years, and asset size of a subset of 110 pairs of fraudulent and non-fraudulent companies which were matched by industry, year, and asset size. Due to space limitations, only a partial matched samples are displays. Columns 1–4 and 5–8 represent the condition of fraud and non-fraud group respectively. We replace non-fraud firms with missing values with another that meets matching conditions. Industry code is based on the 2012 revised "Listed Company Industry Classification Guide" by CSRC

Hong et al. (2012) selected identification variables for Chinese fraudulent enterprises based on the GONE theory, achieving a comprehensive accuracy rate of 79.8% with a Logit model.

In this study, following the GONE theory proposed by Bologua et al. (1993), we categorized 60 initial variables into five categories of Greed, Opportunity, Need, Exposure and Others. Factors of Greed and Need represent internal drivers and Opportunity and Exposure factors incorporates information of external influences, while indicators whose categorical attribution cannot be definitively determined are classified into the category of Others. This classification system provides a comprehensive framework for understanding both the motivational and environmental factors contributing to financial fraud, while acknowledging the complexity of certain indicators that defy simple categorization. Detailed indicator classifications and descriptions are provided in Table 9.2. The following section presents a detailed exposition of variable classification based on the GONE theory, delineating how specific indicators align with each theoretical component (Greed, Opportunity, Need, and Exposure) to create a comprehensive fraud detection framework.

Firstly, Greed, characterized as the propensity to break rules for personal gratification, represents the fundamental driver of financial fraud (Xu et al. 2023). Ethical considerations often prove more effective than monetary penalties in deterring fraudulent financial behavior (Klimczak et al. 2022). Dong (2016) also examined financial statement fraud through the lens of organizational ethics, concluding that ethical corporate culture enhances employee moral awareness and reduces fraudulent activities. Management Hegemony Theory posits that the corporate management level, as both operational leaders and potential fraud perpetrators, exhibit greedy characteristics that determine the sensitivity to economic benefits derived from fraudulent activities as well as the susceptibility to moral losses and shame following fraudulent actions, which will ultimately influence the cost–benefit analysis and subsequent decision-making regarding corporate fraud of management (Chakraborty et al. 2023; Zhang et al. 2022). What is more, the impact of "greed" of the management level on corporate financial fraud is moderated by the ratio of management shareholding (Hong et al. 2012). Meanwhile, the principal-agent problem due to information asymmetry between management and shareholders provide more room for financial fraud since the management is able to "override internal controls", while a higher degree of ownership concentration within the company can alleviate this phenomenon to a certain extent (Zhang et al. 2022). However, when controlling shareholders maintain absolute authority over management, the probability of financial fraud increases significantly (Shen et al. 2019).

Based on the aforementioned research, corporate ownership structure and board characteristics play crucial roles in explaining financial fraudulent behavior, mediating the impact of "greed" characteristics on financial fraud, which aligns with the early research conclusions of Chen et al. (2006). Simultaneously, the research by Ran et al. (2023) reveals a consistent pattern wherein financial fraud typically originates from a select group of powerful stakeholders—the "critical few"—including major shareholders, senior executives, directors, and auditors. The Zeda Yisheng case provides a compelling illustration of this phenomenon, where the convergence

Table 9.2 The detailed definition of initial features

Category	Code	Name	Abbreviation	Description
Need	X31	Net assets per share	NAPS	Total Owner's Equity at the End of the Period/Paid-up Capital at the End of the Current Period
	X37	Is Loss (NP < 0)	IsLoss	Net Profit is Negative, 1; Positive, 0
	X24	Net profit rate on net assets	ROCA	Net Profit/Current Assets
	X3	Cash Ratio	CashRatio	(Current Assets − Inventory)/Current Liabilities
	X6	Profit before interest and tax/ total liabilities	PBIT/L	(Net Profit + Income Tax Expense + Financial Expenses + Long-term Amortization of Intangible Assets + Amortization of Intangible Assets + Depreciation of Fixed Assets + Depletion of Oil and Gas Assets + Depreciation of Productive Biological Assets)/ Average balance of Total Liabilities
	X40	Z-score	ZScore	financial distress condition
	X23	Net profit rate on total assets	NPOA	Net Profit/Total Assets
	X25	Return on equity	ROE	Net Profit/ Shareholder's Equity
	X7	Cash Flow Ratio	CashFlowRatio	Net Cash Flow from Operating Activities/ Average balance of Total Liabilities
	X43	H index	Shrhfd	The square sum of the shareholding proportions of the first major shareholder

(continued)

Table 9.2 (continued)

Category	Code	Name	Abbreviation	Description
	X27	Operating gross margin	OperatingGrossMargin	(Operating Income – Operating Costs)/ Operating Income
	X22	Return of assets	ROA	(Total Profit + Financial Expenses)/ Total Assets
Need	X20	The growth rate of NCF from OA	NCFfromOA_GR	(Net Cash Flow from Operating Activities for the Current Year and Quarter – Net Cash Flow from Operating Activities for the Previous Quarter)/Net Cash Flow from Operating Activities for the Previous Quarter
	X26	Return on invested capital	ROIC	(Net Profit + Financial Expenses)/ (Total Assets – Current Liabilities + Accounts Payable + Short-term Loans + Non-current Liabilities Due Within One Year)
	X18	Operating income growth rate	OI_GR	(Operating Revenue for the Current Year and Quarter – Operating Revenue for the Previous Quarter)/(Operating Revenue for the Previous Quarter)
	X29	Earning per share	EPS	Net Profit for the Current Period/ Paid-up Capital at the End of the Current Period
	X17	Operating profit growth rate	OP_GR	(Operating Profit for the Current Year and Quarter – Operating Profit for the Previous Quarter)/ (Operating Profit for the Previous Quarter)

(continued)

Table 9.2 (continued)

Category	Code	Name	Abbreviation	Description
	X42	Risk coefficient	RiskCoefficient	financial distress condition
	X10	Current assets to income ratio	CA/Income	Current Assets/ Operating Revenue
	X32	NCF per share from OA	NCFfromOA	Net Cash Flow from Operating Activities for the Current Period/Paid-up Capital at the End of the Current Period
	X30	Operating income per share	OIPS	Operating Revenue for the Current Period/Paid-up Capital at the End of the Current Period
	X41	O-score	OScore	financial distress condition
Need	X16	Basic EPS growth rate	EPS_GR	(Basic Earnings per Share for the Current Year and Quarter – Basic Earnings per Share for the Previous Quarter)/ (Basic Earnings per Share for the Previous Quarter)
	X28	OperatingNetProfit	OperatingNetProfit	Net Profit/Operating Income
	X15	Growth rate of total assets	TA_GR	(Total Assets at End of Current Period – Total Assets at Beginning of Current Period)/Total Assets at Beginning of Current Period
	X14	Growth rate of fixed assets	FA_GR	(Net Fixed Assets at End of Current Period – Net Fixed Assets at Beginning of Current Period)/ Net Fixed Assets at Beginning of Current Period

(continued)

Table 9.2 (continued)

Category	Code	Name	Abbreviation	Description
	X21	Equity growth rate	Equity_GR	(Total Owner's Equity at End of Current Period − Total Owner's Equity at Beginning of Current Period)/ Total Owner's Equity at Beginning of Current Period
Exposure	X57	Type of audit opinion	Audittyp	Type of opinion issued by the audit firm. Unqualified opinion: 0, otherwise: 1
	X38	is STPT	STPT	Yes, 1; No, 0
	X61	Is a major litigation or arbitration	IsInvolvedLA	Yes, 1; No, 0
	X59	Is accounting correction	IsCorrection	Yes, 1; No, 0
	X60	Is a major reconstruction	IsMajorRestruction	Yes, 1; No, 0
Opportunity	X45	Nature of property rights	PropertyRightsNature	Whether control is a state-owned enterprise. Non-state-owned enterprise, 0: State-owned enterprise, 1
	X54	Number of board meetings	BoardmeetingNum	Number of board meetings
	X51	Proportion of independent directors	IndDirectorRatio	Ratio of the number of independent directors to the size of the board of directors
	X49	Board size	Boardsize	Number of directors on the board
	X56	Number of shareholder meetings held	GeneralmeetingNum	Average number of times the shareholders' meeting was held in the three years prior to the fraud

(continued)

Table 9.2 (continued)

Category	Code	Name	Abbreviation	Description
	X47	Proportion of institutional investors (%)	InsInvestorProp	Proportion of shares held by institutional investors in the listed company
	X55	Number of supervisory board meetings	SupervisorBoardmeetingNum	Number of supervisory board meetings
	X50	Supervisor size	SupervisorSize	Average size of the board of supervisors in the year of the fraud and the two years prior
Greed	X48	proportion of controlling shareholders (%)	ContrshrProportion	Preference for the shareholding proportion of the controlling shareholder. If the report does not disclose the controlling shareholder, then choose the shareholding proportion of the first major shareholder
Greed	X46	Management ownership ratio (%)	Mngmhldn	Proportion of shares held by the board, supervisors, and senior executives compared to the total number of shares
	X58	Is Chairman changed	ChairChg	If there is a change in the chairman, then 1; otherwise, 0
	X52	Separation rate of actual controller (%)	ControllerSeperation	Percentage of actual control over the controlling rights of the listed company - Percentage of actual ownership of the listed company by the actual controller

(continued)

Table 9.2 (continued)

Category	Code	Name	Abbreviation	Description
	X44	Shares balance	SharesBalance	Shareholding proportion of the 2nd-5th major shareholders / Shareholding proportion of the first major shareholder
	X53	ConcurrentPosition (duality)	ConcurrentPosition	Whether the chairman and general manager are the same person? Yes, 1; No, 0
Others	X4	Asset-liability ratio	AL	TotalLiabilities/ TotalAssets
	X5	Equity to liability ratio	EL	TotalOwner′sEquity/ TotalLiabilities
	X36	Other AR proportion (%)	OtherARProp	Net Other Receivables/Total Assets
	X1	CurrentRatio	CurrentRatio	Current Assets / Current Liabilities
	X2	QuickRatio	QuickRatio	(CurrentAssets − Inventory)/ CurrentLiabilities
	X11	Turnover rate of fixed assets	Faturnover	Operating Revenue/ Net Fixed Assets at End of Period
	X33	Fixed assets proportion(%)	FixedAssetsProp	Net Fixed Assets/ Total Assets
	X9	Inventory turnover ratio	Inventoryturnover	Operating Costs/ Ending Inventory Balance
	X19	Total accruals	TATA	Accruals/Total Assets
	X34	Current assets proportion (%)	CurrentAssetsProp	Net Current Assets/ Total Assets
	X12	Turnover rate of total assets	Taturnover	Operating Revenue/ Net Total Assets at End of Period
	X35	Current liability proportion (%)	CurrentLiabilityProp	Total Current Liabilities/Total Liabilities

(continued)

Table 9.2 (continued)

Category	Code	Name	Abbreviation	Description
Others	X8	Turnover of account receivable	ARturnover	Operating Revenue/ Ending Accounts Receivable Balance
	X13	OperatingIndex	OperatingIndex	Net Cash Flow from Operating Activities/ (Net Profit - Investment Income - Fair Value Change Income - Non-operating Income + Non-operating Expenses + Depreciation of Fixed Assets + Depletion of Oil and Gas Assets + Depreciation of Productive Biological Assets + Amortization of Intangible Assets + Amortization of Long-term Deferred Expenses + Decrease in Deferred Tax Assets + Increase in Deferred Tax Liabilities)

of control through role consolidation—with one individual simultaneously serving as controlling shareholder, chairman, and general manager—exemplified the manifestation of greed-driven governance failures. Based on these considerations, our study classifies indicators that best reflect "greed" characteristics—particularly those related to management, directors, and shareholders—under the "Greed" factor. These indicators include management equity holdings, controlling shareholder ownership concentration, ownership balance indices, chairman turnover indicators, control-cash flow rights separation ratios, and dual role indicators.

Second, Opportunity represents the assessment of fraud feasibility by fraudsters, which is closely linked to the quality of corporate internal controls. In other words, organizational transparency and effective communication can both directly and indirectly prevent fraudulent activities (Hasan et al.2023). Research by Ran et al. (2023) demonstrates that quantitative governance metrics—specifically board and supervisory committee meeting frequencies, independent director proportions, and board size—serve as primary indicators of internal control quality and exhibit the highest predictive power in financial fraud detection models. Zhang et al. (2019) enhanced financial crisis prediction accuracy by incorporating corporate governance indicators alongside traditional financial metrics, including board supervision, audit committee functionality, ownership structure and independent audit systems. Simultaneously, based on Hofstede's Cultural Dimensions Theory, in high power-distance countries like China, power concentration tends to weaken individual moral responsibility consciousness. This cultural context makes financial fraud more difficult to expose, particularly evident in state-controlled companies where fraudulent activities are less likely to be disclosed, thereby creating greater opportunities for manipulation (Perols et al. 2017). Based on these considerations, our study classifies the following indicators under the "Opportunity" factor for measuring financial fraud occurrence, which has been further subdivided into corporate governance indicators encompassing board and supervisory meeting frequencies, independent director proportions, and board size parameters and ownership structure indicators including institutional ownership ratios, ownership concentration (H-index), and property rights.

Thirdly, the "Need" factor, alternatively referred to as "motivation" or "pressure," encompasses the fraud inducement factors related to the maximization of both corporate and individual economic benefits, demonstrating a strong correlation with enterprise profitability. Both the 2005 Administrative Measures for Equity Incentives of Listed Companies marking formal implementation of equity incentive systems in China's capital markets and the 2014 state-owned enterprise compensation reform which further advanced the market-oriented transformation of executive compensation systems in state-owned enterprises established a direct link between personnel remuneration and corporate performance, which provided a novel economic perspective for analyzing corporate fraudulent behavior (Gul et al. 2003; Yao and Zhao 2016). However, previous research findings on the relationship between executive compensation and financial fraud present contrasting perspectives. For example, Zhou et al. (2018) identified a negative correlation between executive compensation and fraud occurrence rates, though this relationship becomes insignificant when companies face delisting pressure. Conversely, Hass et al. (2016) argued that managerial equity incentives actually increase fraud motivation, with this effect being particularly pronounced in state-owned enterprises.

Since 2012, China's delisting system for listed companies has undergone four significant reforms, while net profit indicators, as a reflection of corporate performance and loss-making status, have consistently remained the primary delisting criterion in China. The 2020 delisting regulations introduced stricter and more detailed restrictions on net profit thresholds, elevating the delisting risks of listed companies. This stringent regulatory framework has prompted some listed companies to engage in more sophisticated financial fraud through profit and revenue fabrication to secure additional funding (Xie et al. 2013; Qian and Luo 2015). However, some researches have also revealed positive impacts of delisting regulations on financial fraud. For instance, Lin and Zheng (2016) found that delisting supervision contributes to enhanced corporate performance, mitigated agency problems, and reduced stock crash risks. Xu et al. (2018) demonstrated that the 2012 delisting system reform significantly reduced corporate manipulation of both revenue and expenses. Yu et al.

(2019), examining from an audit perspective, discovered that a strict delisting environment improved the internal management quality of audited entities and reduced audit risks. Beyond regulatory pressures, various other factors may influence corporate financial fraud behavior, including objectives such as stock price enhancement, fulfillment of performance agreements, rights issues, and initial public offering (IPO) financing requirements. Based on these considerations, this research further categorizes the "Need" factor into three secondary classifications: financial risk indicators, stock market indicators, and corporate performance indicators. Corporate performance indicators encompass profit metrics, cash flow indicators, return rates, and growth rates. Financial risk indicators include Z-Score, O-Score, and risk coefficients, providing comprehensive financial status information. Stock market indicators comprise return on equity (ROE), earnings per share (EPS), and operating income per share.

Fourthly, the "Exposure" factor refers to the probability of financial fraud detection. Our research includes several mandatory disclosure items of listed companies under this group, including the type of audit opinion, the status of ST/*ST, major litigation and arbitration cases, error corrections, and significant asset restructuring events. These disclosures, which typically attract significant media attention, have gained enhanced effectiveness following stricter information disclosure standards of the 2019 Securities Law. Specifically, audit opinions are categorized into unqualified standard opinions and non-standard opinions which include qualified opinions, opinions with emphasis of matter (EOM) paragraphs, disclaimers of opinion, and adverse opinions. The issuance of non-standard opinions by auditors represents a significant trigger for listed companies receiving delisting risk warnings (Chen et al. 2023). Companies meeting delisting risk warning criteria have their stocks marked with ST or *ST prefixes and must make public announcements, leading to increased external supervision and higher likelihood of exposing potential financial misconduct (Zhang and Sun 2023). Even after ST status removal, companies continue to face scrutiny regarding their operational sustainability and performance, maintaining elevated exposure risks (Li and Zhang 2014). Similarly, major litigation and arbitration as well as asset restructuring are key requirements for corporate information disclosure that increase the probability of detecting fraudulent activities since major litigation and arbitration events can potentially damage the reputation of defendant companies, increasing their exposure risk and likelihood of regulatory penalties (Liu et al. 2014; Fu and Ji 2017). Additionally, the frequency of accounting error corrections also shows strong correlation with financial fraud (Bertomeu et al. 2021).

Lastly, fundamental financial indicators that cannot be explicitly categorized under any single GONE theory component are classified as "Other" factors. These include total accruals, operating indices, leverage indicators, major asset account proportions and turnover rates, which have been identified as crucial factors in measuring financial fraud (Hong et al. 2012; Li et al. 2023). Figure 9.2 provides a concise summary of variable classification under the GONE theoretical framework.

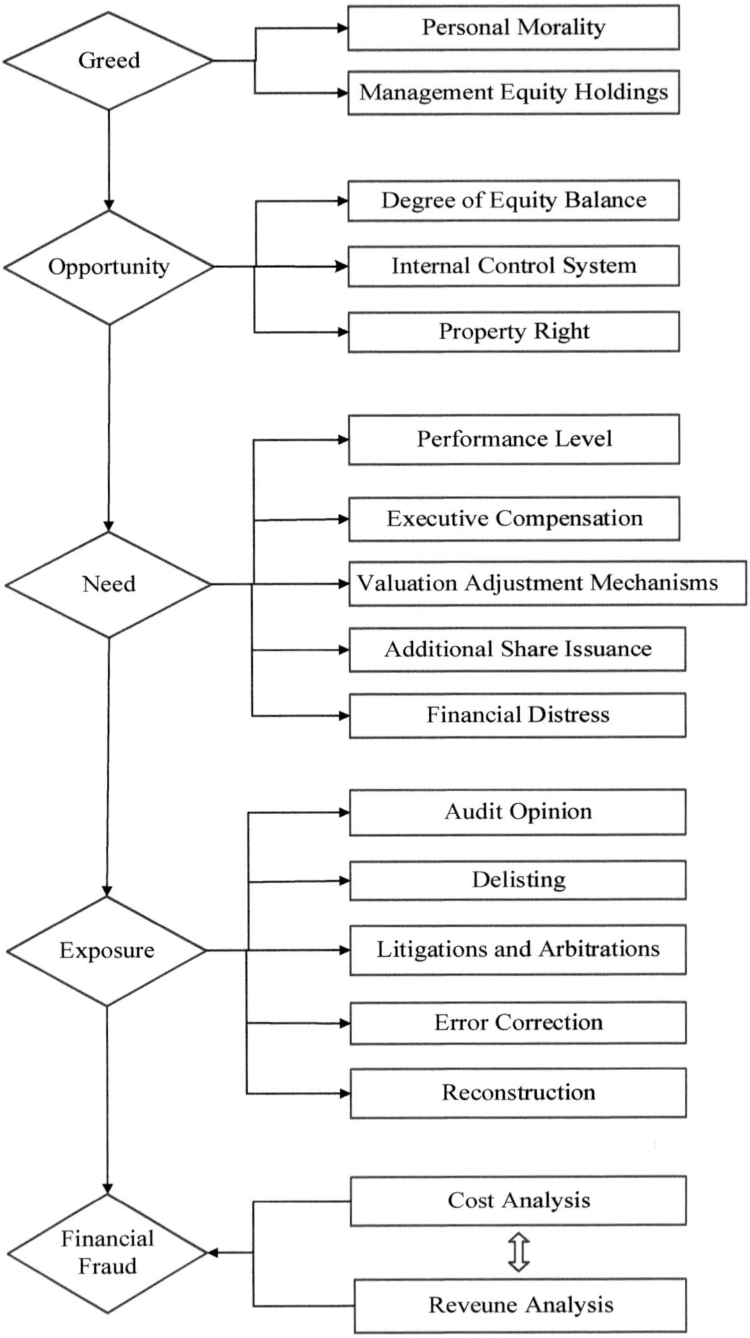

Fig. 9.2 Variable classification based on the GONE theory of financial fraud

9.2 Research Results and Discussion

This research employs a comparative analysis of multiple machine learning approaches for financial fraud detection, incorporating both ensemble learning methods and traditional machine learning models. Specifically, three ensemble learning models—Random Forest (RF), Gradient Boosting Decision Tree (GBDT), and Adaptive Boosting (Adaboost)—are implemented following researches of Bertomeu et al. (2021) and Rahman and Zhu (2023), whishc are evaluated against four traditional machine learning models of Logistic Regression (LR), Support Vector Machine (SVM), Decision Tree (DT), and Gaussian Naive Bayes (GaussianNB) to detect major accounting fraud. To ensure optimal model performance, this study utilizes tenfold cross-validation combined with grid search techniques to identify the optimal parameter combinations for each classifier, with the final parameter configurations detailed comprehensively in Table 9.3.

The post-optimization analysis reveals significant improvements in model performance, particularly evident in the AUC metrics. Among all models, the RF algorithm demonstrates superior performance with the highest AUC score, while the GaussianNB algorithm exhibits the lowest AUC values. To visualize and compare the learning dynamics across models, comprehensive learning curves were generated for all seven algorithms of GaussianNB, DT, SVM, RF, LR, Adaboost, and GBDT, as illustrated in Fig. 9.3, in order to conduct a thorough analysis of computational efficiency across all implemented algorithms. In terms of computational performance, a clear distinction emerges between simple and complex models. The DT and GaussianNB algorithms demonstrate superior computational efficiency with notably shorter execution times. In contrast, the more sophisticated ensemble models such as GBDT, RF, and Adaboost require substantially longer processing times due to their complex architectural nature. The GaussianNB algorithm particularly stands out for its advantageous balance between computational time and operational efficiency.

Table 9.3 Optimal hyperparameters for machine learning algorithms

Algorithms	Optimal hyperparameter combianation
RF	n_estimators = 46, max_depth = 1, min_samples_leaf = 18, min_samples_split = 2
GBDT	learning_rate = 0.01, n_estimators = 400, max_depth = 1, min_samples_leaf = 30, min_samples_split = 10, max_features = 19, subsample = 0.7
Adaboost	algorithm = SAMME.R, learning_rate = 1.0, n_estimators = 50, random_state = 37, threshold = 0.5
DT	min_samples_leaf = 12, max_depth = 19, min_samples_split = 69,
max_features = 34	
LR	C = 0.1, solver = 'lbfgs, max_iter = 10,000,000
SVM	C = 0.8, gamma = 0.001, kernel = linear
GaussianNB	priors = None

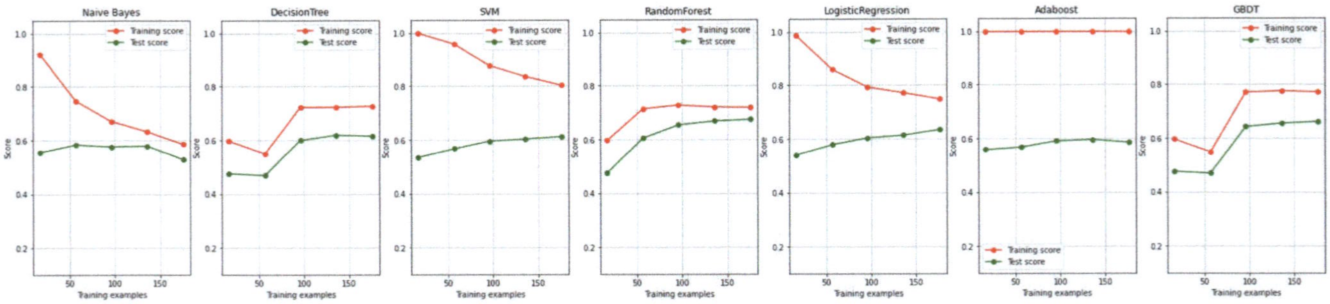

Fig. 9.3 The learning curve of machine learning classifiers with the optimal parameter combinations

Regarding model performance, a significant challenge emerges due to the relatively limited size of the training dataset. The machine learning classifiers generally exhibit overfitting issues on the training samples, making it difficult to simultaneously achieve high generalization capability and identification accuracy. This limitation manifests as a fundamental trade-off in model performance. The overfitting phenomenon, however, demonstrates a gradual amelioration pattern as the training sample size increases. Among the evaluated algorithms, the tree-based ensemble methods, specifically the GBDT and RF, exhibit superior generalization capabilities compared to other machine learning approaches. These ensemble methods are characterized by notably smaller performance disparities between training and test sets, indicating more robust and stable predictive capabilities across different data contexts. In contrast, the traditional machine learning algorithms address the overfitting challenge through a distinct mechanism. These algorithms demonstrate a systematic pattern of overfitting reduction characterized by two simultaneous trends: a gradual decrease in training set accuracy coupled with a progressive increase in test set accuracy. This inverse relationship between training and testing performance demonstrates the ability of these algorithms to achieve better generalization through a natural balance of model complexity and predictive power.

As illustrated in Fig. 9.4, further investigation reveals distinctive patterns in the learning curves of Adaboost and CART (Classification and Regression Tree) decision tree algorithms. Under ten-fold cross-validation, the CART decision tree demonstrates stable performance characteristics, with both training and testing accuracy converging around 0.7 as the sample size increases. The generalization capability of the CART model shows consistent improvement with increasing sample size. This model addresses overfitting through a balanced mechanism where training set accuracy gradually decreases while test set accuracy increases, effectively mitigating the overfitting problem. In contrast, the Adaboost algorithm exhibits perfect performance on the training set but demonstrates relatively weak generalization capabilities, with testing accuracy stabilizing around 0.6. This performance disparity suggests that, within the context of the specific data sample in our study, the single decision tree model demonstrates superior classification performance compared to the ensemble approach of Adaboost. Figure 9.5 provides a comprehensive visualization of how key decision tree parameters including min_samples_leaf, max_features, and min_samples_split influence the model performance. These parameter sensitivity analyses offer crucial insights into the optimization potential of the decision tree model.

9.2.1 Classification Performance of Machine Learning Models

This section synthesizes the empirical results of machine learning methods in financial fraud detection. In terms of feature selection, the importance of features under the GONE theoretical framework is explained, and a novel two-stage feature selection

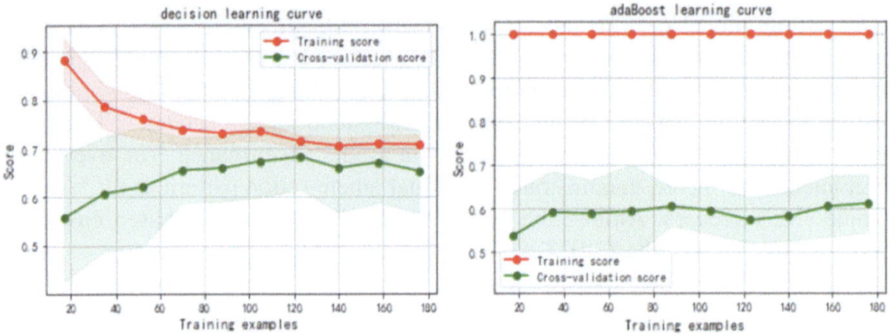

Fig. 9.4 Learning curves of CART and Adaboost classifiers on training and testing sets

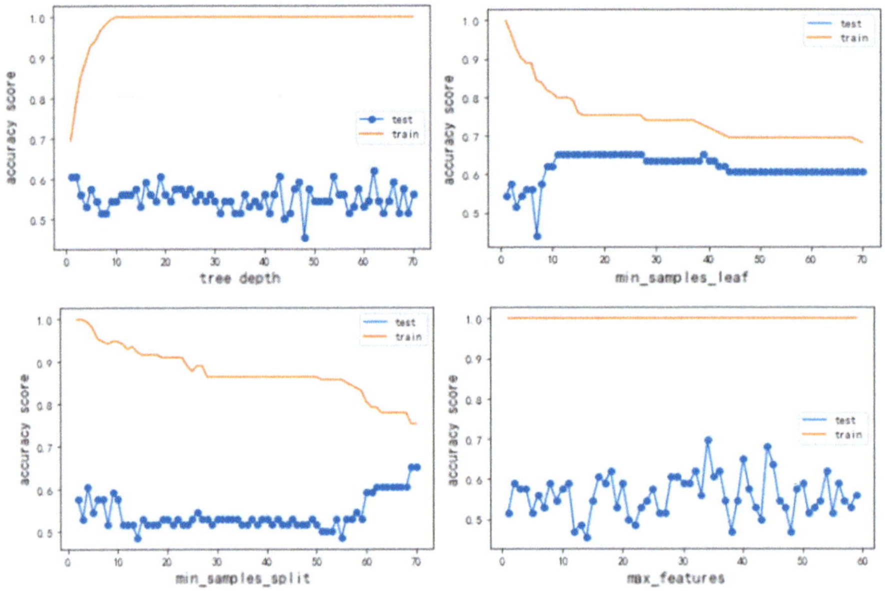

Fig. 9.5 performance changes in the main parameters of the DT algorithm

approach is introduced to further improve the performance advantage of integrated classifiers in financial fraud detection. Moreover, performance evaluation metrics selected in this study include Accuracy, Precision, Recall, Specificity, F1-score and G-means, which are averaged across ten-fold cross-validation to assess model performance across the dataset, with detailed results presented in Table 9.4. Meanwhile, we introduce a sophisticated two-stage feature selection methodology that combines average importance scores computed across different machine learning models and Pearson correlation coefficients, aiming to identify critical discriminative features. This innovative feature selection approach is benchmarked against established feature selection methods including forward stepwise regression, XGBoost and F-statistics, to validate the effectiveness of both the proposed two-stage feature selection method as well as the GONE theoretical framework in financial fraud detection. All the above experiments are implemented on Python 3.6.

It is crucial to understand the cost of classification errors in the context of financial fraud detection research. Type I errors (false positives) occur when non-fraudulent companies are incorrectly classified as fraudulent, while Type II errors (false negatives) happen when fraudulent companies are mistakenly classified as non-fraudulent. The cost implications of Type II errors significantly outweigh those of Type I errors. The primary research objective in financial fraud detection focuses on minimizing Type II error rates while maintaining relatively low levels of both false positives (FP) and false negatives (FN). The experimental results across seven machine learning models reveal the superiority of the RF algorithm in detecting major accounting fraud with the highest scores in accuracy (0.73), recall (0.90), precision (0.73), and F1-score (0.81). Particularly noteworthy is the RF model's exceptional capability in identifying fraudulent samples, successfully detecting 90% of fraudulent cases, which substantially surpasses other models, with DT achieving 0.61, SVM 0.59, GaussianNB 0.59, GBDT 0.80, and Adaboost 0.73. At the same time, the RF model's F1-score of 0.81 also demonstrates superior performance compared to other models (LR 0.76, DT 0.67, SVM 0.63, GaussianNB 0.64, GBDT 0.77, Adaboost 0.70). These findings align with previous research conducted by Barboza et al. (2017) and Yang et al. (2022), confirming the effectiveness of RF in minimizing both false positives and false negatives.

Furthermore, to provide a comprehensive comparison with deep learning approaches, a Convolutional Neural Network (CNN) model was also implemented

Table 9.4 Performance comparison of machine learning algorithms

Algorithm	Accuracy	Precision	Specificity	Recall	F1-score
LR	0.65	0.66	0.24	0.90	0.76
RF	0.73	0.73	0.44	0.90	0.81
DT	0.62	0.74	0.64	0.61	0.67
SVM	0.65	0.69	0.72	0.59	0.63
GaussianNB	0.59	0.71	0.60	0.59	0.64
GBDT	0.70	0.73	0.52	0.80	0.77
Adaboost	0.61	0.67	0.40	0.73	0.70
CNN	0.53	0.71	0.43	0.41	0.53

Notes: This table delineates the performance metrics across multiple classification algorithms. The quantitative evaluation metrics, presented in columns 2–6, encompass accuracy, precision, specificity, recall, and F1-score respectively. The implemented classification methodologies include Logistic Regression (LR), Random Forest (RF), Classification and Regression Tree (CART) Decision Tree (DT), Support Vector Machine (SVM), Gaussian Naive Bayes (GaussianNB), Gradient Boosting Decision Tree (GBDT), Adaptive Boosting (AdaBoost), and Convolutional Neural Network (CNN) under the same fraud dataset. Empirically, the corresponding performance metrics of the CNN model revealed AUC of 0.52, accuracy of 0.53, precision of 0.71, specificity of 0.43, recall rate of 0.41, and F1-score of 0.53, which falls below that of traditional machine learning algorithms in this application scenario. As suggested by Li et al. (2023), this limitation of the CNN model may be attributed to the relatively small sample size, which constrains the training effectiveness of advanced deep learning models. Therefore, it is essential to consider characteristics of dataset when selecting appropriate modeling approaches for financial fraud detection.

Table 9.5 presents the confusion matrices for multiple machine learning algorithms on the testing dataset. The RF algorithm exhibited superior discriminative capability, correctly identifying 37 fraudulent companies and 11 non-fraudulent companies, while it misclassified 14 non-fraudulent companies as fraudulent (Type I errors or false positives) and 4 fraudulent companies as non-fraudulent (Type II errors or false negatives). Closely, the GBDT algorithm achieved correct classification of 31 fraudulent and 14 non-fraudulent entities, while it also produced Type I errors and Type II errors by misclassifying 11 non-fraudulent companies as fraudulent and 10 fraudulent companies as non-fraudulent.

The overall classification accuracy metrics reveal that RF correctly classified a total of 48 companies, while GBDT achieved correct classification for 45 companies, both surpassing the performance of other algorithmic approaches in this study. A notable observation regarding the performance of RF is that despite generating a higher number of false positives compared to other models, it significantly excelled

Table 9.5 Confusion matrix of mahine learning algorithms in the testing samples

LR	RF	Adaboost
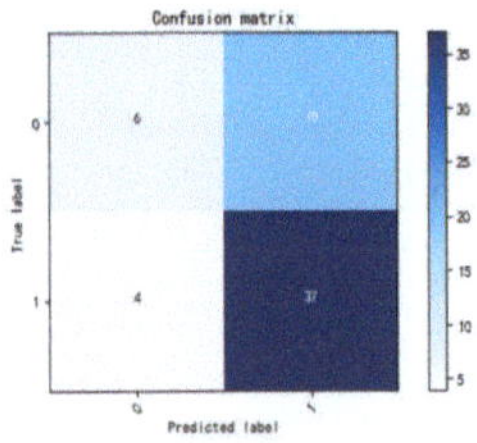	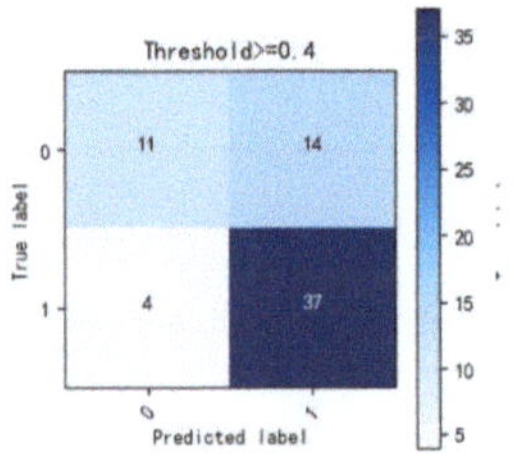	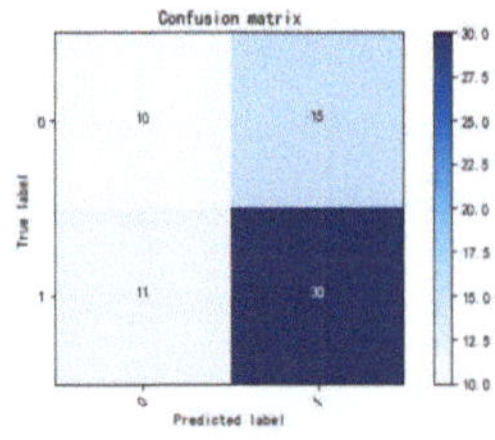
SVM	**GaussianNB**	**GBDT**
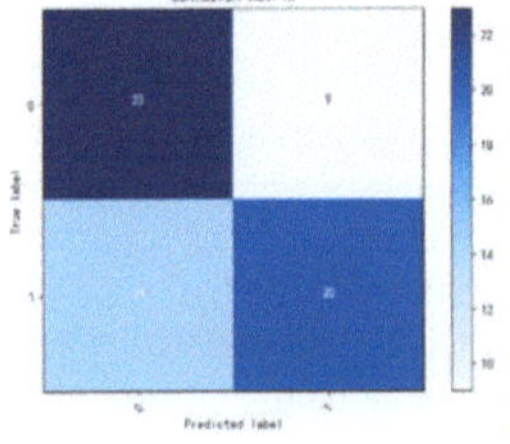	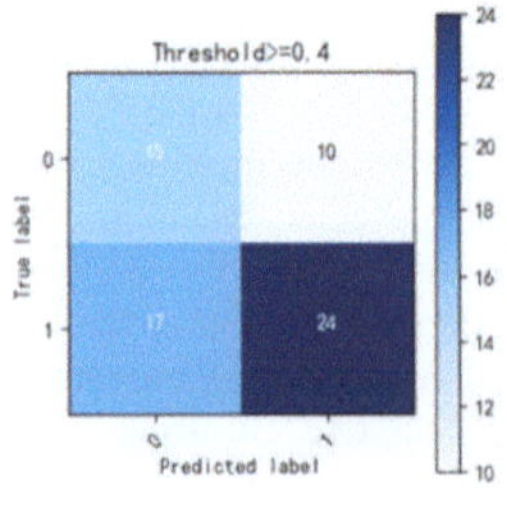	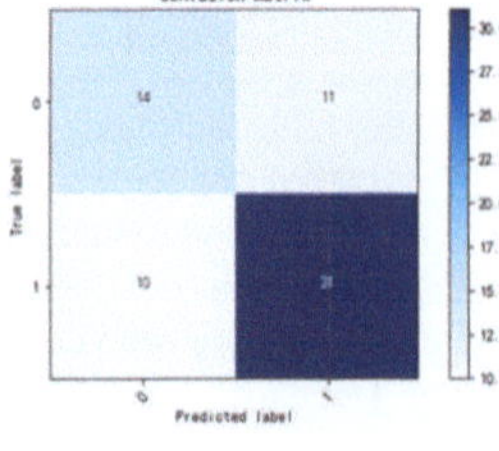

in minimizing Type II errors, misclassifying only 4 fraudulent companies as non-fraudulent. This characteristic is particularly valuable in fraud detection applications, where the cost of failing to identify fraudulent activities typically outweighs the cost of false alerts. Overall, the empirical results conclusively demonstrate the superiority of tree-based ensemble methods in this financial fraud detection context, with RF emerging as the top performer, followed closely by GBDT. This performance hierarchy underscores the effectiveness of ensemble learning approaches, particularly those leveraging decision trees as base learners, in capturing complex, non-linear patterns inherent in financial fraud data. The demonstrated success of these methodologies can be attributed to their robust handling of feature interactions, capacity for managing high-dimensional data structures, and inherent resistance to noise and outliers in the feature space. These findings align with contemporary research in financial fraud detection, highlighting the particular effectiveness of tree-based ensemble methods in addressing the inherent complexities of fraud classification tasks.

9.2.2 Feature Importance Analysis Based on the GONE Theory

The financial fraud detection encompasses a multidimensional feature space characterized by heterogeneous influence variables, wherein the potential interaction effects among independent variables may significantly impact training efficiency and detection precision of classifier. Various classification algorithms implement distinct methodologies for quantifying feature importance. The tree-based ensemble methods, specifically DT, RF, AdaBoost and GBDT, leverage the attribute of Feature_ importances_ embedded within Scikit-learn to compute feature importance scores through Gini Index. Feature importance quantification by GaussianNB is facilitated through the Permutation_importance function provided by Scikit-learn. Additionally, LR and SVM algorithms have no intrinsic feature importance computation mechanisms and this research characterizes feature significance through coefficient analysis, implementing a normalized squared coefficient approach (coefficient^2/ Σcoefficient^2) to neutralize directional effects.

The experimental results demonstrate distinct feature preferences across different machine learning algorithms. The DT algorithm exhibits substantial dependence on three financial indicators including return on total assets (ROA), total asset turnover, and risk coefficient, contributing 64%, 25%, and 11% of the total importance respectively, while other indicators show negligible contributions to the final classification outcomes of DT. In the classification process of the GBDT algorithm, variables representing "Need" emerge as the most significant, accounting for 82.00% of total importance, followed by variables classified as Others with the importance of 15.27%, and "Opportunity" variables with the importance of 2.73%. Detailed feature rankings are presented in Table 9.6.

Table 9.6 Feature importance based on GBDT (importance score > 0.01)

Rank	Name of features	Importance (%)	Cumulative importance (%)	Category
1	Net assets per share	17.70	17.70	Need
2	Cash ratio	11.12	28.82	Need
3	Net profit rate on total assets	8.10	36.92	Need
4	Operating income per share	6.38	43.30	Need
5	Profit before interest and tax/total liabilities	5.77	49.07	Need
6	Net profit rate on net assets	5.17	54.25	Need
7	Growth rate of total assets	4.80	59.05	Need
8	Current assets to income ratio	3.54	62.59	Need
9	Earning per share	3.42	66.01	Need
10	Inventory turnover ratio	3.10	69.10	Others
11	Equity growth rate	3.09	72.19	Need
12	Turnover rate of fixed assets	3.00	75.19	Others
13	Risk coefficient	2.80	78.00	Need
14	Return on equity	2.61	80.61	Need
15	Other AR proportion (%)	2.51	83.12	Others
16	Turnover rate of total assets	1.85	84.97	Others
17	Equity to liability ratio	1.68	86.65	Others
18	Asset-liability ratio	1.63	88.28	Others
19	Board size	1.39	89.67	Opportunity
20	Operating gross margin	1.02	90.69	Need
21	Return of assets	0.95	91.64	Need
22	Operating net profit	0.84	92.48	Need
23	Current assets proportion (%)	0.81	93.29	Others
24	Proportion of institutional investors (%)	0.75	94.04	Opportunity
25	Z-score	0.72	94.76	Need
26	Current liability proportion (%)	0.69	95.45	Others
27	Cash flow ratio	0.60	96.05	Need
28	Nature of property rights	0.60	96.65	Opportunity

For the GaussianNB algorithm, variables with importance scores exceeding 0.01 predominantly fall under the "Need" and "Others" categories. Unlike DT, GBDT, and GaussianNB algorithms which selectively utilize input variables, SVM and LR algorithms incorporate all variables into their classification processes and the cumulative contribution of "Need" variables still remains predominant, further validating the significance of "Need" factors in financial fraud detection, which aligns with the research conclusions of Qian and Luo (2015) and can be corroborated by real fraud cases, exemplified by the Aerospace Communications fraud case, where the founder, under pressure from "Need" motivators such as performance commitments, falsely overstated profits by 2.98 billion yuan during 2016–2018.

However, the LR algorithm, while incorporating all variables, retained over half of the "Exposure" and "Greed" variables, which played crucial roles in its classification process. As shown in Fig. 9.6, within the LR model, audit opinion type (Exposure), dual role occupation (Greed), and chairman turnover (Greed) demonstrate importance values of 21%, 14%, and 12% respectively. In the SVM algorithm (see Fig. 9.7), the audit opinion type, categorized under "Exposure," emerges as the most critical identification variable, followed by ownership structure indicators under the "Opportunity" category. Recent years have witnessed multiple fraudulent enterprises (e.g., Zeda Yisheng, Qibu Holdings, Hiteker) receiving non-standard audit opinions, including qualified opinions or EOM paragraphs from accounting firms within three years prior to regulatory penalties, which empirically validate the correlation between non-standard audit opinions and financial fraud risk.

Table 9.7 presents feature importance rankings based on the RF model, where "Need" variables collectively contribute 86.96% of total importance, exerting the highest impact in the classification process, which is also accordance with the financial fraud detection research conducted by Huang et al (2017), which was similarly based on the fraud triangle theory and identified "pressure/motivation" variables as the most influential factors. However, Xu et al. (2023), also employing GONE theory and RF modeling to investigate variable importance, concluded that "Exposure" variables related to auditors, media, and punitive measures were most crucial in predicting corporate fraud, accounting for 46.22% of total importance.

To sum up, while classification algorithms exhibit heterogeneous variable importance weightings during their training processes, the empirical result demonstrates that the "Need" variables consistently emerge as primary discriminative factors in financial fraud detection. Within the comprehensive set of sixty features, only four fundamental metrics demonstrate universal selection across classification methodologies: operating profit margin (OPM), growth rate of owner's equity, cash ratio, and net assets per share. In actual fraud cases, the artificial inflation of operating revenue and profit constitutes the predominant fraudulent financial manipulation mechanism, directly influencing operating profit margin and owner's equity growth rate metrics, as evidenced in archetypal fraud cases including Kaile Technology and Qixin Holdings. The cash ratio, functioning as a direct quantitative measure of short-term liquidity capacity, frequently serves as a critical indicator, as fraudulent operational activities

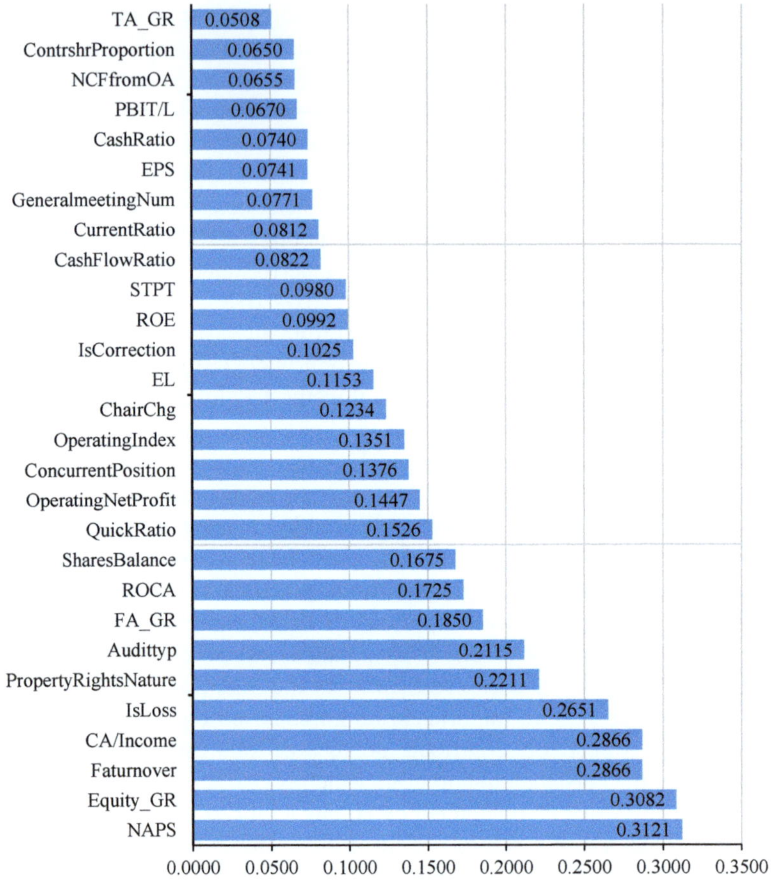

Fig. 9.6 Feature importance based on LR (feature importance score > 0.05)

typically manifest through short-term debt obligation defaults. This pattern is exemplified in the Kangmei Pharmaceutical fraud case, where liquidity metrics, particularly the cash ratio, demonstrated superior efficacy in fraud detection. Moreover, entities under suspicion of financial fraud characteristically exhibit suboptimal operational performance metrics and diminished net asset positions. When analyzed in conjunction with additional risk factors, such as significant management equity holdings or merger-driven incentives, the net assets per share metric demonstrates robust discriminative capability in fraud detection, corroborating the empirical findings of Li et al. (2020).

As previously discussed, different classifiers demonstrate substantial variation in their emphasis on input features. A critical challenge in machine learning feature engineering is determining appropriate feature selection methods to further identify features that contribute significantly to fraud detection while reducing multicollinearity among features. Following the research of Zhuang and Zhang (2023),

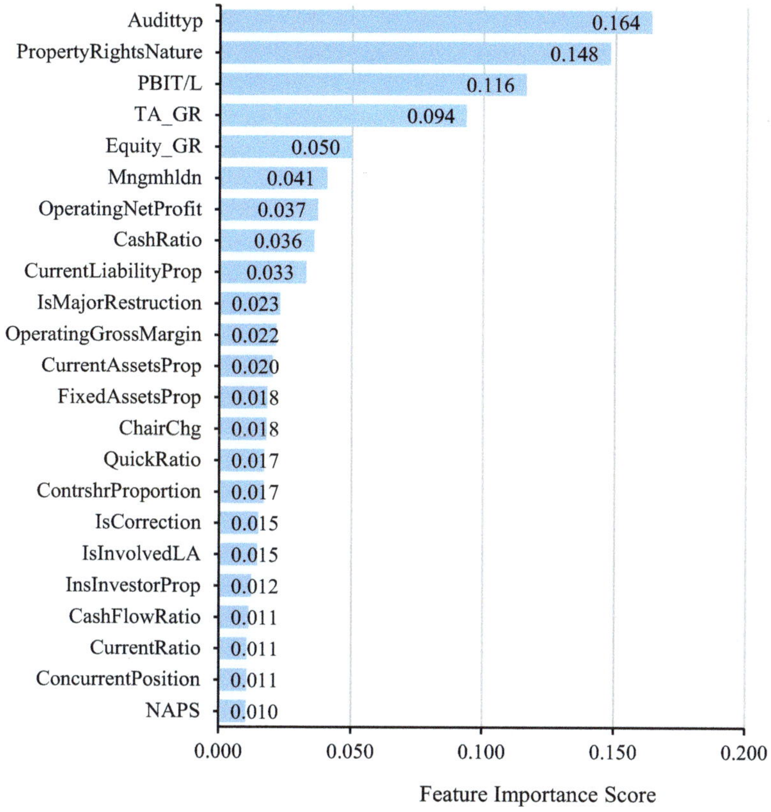

Fig. 9.7 Feature importance based on SVM (feature importance score > 0.05)

this study proposes a two-stage feature selection method based on average feature importance. Initially, the feature importance scores from each classifier are calculated and arithmetically averaged. The average importance for each feature X_i can be expressed as below, where VIM_i represents the feature importance score, ML_j denotes the type of machine learning classifier, encompassing LR, SVM, DT, RF, GBDT, and GaussianNB algorithms, and n denotes the total number of machine learning classifiers.

$$VIM_i = \frac{\sum_{j=1}^{n} VIM_i^{(ML_j)}}{n}$$

Subsequently, to minimize the number of independent variables, we further calculate the Pearson correlation coefficient (PCC) between variables, manually eliminating one variable from each pair where the correlation coefficient exceeds 0.7. For instance, given that the correlation coefficient between X28 (operating profit margin) and X23 (return on total assets) is 0.86, variable X28 is manually excluded.

Table 9.7 Feature importance of the RF classifier (importance score > 1%)

Rank	Feature code	Abbreviations	Importance (%)	Cumulative importance (%)	Category
1	X23	NPOA	21.74	21.74	Need
2	X3	CashRatio	13.04	34.78	Need
3	X31	NAPS	6.52	41.30	Need
4	X25	ROE	6.52	47.83	Need
5	X42	RiskCoefficient	6.52	54.35	Need
6	X5	EL	4.35	58.70	Others
7	X2	QuickRatio	4.35	63.04	Others
8	X29	EPS	4.35	67.39	Need
9	X26	ROIC	4.35	71.74	Need
10	X24	ROCA	4.35	76.09	Need
11	X22	ROA	4.35	80.43	Need
12	X19	TATA	2.17	82.61	Others
13	X36	OtherARProp	2.17	84.78	Others
14	X32	NCFfromOA	2.17	86.96	Need
15	X30	OIPS	2.17	89.13	Need
16	X28	OperatingNetProfit	2.17	91.30	Need
17	X7	CashFlowRatio	2.17	93.48	Need
18	X21	Equity_GR	2.17	95.65	Need
19	X6	PBIT/L	2.17	97.83	Need
20	X15	TA_GR	2.17	100.00	Need

The calculation formula for PCC is shown in the equation below, where n represents the sample size, X_i and Y_i represent the observed values of the two variables, and $\overline{X}$ and $\overline{Y}$ represent their respective mean values.

$$r_{X,Y} = \frac{\sum_{i=1}^{n}\left(X_i - \overline{X}\right)\left(Y_i - \overline{Y}\right)}{\sqrt{\sum_{i=1}^{n}\left(X_i - \overline{X}\right)^2}\sqrt{\sum_{i=1}^{n}\left(Y_i - \overline{Y}\right)^2}}$$

As illustrated in Figs. 9.8 and 9.9, following the average importance ranking and Pearson correlation analysis, the top 30 important features were retained, with correlations between features all below 0.7. Compared to single classifier approaches, this feature selection method preserved varying proportions of the initial feature categories: 80% of Exposure variables, 66.67% of Greed variables, 48.15% of Need variables, 25% of Opportunity variables, and 50% of Other variables, encompassing all categories mentioned in the GONE framework. The top five important indicators include the growth rate of owner equity, turnover on fixed assets, the growth rate of total assets, net assets per share and return on total assets, suggesting that financial anomalies are more readily detectable in asset and profit-related indicators.

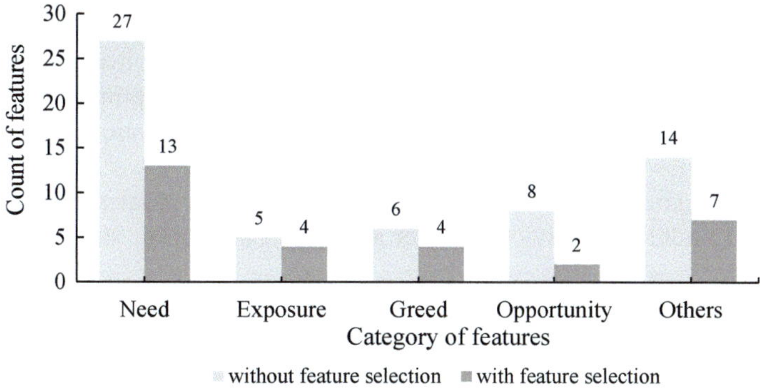

Fig. 9.8 Changes in the number of features with GONE categories with feature selection

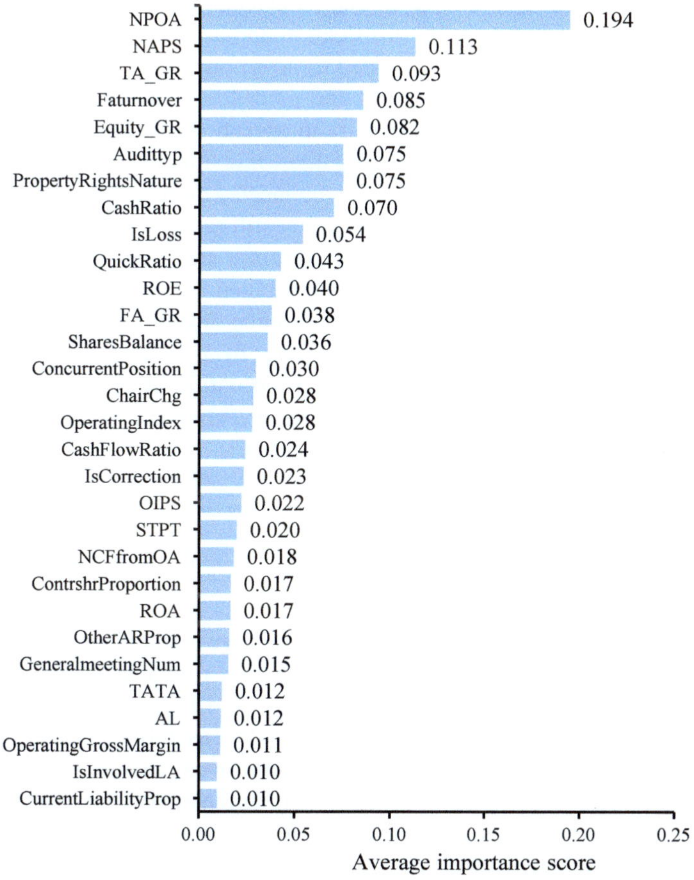

Fig. 9.9 Features based on average importance score and Pearson correlation

Additionally, the type of audit opinion and the nature of property right emerge as key identification variables, reflecting China's unique legal environment and corporate landscape. This finding further validates that auditor opinions have a more pronounced deterrent effect on financial fraud in emerging nations with relatively weak legal frameworks (Chen et al. 2013). Moreover, the lower enforcement rate by the CSRC against State-Owned Enterprises (SOEs) also creates increased opportunities for fraudulent behavior (Hass et al. 2016; Liang et al. 2023; Shahab et al. 2023).

Table 9.8 presents a comparison of descriptive statistics in three kind of groups of fraudulent samples, non-fraudulent samples, and the overall samples based on 30 critical indicators selected through feature selection. The inter-group differences are compared with the most pronounced mean differences observed between fraudulent and non-fraudulent groups. Overall, fraudulent firms exhibit several distinctive characteristics such as deteriorated performance, higher leverage ratios, higher delisting risk, increased probability of litigation and arbitration involvement, more frequent financial restatements, accelerated turnover on chairman, higher likelihood of receiving non-standard audit opinions and more frequent shareholder meetings. Moreover, there is substantial heterogeneity in operational indices between fraudulent and non-fraudulent samples, suggesting that while fraudulent enterprises attempt to create closed-loop false entries across interconnected financial accounts, indicators that genuinely reflect enterprise earnings quality still reveal discrepancies.

Finally, it is observed that non-state-owned enterprises comprise a higher proportion of fraudulent companies, which may be attributed to two potential factors. One is that SOE executives face more deterrents including disciplinary inspection, career considerations, and lifetime accountability to defer from executing fraudulent activities. Another is that fraudulent activities occurred within SOEs are not effectively detected by the public or private enforcement, revealing the potential systematic enforcement disparities between SOEs and non-SOEs.

9.3 Supplementary Analysis

After inputting the 30 features selected through average feature importance and PCC into machine learning models and repeating the experimental process, the empirical results are shown in Figs. 9.10, 9.11, 9.12, 9.13, 9.14. Compared to traditional statistical algorithms (LR, SVM, and GaussianNB), ensemble learning algorithms (GBDT, RF, DT, and Adaboost) demonstrated improved performance post-feature selection. Specifically, the Adaboost algorithm demonstrated the most substantial enhancement, with increases of 7, 6, 5, and 5 percentage points in recall, precision, F1-score, and AUC metrics respectively. GBDT and DT algorithms showed modest improvements, with precision, F1-score, and AUC metrics increasing by 1–2 percentage points. Notably, the G-means metric revealed significant improvements in ensemble learning algorithms, with RF, GBDT, and Adaboost showing increases

Table 9.8 Descriptive statistics of variables after feature selection, by fraud and non-fraud group

Variables	Fraud firms			Non-fraud firms			Overall firms		
	Mean	Std	Number of obs	Mean	Std	Number of obs	Mean	Std	Number of obs
QuickRatio	1.45	2.13	110	2.11	5.24	110	1.78	3.78	220
CashRatio	0.50	0.47	110	0.85	1.18	110	0.68	0.85	220
AL	0.54	0.08	110	0.40	0.04	110	0.47	0.06	220
CashFlowRatio	0.06	0.13	110	0.16	0.12	110	0.11	0.13	220
Faturnover	2.10	6.45	110	1.67	8.99	110	1.88	7.73	220
OperatingIndex	3.26	533.90	110	-0.13	72.76	110	1.57	304.82	220
FA_GR	0.28	1.38	110	0.36	0.93	110	0.32	1.15	220
TA_GR	0.26	0.34	110	0.33	0.95	110	0.29	0.64	220
TATA	-0.02	0.03	110	-0.01	0.01	110	-0.02	0.02	220
Equity_GR	0.27	4.91	110	0.37	1.05	110	0.32	2.97	220
ROA	0.00	0.03	110	0.04	0.02	110	0.02	0.03	220
NPOA	-0.03	0.03	110	0.03	0.02	110	0.00	0.03	220
ROE	-0.14	0.52	110	0.03	0.08	110	-0.05	0.31	220
OperatingGrossMargin	0.24	0.03	110	0.30	0.03	110	0.27	0.03	220
OIPS	5.38	281.00	110	5.83	45.65	110	5.61	162.63	220
NAPS	2.95	6.52	110	4.58	8.90	110	3.77	8.35	220
NCFfromOA	0.18	3.14	110	0.38	0.70	110	0.28	1.92	220
CurrentLiabilityProp	0.85	0.03	110	0.85	0.03	110	0.85	0.03	220
OtherARProp	0.05	0.01	110	0.02	0.00	110	0.03	0.01	220
IsLoss	0.28	0.20	110	0.13	0.11	110	0.20	0.16	220
STPT	0.11	0.10	110	0.00	0.00	110	0.05	0.05	220
SharesBalance	0.77	0.38	110	0.74	0.43	110	0.75	0.40	220
PropertyRightsNature	0.22	0.17	110	0.36	0.23	110	0.29	0.21	220
ContrshrProportion	0.31	0.02	110	0.37	0.03	110	0.34	0.03	220
ConcurrentPosition	0.27	0.20	110	0.26	0.20	110	0.27	0.20	220
GeneralmeetingNum	3.75	3.40	110	3.41	2.98	110	3.58	3.20	220
Audittyp	0.79	0.17	110	0.97	0.03	110	0.88	0.11	220
ChairChg	0.17	0.14	110	0.15	0.13	110	0.16	0.13	220
IsCorrection	0.22	0.17	110	0.12	0.11	110	0.17	0.14	220
IsInvolvedLA	0.35	0.23	110	0.22	0.17	110	0.29	0.21	220

Notes: The table reports the mean, standard deviation, the number of observations of 30 top variables after feature selection. The selection method is based on the average feature importance ranking and Pearson correlation coefficient. Column (1) is the abbreviation of variables. Columns (2)–(4) pertain to the fraud group, columns (5)–(7) pertain to the non-fraud group and columns (8)–(10) pertain to the entire sample group. The sample period is from 2006 to 2021, and the detailed definitions of each variable can be found in Table 9.2

of 3, 3, and 5 percentage points, respectively. Conversely, traditional statistical algorithms (LR, SVM, and GaussianNB) exhibited performance deterioration of 7, 5, and 3 percentage points, respectively, suggesting enhanced sensitivity to feature space modifications. Comparative analysis employing alternative feature selection methodologies (forward stepwise regression, XGBoost, and F-statistics) consistently demonstrated the predominant contribution of "Need" variables in financial fraud detection, providing robust validation of the superiority of the GONE theoretical framework in financial fraud detection indicator system construction and model interpretability enhancement. Performance comparison of machine learning algorithms documented in Table 9.9 underscore the differential impact of feature selection across algorithmic classes.

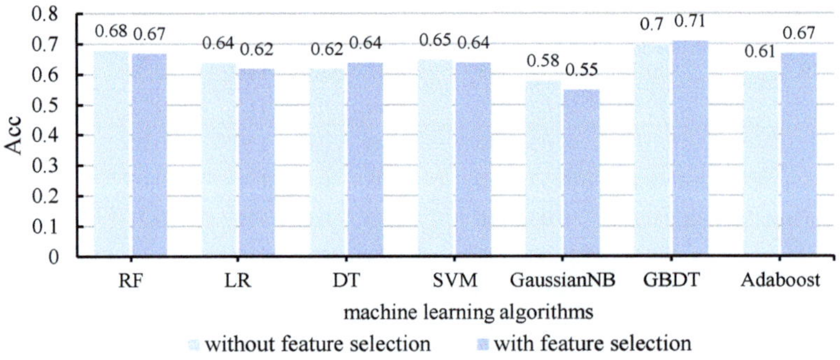

Fig. 9.10 Accuracy of machine learning algorithms before and after feature selection

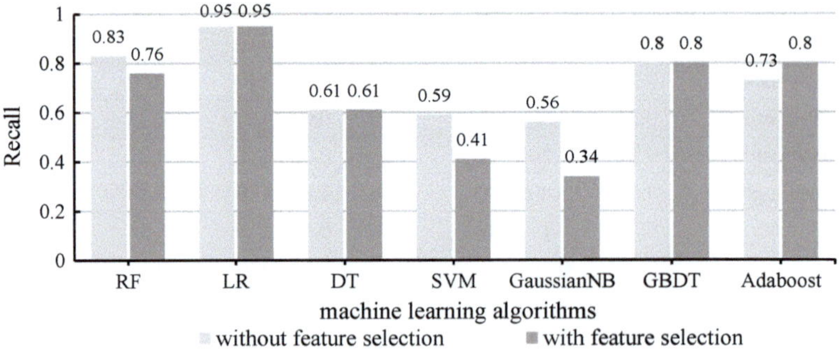

Fig. 9.11 Recall rate of machine learning algorithms before and after feature selection

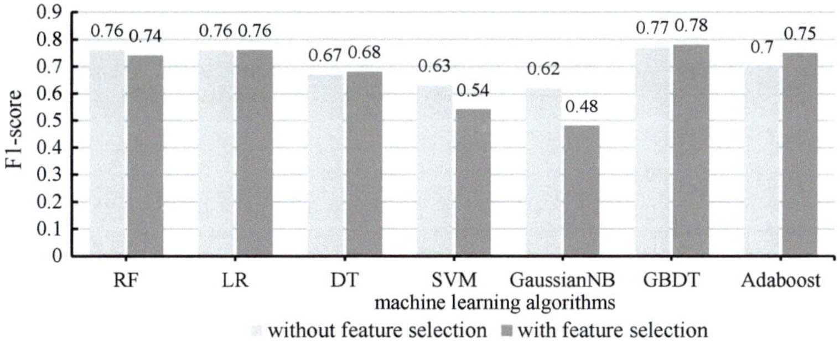

Fig. 9.12 F1-score of machine learning algorithms before and after feature selection

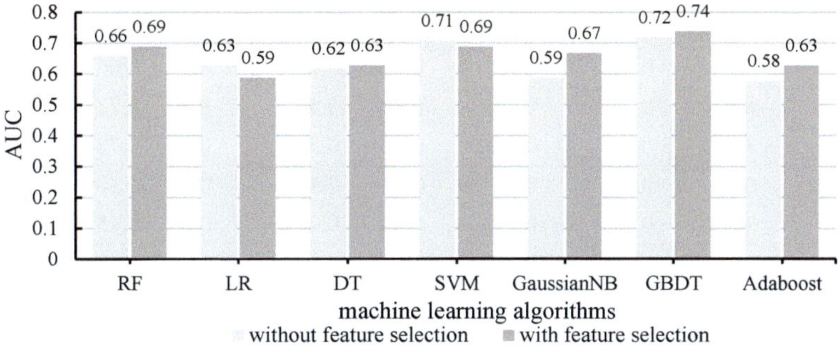

Fig. 9.13 AUC of machine learning algorithms before and after feature selection

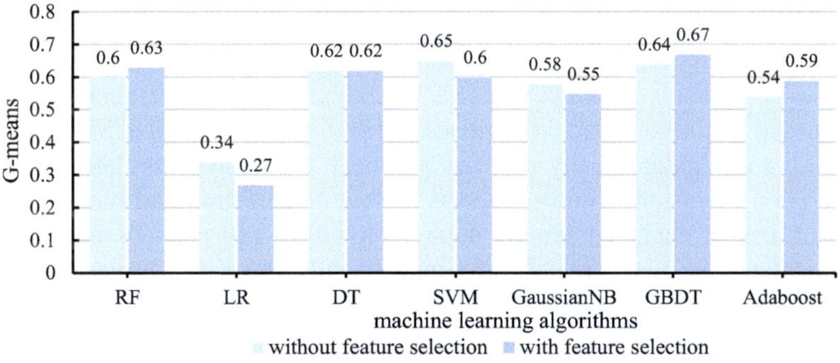

Fig. 9.14 G-means of machine learning algorithms before and after feature selection

Table 9.9 Performance comparison of machine learning algorithms with 60 and 30 features

Algorithms	Number of features	Accuracy	Precision	Recall	Specificity	AUC	F1-score	G-means
LR	60	0.65	0.66	0.90	0.24	0.64	0.76	0.46
	30	0.61	0.64	0.85	0.20	0.58	0.73	0.41
DT	60	0.62	0.74	0.61	0.64	0.62	0.67	0.62
	30	0.64	0.76	0.61	0.64	0.63	0.68	0.62
SVM	60	0.65	0.69	0.59	0.72	0.71	0.63	0.65
	30	0.64	0.78	0.41	0.88	0.69	0.54	0.60
GaussianNB	60	0.58	0.70	0.56	0.60	0.59	0.62	0.58
	30	0.55	0.82	0.34	0.88	0.67	0.48	0.55
RF	60	0.68	0.73	0.78	0.52	0.73	0.75	0.64
	30	0.62	0.75	0.59	0.68	0.74	0.66	0.63
GBDT	60	0.70	0.73	0.80	0.52	0.72	0.77	0.64
	30	0.71	0.75	0.80	0.56	0.74	0.78	0.67
Adaboost	60	0.61	0.67	0.73	0.40	0.58	0.70	0.54
	30	0.67	0.70	0.80	0.44	0.63	0.75	0.59

Notes: Column 1 represents the seven machine learning classifiers. Column 2 indicates the number of input variables before and after feature selection, with 60 initial features reduced to the top 30 features ranked by importance scores, where Pearson correlation coefficients between variables are all below 0.7. Columns 3–9 present the values of different evaluation metrics, with precision, recall, and F1-score calculated specifically for fraudulent samples

9.4 Summary

This chapter presents a comprehensive investigation of severe accounting fraud cases among Chinese listed enterprises subject to substantial CSRC penalties, employing a methodologically rigorous approach to enhance regulatory efficiency and detection precision from the aspects of feature selection and model combination. It utilized a balanced sample dataset including 110 pairs of fraudulent and non-fraudulent companies matched by industry classification, temporal alignment, and firm size. A comprehensive feature system encompassing 60 financial and non-financial variables was developed and systematically categorized according to the GONE theoretical framework (Greed, Opportunity, Need, Exposure, and residual categories). Then seven machine learning models including Logistic Regression, Decision Tree, Gaussian Naive Bayes, Support Vector Machine, Random Forest, Adaboost, and Gradient Boosting Decision Tree were implemented with hyperparameter optimization through k-fold cross-validation and grid searching.

Empirical findings revealed that Random Forest outperformed other financial fraud detection model, followed by GBDT, while the motivation related to "Need" emerged as primary fraud determinants. Notably, only four features (6.67%) demonstrated universal selection across algorithmic implementations and these features aligned with common fraudulent methods including revenue and profit overstatement, the fabrication of cash and cash equivalents, and asset misrepresentation in the real fraud scandals. Furthermore, it developed a novel two-step feature selection method integrating feature importance score and Pearson correlation analysis, which maintained GONE theoretical framework coverage while enhancing ensemble learning algorithm performance. While acknowledging potential sample selection bias inherent in matched-pair sampling versus large-scale resampling methodologies, this research establishes a foundation for future enhancement of detection precision through advanced econometric methodologies.

References

Barboza F, Kimura H, Altman E (2017) Machine learning models and bankruptcy prediction. Expert systems with applications 83: 405-417

Beaver WH (1966) Financial ratios as predictors of failure. J Account Res 4:71–111

Bertomeu J, Cheynel E, Floyd E, Pan W (2021) Using machine learning to detect misstatements. Rev Account Stud 26(2):468–519

Bologna J, Lindquist RJ, Wells JT (1993) The accountant's handbook of fraud and commercial crime. Wiley, New York, NY

Chakraborty A, Gao LS, Musa P (2023) Corporate social responsibility and litigation risk: evidence from securities class action lawsuits. Account Finance 63(2):1785–1819

Chen G, Firth M, Gao DN, Rui OM (2006) Ownership structure, corporate governance, and fraud: evidence from China. J Corp Finan 12(3):424–448

Chen J, Cumming D, Hou W, Lee E (2013) Executive integrity, audit opinion, and fraud in Chinese listed firms. Emerg Mark Rev 15:72–91

Chen S, Pan Y, Wu D, Yang S (2023) In-house versus outsourcing collection in a closed-loop supply chain with remanufacturing technology development. Int J Prod Res 61(6):1720–1735

Dong H (2016) An organizational ethics analysis of financial reporting fraud. Account Res (09):11–16

Farrar J, King T (2023) To punish or not to punish? The impact of tax fraud punishment on observers' tax compliance. J Bus Ethics 183(1):289–311

Fu C, Ji L (2017) Litigation risk and corporate charitable donations: an explanation from the perspective of "reputation insurance." Nankai Bus Rev 20(02):108–121

Gul FA, Chen CJP, Tsui JSL (2003) Discretionary accounting accruals, managers' incentives, and audit fees. Contemp Account Res 20(3):441–464

Hasan I, Noth F, Tonzer L (2023) Cultural norms and corporate fraud: evidence from the Volkswagen scandal. J Corp Finance 82:102443

Hass LH, Tarsalewska M, Zhan F (2016) Equity incentives and corporate fraud in China. J Bus Ethics 138:723–742

Hong H, Hu H, Guo C (2012) Research on financial reporting fraud identification of listed companies based on GONE theory. Account Res (08):84–90+97

Huang S, Zhou S, Ye F, Chen C (2021) Research on enterprise financial performance recognition under major public health emergencies: theoretical analysis of depreciation issues in the context of COVID-19. Account Res (03):3–10

Huang SY, Lin CC, Chiu AA, Yen DC (2017) Fraud detection using fraud triangle risk factors. Inform Syst Front 19(6): 1343-1356

Huang SY, Lin CC, Chiu AA, Yen DC (2017) Fraud detection using fraud triangle risk factors. Inf Syst Front 19:1343–1356

Klimczak KM, Sison AJG, Prats M, Torres MB (2022) How to deter financial misconduct if crime pays? J Bus Ethics 179(1):205–222

Li C, Jia H, Zhao G et al (2023) Credit risk early warning of listed companies based on information disclosure text: Empirical evidence from Chinese annual report management discussion and analysis. Chin J Manag Sci 31(02):18–29

Li J, Sun H, Chang Y et al (2024) Financial fraud identification considering multiple semantic associations of audit elements. J Manag Sci 27(03):58–70

Li J, Wu Y, Lei Y, Huang Y (2020) Effective early warning indicators and artificial intelligence models for listed companies' violations based on deferred tax changes. J of Financ Res 8: 149-168

Li W, Zhang Y (2014) New CEO characteristics, management team adjustment and corporate performance: empirical evidence from ST listed companies. Chin J Manag Sci 22(08):47–55

Liang Q, Wang Z, Guan X, Wang D (2023) Party direct control and corporate fraud: Evidence from China. Q Rev Econ Finance 92:274–290

Lin L, Zheng D (2016) Delisting regulation and stock price crash risk. China Ind Econ (12):58–74

Liu Q, Li H, Zhao C et al (2014) Media negative coverage, litigation risk and audit fees. Account Res (06):81–88+97

Perols JL, Bowen RM, Zimmermann C, Samba B (2017) Finding needles in a haystack: using data analytics to improve fraud prediction. Account Rev 92(2):221–245

Qian P, Luo M (2015) Financial fraud prediction model for Chinese listed companies. Account Res (07):18–25+96

Rahman MJ, Zhu H (2023) Predicting accounting fraud using imbalanced ensemble learning classifiers–evidence from China. Account Finance 63(3):3455–3486

Ran M, Yu L, Wang J (2023) Can CSRC's comprehensive inspection of accounting firms improve audit quality? A quasi-natural experiment based on "double random, one public". Audit Res (06):35–47

Shahab Y, Wang P, Gull AA, Ullah F (2023) Social trust and environmental performance in China: does state ownership matter? Econ Model 124:106328

Shen Y, Gao D, Bu D, Yan L (2019) CEO hometown ties and tax avoidance-evidence from China's listed firms. Account Finance 58(5):1549–1580

Wei L, Xu L, Liu J (2011) Identification of financial reporting fraud in listed companies: an empirical study based on triangle theory. Audit Res (02):98–106

Wu DD, Mitchell J, Lambert JH (2021) Global systemic risk and resilience for novel coronavirus and COVID-19. Risk Anal 41(5):701–704

Xie L, Zhu R, He K (2013) The impact of delisting system on earnings management behavior of GEM listed companies: analysis based on accrual and real earnings management. Audit Res (01):95–102

Xu W, Su L, Lv P et al (2018) The impact of delisting system reform on earnings management behavior of listed companies. Account Res (06):32–38

Xu X, Xiong F, An Z (2023) Using machine learning to predict corporate fraud: evidence based on the gone framework. J Bus Ethics 186(1):137–158

Yang ZH, Zhang PM, Lin SH (2022) Systemic risk and corporate financial crisis early warning: A new perspective based on cutting-edge machine learning. J Financ Res 8: 152–170

Yao Y, Zhao M (2016) Chinese-style risk disclosure, disclosure level and market reaction. Econ Res J 51(07):158–172

Yu P, Song Y, Fan Y (2019) Delisting system and audit delay. Audit Res (06):96–104

Zhang HL, Wang Y, Wang JY (2019) Does the social relationship between external auditors and independent directors affect audit quality? Account Res, 4: 92–100

Zhang Q, Sun X (2023) Research on material misstatement risk in government financial report audit: analysis based on audit report text from multiple countries. Account Res (06):136–149

Zhang X, Du Q, Zhang Z (2022) A theory-driven machine learning system for financial disinformation detection. Prod Oper Manag 31(8):3160–3179

Zhou F, Zhang Z, Yang J, Chen R (2018) Delisting pressure, executive compensation, and corporate fraud: evidence from China. Pac Basin Financ J 48:17–34

Zhuang R, Zhang H (2023) Anomaly detection based on average feature importance and ensemble learning. Comput Syst Appl 32(06):60–69

Chapter 10
The Classical Case of Financial Fraud

This chapter analyzes seven landmark financial fraud cases including LeTV and Luckin Coffee, detailing corporation background, financial fraud behavior identified by regulators, fraudulent methods, regulatory responses penalties imposed on both corporate and individual levels and finally the management implications for each case. The cases reveal distinctive patterns in Chinese financial fraud such as extended timeframes, extensive record falsification, and multi-stakeholder involvement. This chapter concludes with context-specific prevention recommendations tailored to the unique market environment and institutional framework in China.

10.1 Case Study 1: Xingxing Technology (300256.SZ)

(1) Corporate Background

Established in September 2003 in Taizhou, Zhejiang Province, Xingxing Technology was subsequently listed on the ChiNext board of the Shenzhen Stock Exchange in August 2011. The company primarily engages in the research, development, production, and distribution of protective window screens, touch display modules, precision structural components, and electric two-wheeled vehicles. Prior to its public listing, the product portfolio of this company was predominantly focused on mobile phone components and accessories. In 2019, the Pingxiang Economic Development Zone Administration Committee acquired controlling interest from the original controlling shareholder, Ye Xianyu, of Xingxing Technology. However, following this state-owned asset acquisition, significant fraudulent activities were revealed and disclosed within Xingxing Technology, with several subsidiaries subsequently filing for bankruptcy reorganization or liquidation. By late 2021, Lima Group, an enterprise specializing in electric vehicle research, manufacturing, and sales, assumed control of Xingxing Technology. In August 2022, the actual controlling entity of Xingxing

X. Ma and D. Wu, *Financial Fraud Detection Using Machine Learning*, AI for Risks,
https://doi.org/10.1007/978-981-95-0840-2_10

Technology transitioned from Pingxiang state-owned assets to the married couple Ying Guangjie and Luo Xueqin.

(2) Financial Fraud Behavior

In November 2022, the China Securities Regulatory Commission (CSRC) issued a "Notice of Administrative Penalties and Market Entry Prohibition" to Xingxing Technology and relevant parties involved. Subsequently, in August 2023, the CSRC delivered an "Administrative Penalty Decision" [No. (2023) 56] to the company and it determined that the company had artificially inflated its operating revenue and profits, with a cumulative falsified revenue of 4.576 billion yuan across the fiscal years 2019 and 2020.

According to the investigation, in April 2020, Xingxing Technology disclosed its annual financial report for fiscal year 2019 with operating revenue of 6.34 billion yuan, operating costs of 5.32 billion yuan, and total profit of 150 million yuan for the whole reporting period. In actuality, the corporation engaged in substantial financial manipulation by fraudulently reporting approximately 1.4 billion yuan in operating revenue, 270 million yuan in operating costs, and 1.17 billion yuan in total profit for this fiscal year. In the following year, it continued this kind of number-cooking behavior by overstating 3.26 billion yuan in operating revenue, 1.59 billion yuan in operating costs, and 1.66 billion yuan in total profit for the 2020 fiscal year. In April 2021, Xingxing Technology released its annual financial statements for fiscal year 2020, in which the company reported operating revenue of 8.30 billion yuan, operating costs of 7.18 billion yuan, and total profit of 40 million yuan for the reporting period. There is obviously systematic financial fraud through a complex dual manipulation technique, paradoxically understating its operating profits while simultaneously overstating both revenue and operating costs.

We will describe several significant financial fraud activities perpetrated by Xingxing Technology in detail, which have been confirmed by regulatory authorities and have substantially distorted the financial performance of the company during the 2019–2020 fiscal periods. These financial fraud activities are systematically categorized as follows.

First is the fabrication of sales transactions to inflate revenue. In 2019, Xingxing Technology subsidiaries, including Jiangxi Yihong Electronic Technology Co., Ltd. and Pingxiang Xingxing Touch Control Technology Co., Ltd., engaged in the fabrication of sales operations, resulting in artificially inflated operating revenue of 1.38 billion yuan. This practice intensified in 2020, with subsidiaries including Jiangxi Xingxing, Xingxing Touch Control, Xingxing Precision Technology (Shenzhen) Co., Ltd., and Guangdong Xingchi Optoelectronic Technology Co., Ltd. collectively fabricating sales operations that inflated operating revenue by 3.19 billion yuan. Second is the invention of leasing and processing operations to increase operating revenue. The investigation revealed that its subsidiaries, primarily Xingxing Precision and Xingxing Touch Control, fabricated leasing and processing operations, thereby artificially increasing operating revenue by 50 million yuan in 2019. This fraudulent activity continued in 2020, resulting in falsely inflated operating revenue of 70 million yuan during that fiscal year.

Third is the manipulation of procurement activities and the overstatement of operating costs. For the fiscal year 2019, Xingxing Technology subsidiaries—notably Xingxing Touch Control and Jiangxi Xingxing—engaged in fictitious procurement activities totaling 400 million yuan. This practice expanded significantly in 2020, with subsidiaries including Xingxing Touch Control, Xingxing Precision, Jiangxi Xingxing, and Guangdong Xingxing participating in fabricated procurement transactions aggregating 1.57 billion yuan. The forth main fraudulent means is understating operating costs through fraudulent procurement discounts. In both year of 2019 and 2020, Xingxing Touch Control, as one subsidiary of Xingxing Technology, made collusion with suppliers for more fictitious discount arrangements to smoothing the purchase costs. Through these fraudulent discount schemes, the company artificially reduced operating costs by 4.19 million yuan in 2019 and 1.55 million yuan in 2020.

Through the aforementioned methods including fabricated sales, fictitious leasing and processing operations, fabricated procurement, and fraudulent procurement discounts, financial statements were significantly distorted. Consequently, in the fiscal year of 2019, the company artificially inflated operating revenue by 1.44 billion yuan, operating costs by 270 million yuan, and total profit by 1.17 billion yuan (excluding adjustments for taxation, periodic expenses, and other factors). These misrepresentations constituted 23% of reported operating revenue, 5% of operating costs, and a remarkable 780% of total profit for the period. In the fiscal year of 2020, financial falsification escalated further with artificially inflated operating revenue of 3.26 billion yuan, operating costs of 1.59 billion yuan, and total profit of 1.66 billion yuan (excluding adjustments for taxation, periodic expenses, and other factors). These falsifications represented 39% of reported operating revenue, 22% of operating costs, and an extraordinary 4150% of reported total profit.

Additionally, inadequate recognition of goodwill impairment losses is also a concealed path to overstate revenue in financial statements. Xingxing Technology completed the acquisition of 100% equity in Xingxing Touch Control and Xingxing Precision in December 2013 and July 2015, respectively. As of December 31, 2019, the book value of goodwill formed by these acquisitions amounted to ¥305.94 million for Xingxing Touch Control and ¥569.98 million for Xingxing Precision. In both the 2019 and 2020 annual reports, Xingxing Technology disclosed that no impairment had occurred in the goodwill resulting from these acquisitions. Through various fraudulent practices, including fabricated sales, fictitious leasing, and processing operations, Xingxing Touch Control artificially inflated its revenue by ¥200.33 million in 2019 and ¥1.89 billion in 2020. Similarly, Xingxing Precision falsely inflated its revenue by ¥2.82 billion in 2019 and ¥490 million in 2020. Consequently, the financial data underpinning Xingxing Technology's goodwill impairment tests for Xingxing Touch Control and Xingxing Precision in 2019 and 2020 was fundamentally flawed, resulting in significant understatement of goodwill impairment losses. On December 30, 2021, Xingxing Technology issued an announcement of accounting error correction, acknowledging that the goodwill from the acquisitions of Xingxing Touch Control and Xingxing Precision had indeed been impaired as of December 31, 2019, and December 31, 2020. According to the corrected statements, Xingxing Technology supplementarily recognized goodwill impairment losses of ¥150 million for fiscal year 2019, comprising ¥49.01 million for Xingxing Touch Control and ¥97.71 million for Xingxing Precision. For fiscal year 2020, additional goodwill impairment losses of ¥729.20 million were recognized, consisting of ¥256.93 million for Xingxing Touch Control and ¥472.27 million for Xingxing Precision.

(3) Regulatory Violations and Penalties

The aforementioned financial fraud and disclosure violations by Xingxing Technology contravened Article 78, Paragraph 2 of the Securities Law, which stipulates that "information disclosed by obligated parties shall be authentic, accurate, complete, concise, clear, and comprehensible, without any false records, misleading statements, or significant omissions." These actions constituted violations under Article 197, Paragraph 2 of the Securities Law regarding "reports submitted or information disclosed by obligated parties containing false records, misleading statements, or significant omissions."

Finally, the imposed sanctions by the CSRC comprehensively cover all relevant stakeholders implicated in these violations, including the corporate entity, senior executives, and other responsible individuals. This multi-tiered enforcement approach actually establishes accountability at every organizational level. The detailed sanctions are listed. 1) The CSRC issued a warning to *ST Xingxing and imposed a fine of ¥6 million. 2) Each involved executive received warnings, lifetime market bans, and individual fines of ¥4.5 million, including Chairman of the Board Liu Jianxun, Director and General Manager Pan Qingshou, and Deputy General Manager Liu Langwen. 3) Yang Shuming, as a responsible party, received a warning, a 10-year market ban, and a fine of ¥3 million. 4) Additional responsible parties received warnings and varying fines ranging from ¥500,000 to ¥800,000, including Zhang Shaohuai, Chen Meifen, Li Juan, Wang Jun and Dong Shenglian.

(4) Case Implications

In the case of Xingxing Technology, financial fraudulent behavior was primarily driven by the capital requirements of the company. Despite its main traditional business sectors have experienced rapid technological advancement, it failed to accurately anticipate future product trends and market directions, resulting in innovation stagnation and diminished competitiveness. Concurrently, the excessively high debt-to-asset ratio within the company created severe liquidity constraints and erected additional barriers to accessing debt financing, further reducing research and development (R&D) investments and triggering a downward spiral. Against this backdrop of financial misrepresentation, executive management underwent frequent changes, undermining operational stability and continuity, which exacerbated the performance decline of the company.

To prevent similar financial fraud cases, regulatory oversight must be strengthened and punitive measures refined. The current earnings forecast disclosure system in China employs various disciplinary actions for violations, including rectification orders, regulatory interviews, warning notices, public explanation mandates, periodic reporting requirements, suspension or termination of merger and acquisition activities, and monetary penalties. However, in practice, the fines imposed on companies of violation often appear insignificant compared to the benefits derived from fraudulent activities, potentially diminishing their deterrent effect.

Therefore, regulatory authorities should consider establishing graduated penalty structures based on the magnitude of discrepancies between initial earnings forecasts and subsequent corrections. These refined punishment protocols should be detailed and publicly disclosed. Companies with repeated instances of financial fraud should face substantially enhanced penalties. Furthermore, corporate governance structures in listed companies require reinforcement. Financial misrepresentation essentially stems from operational deficiencies and governance inadequacies, which necessitates further refinement of the independent director system. Additionally, comprehensive internal monitoring systems must be established and perfected to mobilize all corporate departments to function not only with operational coordination and resource integration but also with appropriate checks and balances through separation of powers and responsibilities. By implementing these multifaceted measures referring to enhanced regulatory enforcement, governance restructuring, and strengthened internal controls, similar instances of financial misconduct can be more effectively prevented.

10.2 Case Study 2: Qixin Corporation (002781.SZ)

(1) Corporate Background

Established in 1995, Qixin Shares developed into a diversified enterprise group integrating building decoration design and construction, IoT platform applications for decoration, and new materials research and development. The company pursued a strategic industrial layout that balanced IoT platform development with decoration materials research, establishing multiple specialized subsidiaries for coordinated development and positioning itself as a comprehensive solutions provider. It was listed on the Shenzhen Stock Exchange on December 22, 2015, with Ye Jiahao as the actual controller. This company primarily engaged in building decoration engineering design and construction services, with public building decoration construction as its principal revenue source.

During the period between its initial public offering (IPO) in December 2015 and its delisting in July 2023, Qixin Shares raised a total of ¥799 million through direct financing which was comprised by ¥599 million from its initial public offering and ¥200 million from bond issuance. During this period, the company recorded a cumulative net loss of ¥3.794 billion while distributing ¥64.8 million in cash dividends. This financial trajectory, characterized by substantial capital raising followed by significant cumulative losses, presents striking similarities to other cases of corporate financial distress. When one firm experiencing operational deterioration is still urgent to find external financing, it often face heightened pressure to maintain appearances of financial health, potentially creating conditions conducive to accounting irregularities. What is more, this company still made continued dividend payments under this kind of operational losses, inevitably raising questions from investors about the validity of its capital allocation decisions and the reliability of financial reporting practices during the public market tenure.

(2) Financial Fraud Behavior

In April 2023, the CSRC issued an "Administrative Penalty and Market Entry Prohibition Prior Notice" to Qixin Shares for the determination that it had engaged in eight-year continuous financial fraud spanning from 2012 to 2019—a period encompassing both pre-IPO and post-IPO operations. The cumulative falsified profits amounted to an extraordinary magnitude of ¥2.81 billion. According to the CSRC investigation, Qixin Shares committed information disclosure violations on both its IPO prospectus and subsequent periodic reports. Before the IPO, the prospectus disclosed on December 11, 2015 has made significant misrepresentations on revenue, costs and profits from the year of 2012 to 2015.

The systematic financial manipulation began in 2012, when Qixin falsified ¥256 million in revenue and ¥224 million in profits (127.21% of reported profit) through fictitious contracts and cost underreporting. This pattern intensified in 2013, with the company artificially inflating revenue by ¥134 million and profits by ¥251 million (131.96% of reported profit) using similar tactics while adding off-book payments to conceal expenses. By 2014, the fraud reached its peak, with ¥125 million in fabricated revenue supporting a staggering ¥370 million in falsified profits (162.94% of reported profit)—achieved through an elaborate scheme of fraudulent contracts, deliberately underreported costs totaling ¥340 million, and concealed expenses of ¥5.21 million. The escalating proportion of falsified profits to reported profits (from 127% to nearly 163%) demonstrates how the company became increasingly dependent on accounting manipulation to maintain its apparent financial health as it approached its public offering.

After its IPO, Qixin Shares continued its fraudulent practices by whitewashing financial statements in the following consecutive five years from 2015 to 2019. Similarly, the pattern of financial manipulation continued aggressively post-IPO, with the 2015 annual report reflecting ¥437 million in fabricated revenue supporting ¥371 million in falsified profits (179.68% of reported profit). In 2016, the company further inflated revenue by ¥287 million while manufacturing ¥325 million in artificial profits (203.47% of reported profit). By 2017, while the revenue inflation decreased to ¥22.34 million, the underreported costs ballooned to ¥381 million, resulting in ¥397 million of falsified profits (201.35% of reported profit). The 2018 report contained ¥43.32 million in fictitious revenue and ¥379 million in fabricated profits (158.94% of reported profit), while the 2019 report, though showing reduced revenue manipulation at just ¥4.41 million, still presented ¥312 million in fraudulent profits—a staggering 242.64% of reported profit, the highest percentage across all years.

The fraudulent techniques utilized by Qixin remained consistent throughout this period, primarily involving: (1) executing fictitious construction contracts or inflating contract values, (2) deliberately underreporting costs for internally contracted projects, and (3) making off-book payments to conceal expenses. Through these systematic accounting manipulations, the company cumulatively fabricated ¥1.026

billion in profit, representing between 127 and 162% of the profits disclosed during the corresponding periods.

This case exemplifies a type of sustained accounting manipulation, wherein initial fraudulent misrepresentations necessitate increasingly aggressive manipulations in subsequent periods to maintain the appearance of financial health. The dramatic escalation in the proportion of falsified profits to reported profits—peaking at over 242% in 2019—suggests the actual operations within the company were deteriorating significantly while management attempted to mask this reality through increasingly desperate accounting maneuvers. Such extensive, multi-year fraud schemes typically collapse under their own weight as the divergence between reported performance and economic reality becomes unsustainable (Beneish 1999), ultimately leading to regulatory intervention and market penalties.

(3) Regulatory Violations and Penalties

In response to the extensive financial fraud perpetrated by Qixin Shares, regulatory authorities imposed a comprehensive set of penalties targeting the company, key executives, and their auditor: (1) The CSRC issued a rectification order and warning, alongside a substantial fine of ¥50 million on the company. (2) Ye Jiahao, the actual controller of the company during the relevant period, received a personal penalty of ¥14 million. (3) Three senior executives including Ye Hongxiao (former director, vice chairman, and chairman), Yu Shaoxiong (former president and director), and Qiao Feixiang (former CFO, vice president, and senior vice president) received warnings and fines of ¥7 million/person.

Mid-level executives and supervisory personnel faced proportionally lower but still significant penalties: (1) Song Xueshan (former supervisor), Zhang Cuilan (former vice president), and Luo Weimin (former vice president, senior vice president, and executive president) each received warnings and fines of ¥3.5 million. (2) Seven other executives and staff members including He Dingtao (former board secretary), Ye Xiaojin (former vice president and executive president), Zhu Yongzhen (former vice president), Xie Zhipan (former vice president), Wang Hui (former supervisor), Su Lijun (former supervisor), and Wu Xiaoyong (finance department staff) received warnings and individual fines of ¥2 million each.

Notably, the regulatory response extended beyond the company to include Tianfu International Accounting Firm (Special General Partnership), which was ordered to implement corrections, received a warning, had business income of ¥3.68 million confiscated, was fined ¥23.4 million, and was suspended from providing securities services for six months. The culmination of these regulatory actions resulted in Qixin Shares being delisted from the Shenzhen Stock Exchange in August 2023.

(4) Case Implications

This enforcement approach aligns with research on optimal deterrence theory in financial markets (Becker 1968; Karpoff et al. 2008), which suggests that effective sanctions should target both the corporate entity and the individual decision-makers responsible for fraudulent activities. Optimal enforcement regimes must balance both institutional penalties and individual accountability (Dyck et al. 2010). The proportional penalties—with the controller receiving the largest individual fine and descending amounts for executives based on their hierarchical positions—reflect an attempt to calibrate punishment according to responsibility and decision-making authority. The significant penalties imposed on the external auditor also underscore regulatory recognition of gatekeepers' critical role in preventing financial fraud, consistent with post-Enron regulatory frameworks worldwide that emphasize auditor accountability (Coffee 2004).

The eight consecutive years of financial fraud in Qixin Shares centered on the systematic misappropriation of over ¥2 billion through manipulations of the "construction in progress" accounting item, creating an asset black hole substantial enough to consume all net profits generated after its public listing. To secure its initial public offering, the company engaged in prolonged and continuous financial fabrication—a stark reality that became evident when its financial performance dramatically deteriorated after the Jiangxi state-owned assets investment, resulting in aggregate losses of ¥2.3 billion in 2020 and 2021 alone. This extensive fraud was principally orchestrated by its senior management team, but enabled by the serious dereliction of duty among gatekeeping institutions including the sponsoring securities firm, legal counsel, and accounting firm. This collective failure of market safeguards permitted the company to perpetrate its deception in the capital markets for an extended period.

To fundamentally address such systemic issues, more stringent measures must be implemented. Firstly, the punishment costs of violations should be significantly emphasized and the regulators should ensure that perpetrators face financial penalties severe enough to deter the occurrence of financial fraud. Secondly, the accountability of intermediary institutions should also be strengthened by imposing career-ending consequences such as the professional disqualification for professionals who neglect their duty. Thirdly, the regulatory oversight mechanisms should also be enhanced to ensure market fairness and transparency, with particular emphasis on early detection systems for accounting anomalies in high-risk sectors.

10.3 Case Study 3: Aerospace Communications Holdings (600677.SH)

(1) Corporate Background

Aerospace Communications traces its origins to Zhejiang Textile Co., Ltd., established in February 1987. The company evolved from Zhejiang Zhonghui (Group) Co., Ltd. in the 1990s, initially focusing on communications industry investment and asset management. It achieved a significant milestone in September 1993 when it listed on the Shanghai Stock Exchange with a registered capital of ¥522 million. The company held a distinguished position as a reform pilot unit under the National Defense Science and Technology Commission and became the first listed company possessing a missile assembly system in China. Its core business operations encompassed information communication, aerospace defense, and equipment manufacturing. Through multiple rights issues, bonus shares, and conversions, the company gradually expanded its business scope to include communications engineering, communications equipment maintenance, and computer network services.

China Aerospace Science and Industry Corporation emerged as its largest shareholder, with the State-owned Assets Supervision and Administration Commission of the State Council serving as the actual controller, positioning Aerospace Communications as a pivotal subsidiary of a major state-owned enterprise. In 2015, the company issued shares to Zou Yonghang and other counterparties in a significant asset restructuring transaction to acquire 51% equity in Wisdom Hipad Technology Co., Ltd. (referred to as "Wisdom Hipad"). This acquisition, which included substantial performance commitments, established Wisdom Hipad as a controlled subsidiary of Aerospace Communications.

(2) Financial Fraud Behavior

According to Shanghai Stock Exchange Disciplinary Decision No. [2021]142 and CSRC Administrative Penalty Decision No. (2023)9, Aerospace Communications committed multiple regulatory violations: (1) False and inaccurate financial disclosures (2016-Q3 2019). Subsidiary Wisdom Hipad fabricated procurement and sales operations, creating ¥6.574 billion in fictitious revenue and generating ¥2.246 billion in false profits. (2) Inaccurate performance forecasts without timely corrections. Wisdom Hipad inflated overseas consignment processing sales revenue and profits. Between 2016 and 2018, Wisdom Hipad and its subsidiaries falsely increased R&D revenue and profits by ¥328 million. (3) Material internal control weaknesses. Its internal control report in 2019 received a adverse opinion. (4) Improper guarantees for related parties. The company provided substantial unauthorized guarantees to related entities. (5) Failure to follow related-party transaction procedures. It neglected to properly review related-party transactions or fulfill disclosure obligations.

Aerospace Communications employed multiple sophisticated financial fraud techniques: (1) Off-book fund cycling to inflate revenue and profits. On November 6, 2007, the 13th Accounting Information Quality Inspection Bulletin enacted by Ministry of Finance of China determined that between 2003 and 2005, the company diverted funds through external entities in circular transactions, artificially inflating profits by ¥31.10 million, which represents a classic "round-trip" fraud scheme where funds leave and return to create the illusion of legitimate business activity. (2) Related-party transactions to fabricate revenue and profits. During an on-site inspection on August 18, 2010, the Zhejiang Securities Regulatory Bureau discovered that two subsidiaries named as Chengdu Aerospace Communications Equipment Co., Ltd. and Shenyang Aerospace Machinery Co., Ltd. had falsely inflated their revenues for the year of 2009 by ¥20.21 million and ¥10.92 million respectively. This is an effective fraudulent method due to the decreased scrutiny applied to intra-group dealings. (3) Adjustment of accounting measurement on assets to understate costs and overstate profits. On December 10, 2012, the Zhejiang Securities Regulatory Bureau issued an administrative regulatory measure decision against Aerospace Communications for its significant deficiencies in the measurement on inventory and fixed asset of its newly acquired controlling subsidiary, Zhang Jiagang Free Trade Zone Xinle Wool Textile Co., Ltd. on the time of acquisition. The choice of accounting policy can be utilized to artificially enhance financial results. (4) Fictitious transactions through reciprocal invoice issuance. On September 20, 2014, Aerospace Communications announced that it received "Decision on Ordering Aerospace Communications Holdings Group Co., Ltd. to Take Corrective Measures" (No. [2014]12) from the Zhejiang Securities Regulatory Bureau. The regulatory authority determined that its subsidiary, Yixun Technology, had inflated its 2013 operating revenue by ¥45.56 million, overstated operating costs by ¥36.85 million, and artificially increased administrative expenses by ¥3.52 million, resulting in fabricated net profits of ¥4.41 million. Additionally, this subsidiary also engaged in fictitious business transactions and improper revenue recognition from agency businesses. In general, the accrual-based earnings management techniques are popular in this case (Perols 2011). Meanwhile, the progression from simpler schemes (fund cycling) to more complex arrangements (reciprocal invoicing) demonstrates the evolutionary nature of financial fraud (Perols and Lougee 2011).

(3) Regulatory Violations and Penalties

Regulators imposed severe sanctions on Aerospace Communications and its leadership, including public condemnations for the company and multiple executives such as former Chairmen Ao Gang and Yu Dehai, former CFO Zhao Shufei, and others in senior positions. Notably, Ao Gang received a 10-year disqualification from serving as an officer in any listed company, while a broader circle of directors, independent directors, supervisors, and executives received official reprimands. The culmination of these regulatory actions led to Aerospace Communications voluntarily delisting from the A-share market in March 2021, subsequently transferring to the New Third Board market (NEEQ).

(4) Case Implications

The case reveals crucial governance failures. Aerospace Communications exercised inadequate oversight of its subsidiary Wisdom Hipad while disregarding warning signs raised by auditors and internal personnel regarding the acquisition and operations. Under pressure to meet aggressive performance commitments, Wisdom Hipad engaged in systematic business fraud by effectively circumventing the internal control system established by the parent company. The involvement of a state-owned enterprise parent company adds a distinctive dimension to this case, suggesting potential weaknesses in oversight mechanisms within China's mixed-ownership reform initiatives (Lin and Milhaupt 2013). The substantial scale of the fictitious transactions makes this case among the more significant accounting frauds in recent Chinese corporate history, comparable in scope to other major cases documented in emerging markets (Claessens and Fan 2002). Finally, this case also demonstrates how performance-based acquisition incentives can create heightened fraud risks that ultimately lead to market expulsion when misconduct becomes unsustainable.

10.4 Case Study 4: Kaile Technology (600260.SH)

(1) Corporate Background

Kaile Technology was established in February 1993, headquartered in Gong'an County, Hubei Province, primarily engaging in network systems R&D, electronic product services, and telecommunications services. It successfully listed on the Shanghai Stock Exchange in July 2000 under the stock code 600260. Following its public listing, Kaile Technology began frequently shifting its core business, venturing into optical communications, real estate, education, and liquor industries, though most of these transformation attempts failed to achieve expected results. In 2015, Kaile Technology officially entered the private network communications sector (专网通信业务), collaborating with Sui Tianli to develop projects named as "specialized network communication" that provided dedicated communication networks for government agencies and institutional clients. Subsequently, private network communications became Kaile's cash cow, representing 60.77%, 73.46%, 86.88%, 86.36%, and 91.51% of total revenue from 2016 to 2020 respectively.

(2) Financial Fraud Behavior

The superficial success masked systematic financial fraud between 2016 and 2020, during which the company fraudulently inflated its operating revenue by ¥51.225 billion and total profits by ¥5.936 billion. According to the Administrative Penalty and Market Entry Prohibition Pre-notification, during the accounting period between 2016 and 2020, Kaile Technology deliberately overstated operating revenue, operating costs, R&D expenditures and total profits by ¥51.225 billion, ¥44.352 billion, ¥937 million and ¥5.936 billion respectively, which presents staggering scale of fraud.

Though the Shanghai Stock Exchange issued inquiry letters in 2017 and 2019 regarding financial anomalies in the specialized communications business and supplier-customer relationships, key personnel including CFOs Liu Lianchun and Zhang Jian, along with Vice President/Director Duan Heping, continued signing in fraudulent annual reports. Meanwhile, despite reporting explosive growth in operating cash flow after entering specialized communications in 2016, its cash and cash equivalents in book (¥1.465 billion in 2018) was largely restricted as "acceptance guarantee deposits," forcing reliance on bank borrowings and creating a problematic "high borrowing, high lending" financial structure that masked the company's actual negative performance.

The main fraudulent means are summarized in three aspects. First, it fabricated the majority of its specialized network communications business and actually it conducted only minimal legitimate specialized network communications activities during its collaboration with Sui Tianli (the actual controller of Hongda New Materials). To support this deception, the company forged documentation for contractually stipulated procurement receipts, production entries, and sales deliveries, despite never fulfilling these obligations in reality. Recalculations revealed that net profits during this period attributable to the parent company was actually negative. The company never engaged in actual production or logistics for these purported operations, instead systematically forging documentation according to contractual specifications. The detailed fraudulent behavior occurred in contract formulation, contract execution, and financial processing. Company Vice Presidents Wei Kai or Zhu Houli would draft contracts inserting fabricated business volumes, handle the contract signing process, and subsequently process these fictional volumes in the accounting records to reflect non-existent business activities in the financial statements. The case exemplifies how companies can exploit business transformation and technical complexity to cover up financial manipulation, particularly when a single business segment grows to become a cash cow following multiple unsuccessful business pivots.

Second, the company failed to properly review and disclose the changes in accounting policy when it adjusted its specialized network communications revenue recognition method from gross method to net method in its 2021 annual report without issuing an interim report as required by regulations. Additionally, this systematic deception extended to R&D expenditures, with artificial inflation of ¥337 million in 2018, ¥393 million in 2019, and ¥207 million in 2020. As a self-proclaimed high-tech enterprise focused on communications and internet sectors, Kaile exaggerated its R&D investments to enhance its technological credibility, cook financial reporting, boost stock prices, and attract investors.

(3) Regulatory Violations and Penalties

In December 2022, the CSRC issued an "Administrative Penalty and Market Entry Prohibition Pre-notification" to Kaile Technology, proposing corrective orders, a formal warning, and a significant ¥10 million fine as administrative penalties against the company. Notably, the CSRC also recommended severe individual sanctions against Zhu Dixiong, Kaile's legal representative and board chairman, including a securities market ban and a substantial ¥3 million personal fine. The regulatory action extended to eight other senior executives who faced varying degrees of administrative penalties and securities market exclusions based on their involvement in the fraud scheme. The final regulatory consequence came on February 15, 2023, when the company was delisted from the exchange, completing the company's fall from grace.

(4) Case Implications

Financial fraud in Kaile Technology stemmed from four fundamental issues. First, the company failed to implement effective testing on the internal control system for its sales and collection cycle. Therefore, while Kaile had designed segregation of incompatible duties for requisition, approval, purchasing, acceptance, and inventory management to theoretically mitigate risks, these internal controls were not effectively executed with certain business processes exhibiting a "one-man rule" phenomenon. Second, executive leadership actively connived financial fraud. Chairman Zhu Dixiong, who exercised actual control over Kaile's operations, personally directed and organized the financial deception, instructing subordinates to conduct fictitious business activities with extraordinary severity. The risk of management override of controls went undetected as auditors failed to properly assess how suspected violations affected the company's control environment, risk assessment, and control activities. Third, audit procedures were inadequately executed, with violations of basic auditing standards occurring during control testing, such as failing to implement alternative procedures when sufficient appropriate audit evidence cannot be obtained. Finally, auditors lack professional ethics. Zhongtian Accounting Firm has provided internal control audit reports for Kaile Technology for six consecutive years without identifying control deficiencies, suggesting audits were merely perfunctory or potentially involved collusion for mutual benefit.

This fraud case highlight the need for regulators to: (1) improve internal control disclosure policies by establishing effective mechanisms and clear standards for internal control, which also requires regulators to perform follow-up verification; and (2) increase the costs of information disclosure violations, as current penalties (public condemnation, 5-year market bans, and credit file notations for executives; warnings and criticism for accountants) lack substantive impact and deterrent effect. Comprehensive legislative reform is needed to enable administrative, civil, and criminal penalties against companies with material control deficiencies and accounting firms issuing materially false control reports, ensuring accountability and restoring investor confidence in internal control reporting.

10.5 Case Study 5: Hontom High-Tech (600122.SH)

(1) Corporate Background

Hontom High-Tech was established in 1998 with a registered capital of ¥1.15 billion. The company operates as a comprehensive large-scale listed enterprise integrating five major business segments: retail chain operations, financial services, art auctions, technology manufacturing, and real estate development, alongside equity investments in financial institutions. Recognized as a high-tech enterprise by the Jiangsu Provincial Science and Technology Department, Hontom High-Tech specializes in computer systems integration, building automation, video-on-demand systems, and software development within the high-tech information industry. As one of Jiangsu Province's first designated software development enterprises, its technical expertise spans information management ERP systems, software development, networking and communications, automatic control, security monitoring, and intelligent building engineering. Its product has a diverse client base including government agencies, military units, public security departments, financial institutions, securities firms, tax authorities, telecommunications providers, universities, transportation systems, petroleum companies, and healthcare organizations.

(2) Financial Fraud Behavior

There are three major violations identified by regulatory authorities. First, the company fabricated transactions with relates parties to artificially increase revenue and profits. During the year of 2017 and 2018, Hongtu High Technology, through its thirty-two subsidiaries including Hongtu Sanbao and three branches, made fictitious business transactions with eighteen companies. These eighteen companies were established, borrowed, or controlled by Sanbao Group. These purchase and sales operations resulted in false financial reporting in the annual financial reports in 2017 and 2018.

Second, Hongtu High Technology dramatically understated its liabilities between 2017 and 2018. This company (including Hongtu Sanbao) conducted numerous large-scale commercial factoring and bill discounting transactions that led to understated liabilities in its financial statements from 2017 to 2021 amounting to ¥9.063 billion, ¥9.820 billion, ¥9.801 billion, ¥9.748 billion, and ¥9.748 billion respectively, totaling ¥48.18 billion. These undisclosed liabilities represented 81.28%, 104.73%, 106.40%, 103.34%, and 101.75% of the reported liabilities for each current period, constituting material misrepresentation of the financial position. Third, This company made material omissions by failing to disclose factoring contracts signed with Shanghai Yueshen and Haitong Hengxin in annual reports from 2017 to 2021. As a consequence of these serious violations, Hongtu High Technology triggered mandatory delisting conditions for major legal violations and subsequently delisted from the Shanghai Stock Exchange.

(3) Regulatory Violations and Penalties

As punishment, the CSRC fined Sanbao Group ¥4 million, fined actual controller Yuan Yafei ¥2 million with a 10-year market ban, and fined former Supervisory Board Chairman Tan Jiamin ¥1 million. The Shanghai Stock Exchange implemented delisting procedures, and ST Hongtu was officially delisted on May 29, 2023.

(4) Case Implications

The financial fraud of Hongtu High Technology was shocking both in its duration and magnitude, stemming from major shareholder Yuan Yafei's excessive ambition, extreme financial leverage, and neglect of core business operations. Its continuous fraudulent practices thorough the overstatement of revenues and profits and understatement of liabilities resulted in penalties and market exclusion for both the company and its controlling shareholder. These violations went beyond simple administrative penalties, triggering mandatory delisting for severe legal violations. In 2020 and 2021 alone, Hongtu High Technology understated liabilities by nearly ¥19.5 billion, representing an astounding 4107% of its reported net assets during those years. This situation constituted fraudulent balance sheets for two consecutive years, with misrepresentations exceeding ¥500 million and surpassing 50% of the company's reported net assets, which met the criteria for mandatory delisting under the Shanghai Stock Exchange's Listing Rules (February 2023 revision).

Under comprehensive registration-based system in China, the importance of accurate information disclosure has reached unprecedented levels, with financial fraud facing increasingly severe consequences. Regulatory authorities maintain high pressure on violators, implementing "sharp-toothed" oversight with clear boundaries. They continue to intensify investigation and punishment of financial fraud in capital markets and accounting firms that fail to fulfill due diligence obligations. These efforts ensure that those who "tell lies," "create false accounts," or "hide truths" face comprehensive penalties affecting both personal and financial interests. By maintaining stable capital market operations, protecting investor rights, and providing strong safeguards for high-quality market development, regulators are fostering a healthy market ecosystem where only the most compliant and well-managed companies can thrive.

10.6 Case Study 6: LeTV (300104)

(1) Corporate Background

LeTV (originally known as LeTV Network) was founded in Beijing in 2004 with the ambitious vision of creating a comprehensive ecosystem built around "platform + content + terminal + applications" within the video industry, content production, and smart devices sectors. On August 20, 2010, this company achieved a significant milestone by completing its initial public offering on the Shenzhen ChiNext board, becoming the world's first publicly listed online video company. It developed a vertically integrated business model spanning multiple sectors including internet video streaming, film production and distribution, smart terminals, application marketplaces, e-commerce, and even internet-connected electric vehicles. Under the actual controlling of Jia Yueting, this corporation encompassed numerous subsidiaries including LeTV Network, LeTV Zhixin, LeTV Mobile, LeTV Pictures, LeTV Sports, WineNetwork, and LeTV Holdings. LeTV initially gained prominence as an innovative player in technology landscape of China, attempting to build an ecosystem similar to major global tech conglomerates but with distinctly Chinese characteristics, before encountering the significant operational and financial challenges.

(2) Financial Fraud Behavior

In April 2021, the CSRC issued an Administrative Penalty Decision to LeTV, exposing a decade-long financial fraud scheme from 2007 to 2016 that LeTV had falsified its IPO documentation and annual reports, failed to disclose related-party transactions, concealed guarantees for affiliated companies, misrepresented loan commitment fulfillments by Jia Moefang and Jia Yueting, and engaged in fraudulent issuance during its 2016 private placement. The extent of the fraud was staggering: in 2007, LeTV inflated revenue by ¥9.40 million and profit by ¥8.70 million (59.27% of reported profit); by 2015, these figures had ballooned to ¥399.22 million in inflated revenue and ¥382.95 million in inflated profit (516.32%). The details of fraudulent financial reporting from 2007 to 2016 is listed as Table 10.1.

Numerous fraudulent methods are employed by this company, including making fictional business with fake invoices and fund transfers, falsifying customer payments, offsetting accounts receivable with intangible assets without actual cash

Table 10.1 The condition of overstated profits and revenue for ten years in LeTV

Year	Revenue overstatement (¥Million)	Profit overstatement (¥Million)	Proportion of reported profit (%)
2007	9.4	8.7	59.27
2008	46.16	43.08	136.00
2009	93.76	88.83	186.22
2010	99.62	94.43	126.19
2011	69.38	65.29	39.75
2012	89.65	84.45	37.04
2013	199.98	193.4	78.49
2014	351.94	342.7	470.11
2015	399.22	382.95	516.32
2016	512.47	432.76	131.66

Notes: Proportion of reported profit represents the percentage of the overstated profits of the total reported profits for that period (similar percentage calculations apply to subsequent years)

receipts, manipulating related-party transactions through advertising fees and technology usage fees, creating off-book circulation of funds, improperly expensing R&D costs, and using straight-line amortization for media copyrights instead of the industry-standard accelerated depreciation.

(3) Regulatory Violations and Penalties

In April 2021, the CSRC imposed a substantial penalty of ¥240 million on LeTV and an identical ¥240 million fine on Jia Yueting personally for their decade-long financial fraud. The consequences extended further when, in September 2023, the Beijing Financial Court delivered a landmark judgment ordering LeTV to pay compensation totaling ¥2.04 billion to plaintiff investors, covering investment losses, commissions, stamp duties, and other damages. Jia Yueting was held jointly liable for this massive compensation amount. Additionally, thirteen former executives, including Yang Lijie (LeTV's former CFO), received fines ranging from ¥30,000 to ¥600,000. The ripple effects of this fraud case continue, as its intermediary agencies, including auditors and financial advisors, may potentially face joint liability for their roles in facilitating or failing to detect the extensive financial misrepresentations that spanned a decade and significantly harmed investors.

(4) Case Implications

After its successful IPO, LeTV engaged in prolonged financial fraud through fictitious advertising business, inflated intangible assets, and fabricated cash flow cycles, severely harming investors and undermining capital market integrity. Several lessons can be drawn from this series of fraudulent practices. First, when conducting audit risk identification and assessment, auditors must consider the operational risks stemming from aggressive investment strategies. LeTV's eventual liquidity crisis primarily resulted from overextension across too many investment sectors. When evaluating similarly aggressive companies, certified public accountants should focus particularly on financial indicators such as free cash flow and short-term interest-bearing debt. Second, auditors should attach more importance to frequent and high-value related-party transactions within the company, which is an effective path for fraudulent companies to fabricate business activities through making collusion with related parties or controlled entities. Third, auditors must thoroughly examine the revenue structure as well as aging and bad debt provisioning ratios of accounts receivables for their audit clients.

10.7 Case Study 7: Luckin Coffee (LKNCY)

(1) Corporate Background

Luckin Coffee was established in June 2017 and went public on the NASDAQ in May 2019 as a Chinese chain coffee brand. The company leveraged technological innovation by integrating mobile internet and big data technologies to implement a fully online ordering and offline delivery model, which reduced labor costs while meeting the needs of university students and urban white-collar workers. Luckin rapidly expanded its store network, strategically locating outlets in community commercial areas, office districts, and near university campuses to effectively lower delivery and advertising costs. During its trial operation in 2018, the company processed 4 million orders, sold over 5 million cups of coffee, and served more than 1.3 million customer visits. Following this initial success, Luckin quickly established a presence in multiple cities nationwide, with its store count exceeding 500 locations. By December 2019, Luckin operated more than 4500 company-owned stores, with nearly a thousand additional locations in preparation. Through its new retail model that fully utilized mobile internet and big data technologies, Luckin Coffee committed to providing customers with high-quality, cost-effective, and convenient products. By January 2020, its directly-operated store count reached 4507, making it the largest coffee chain brand in China. Luckin Coffee underwent multiple rounds of financing throughout its development, using powerful capital infusions to fuel its rapid growth and expansion.

(2) Financial Fraud Behavior

In January 2020, short-seller Muddy Waters released a report exposing financial fraud of Luckin Coffee through several deceptive practices. First, this company overstated sales volumes by approximately 12% through creating phantom orders, evidenced by discontinuous order numbering with missing sequences representing fabricated transactions. Luckin also exaggerated selling prices of its product on financial statements by recording pre-discount prices rather than the actual promotional prices paid by consumers, thereby increasing reported sales revenue. Second, Luckin engaged in undisclosed related-party transactions by purchasing large quantities of vouchers through companies connected to Chairman Lu Zhengyao. These vouchers, redeemable for coffee, created the appearance of legitimate sales revenue. The company also transferred its own funds to Beijing Hydrogen Yiwei Technology Co., Ltd. (a subsidiary of China Auto Rental Inc.), which were then returned as sales revenue to fabricate transactions.

Third, Lu Zhengyao transferred assets through related-party channels, notably transferring assets valued at ¥137 million to his former classmate Wang Baiyin through the acquisition of Borgward Automotive. Wang established Zhengzhe International Trading Company which primarily sold coffee machines and raw food materials, creating opportunities for undisclosed related-party transactions and inflated advertising expenses. In April 2020, Luckin Coffee admitted to overstate ¥2.18 billion in operating income from the second through fourth quarters of 2019, causing its stock price to plummet 75.6% and wiping out ¥35.4 billion in market value. Chief Operating Officer (COO) and Director Liu Jian and several subordinate employees had engaged in most of these misconducts.

(3) Regulatory Violations and Penalties

Following the revelation of the extensive financial fraud by Luckin Coffee, severe punitive measures were imposed on the company. In June 2020, Luckin was forcibly delisted from NASDAQ. The following month, in July 2020, the CSRC launched its own investigation and by September 2020, State Administration for Market Regulation and local regulatory authorities in China levied fines totaling ¥61 million against 45 companies implicated in the Luckin Coffee fraud scheme. Additionally, multiple law firms initiated class-action lawsuits against Luckin Coffee on behalf of defrauded investors who had suffered significant financial losses when the stock price collapsed following the admission of its accounting irregularities. This comprehensive response reflected the serious nature of violations in Luckin and the determination of both Chinese and American authorities to address corporate financial misconduct in the increasingly interconnected global capital markets.

(4) Case Implications

In its pursuit of a successful NASDAQ listing, Luckin Coffee urgently needed to improve its price-to-sales ratio and expand its revenue growth to attract investors, ultimately resorting to financial fraud to enhance company valuation and meet performance commitments. From an objective perspective, the governance structure of this startup suffered from significant deficiencies when the audit committee failed to promptly identify and disclose problems and fulfill their proper oversight functions. Furthermore, the internal control processes also showed major flaws in sales operations, procurement activities, and cash management. So that this company can deliberately fabricated financial and operational data, exaggerating metrics such as daily order volume per store, number of items per order, and net selling price per product to create an illusion of store-level profitability.

From a regulatory standpoint, this case highlights the need for more rigorous financial and operational data verification for companies in early development stages. Regulators should implement more comprehensive due diligence requirements for newly established companies seeking public listings, particularly those demonstrating unusually rapid growth trajectories or operating in highly competitive markets. The Luckin case serves as a cautionary example of how governance weaknesses and growth pressures can lead to systematic financial misrepresentation when proper checks and balances are absent.

10.8 Practical Suggestions

Drawing from empirical analyses and China's current capital market conditions, we propose locally-adapted recommendations to prevent the occurrence of financial fraud scandals as analyzed before. First, we advocate establishing a China-specific financial risk assessment and monitoring framework through government-enterprise-academic partnerships. This system would serve as a comprehensive tool for preventing and managing capital market risks, requiring interdisciplinary teams that merge artificial intelligence capabilities with financial expertise. The focus should be on leveraging AI technology to capture complex, traditionally hard-to-observe market factors. Second, Chinese regulatory authorities should grant appropriate regulatory powers to industry associations and professional bodies to innovate supervision models. This strategic distribution of regulatory duties would create an effective decentralized system where official institutions collaborate with private sector entities, such as audit firms and valuation specialists to strengthen risk monitoring, enhance early warning mechanisms, enable continuous refinement of industry-specific metrics and ultimately improve the detection of financial fraud among listed companies while maintaining industry-specific oversight.

Thirdly, we advocate for developing industry-specific guidelines for financial statement reporting and interpretation to guide differentiated information disclosure by listed companies in different industries. Given that the problem of financial fraud is primarily related to information disclosure issues and different industries have varying disclosure priorities and indicator ranges, it is essential to further improve industry-specific regulatory mechanisms for listed company information disclosure to guide listed companies to differentiate financial reporting content based on industry characteristics, focusing on key areas such as revenue recognition, cost allocation, asset impairment provisions, and fair value measurement of high-risk operations, while fully disclosing industry-specific potential risks. Fourthly, we suggest to normalize information disclosure systems of listed companies and standardize databases construction of basic data and information output, which is also supported by the rigorously theoretical and legal standards establishment for defining "financial falsification," "financial fraud," and "earnings management" published and explained by official authoritative institutions with timely updates based on market conditions. Due to the flexibility of these definition, the use of consistent terminology and standards in both academic and business activities by research institutions and industry associations should be encouraged to enhance research comparability. Finally, it is urgent to establish multi-level forensic accounting specializations to strengthen the theoretical framework of forensic accounting and cultivate legal expertise, leveraging the crucial role of forensic accounting in corporate management, tax planning, and fraud control. Financial fraud detection and false information disclosure problem in listed companies requires multi-angle contribution from legal, accounting, and auditing perspectives as well as the collaborations between securities analysts, asset appraisers, auditors, and other capital market participants to promote stable market economic development.

The following governance insights are proposed for listed companies in China. First of all, large-scale listed companies should engage accounting firms with diverse client portfolios and larger scale of operation for internal or external audits, since these auditing teams typically deliver higher quality auditing service based on complete financial examinations of audit clients, which will help companies effectively prevent or timely detect financial fraud. Moreover, the educational expenditures on law and accounting should be expanded to cultivate interdisciplinary professionals who can apply integrated approaches combining accounting, forensic investigation, and legal knowledge to resolve disputes between parties regarding loss quantification and causation, evaluate the economic implications of court decisions, and minimize litigation-related compensation risks in securities civil litigations involving financial fraud.

Additionally, different departments in one corporation should collaborate to establish a comprehensive and professional risk management system encompassing decision-making strategies, management policies, risk appetite frameworks, risk modeling, and performance evaluation metrics. Meanwhile, directors, supervisors, and executives should strengthen their due diligence to enhance internal governance and risk control capabilities in response to routine regulatory inquiries. Furthermore, companies should establish robust cash flow management and control systems by strengthening inventory management, optimizing accounts receivable and payable, enhancing risk resilience while pursuing business growth, and supporting sustainable long-term development.

References

Becker GS (1968) Crime and punishment: an economic approach. J Polit Econ 76(2):169–217

Beneish MD (1999) The detection of earnings manipulation. Financ Anal J 55(5):24–36

Claessens S, Fan JPH (2002) Corporate governance in Asia: a survey. Int Rev Finance 3(2):71–103

Coffee JC Jr (2004) Gatekeeper failure and reform: the challenge of fashioning relevant reforms. BUL Rev 84:301

Dyck A, Morse A, Zingales L (2010) Who blows the whistle on corporate fraud? J Finance 65(6):2213–2253

Karpoff JM, Lee DS, Martin GS (2008) The cost to firms of cooking the books. J Financ Quant Anal 43(3):581–611

Lin LW, Milhaupt CJ (2013) We are the (national) champions: understanding the mechanisms of state capitalism in China. Stanf Law Rev 65(4):734–760

Perols J (2011) Financial statement fraud detection: an analysis of statistical and machine learning algorithms. Audit J Pract Theory 30(2):19–50

Perols JL, Lougee BA (2011) The relation between earnings management and financial statement fraud. Adv Account 27(1):39–53

MIX
Papier aus verantwortungsvollen Quellen
Paper from responsible sources
FSC® C105338

If you have any concerns about our products,
you can contact us on
ProductSafety@springernature.com

In case Publisher is established outside the EU,
the EU authorized representative is:
Springer Nature Customer Service Center GmbH
Europaplatz 3, 69115 Heidelberg, Germany

Printed by Libri Plureos GmbH
in Hamburg, Germany